JUSTICE IN A PLURALISTIC SOCIETY

A READER

FOURTH EDITION

INST 270

■ ■ ■

Edited by
Dr. Sandy Bauer
Dr. Drick Boyd
Rev. Nate Coleman
Dr. Bret Kincaid
Dr. Kathy Lee
Monica Smith, MSW
Dr. Van Weigel

Tapestry Press, Ltd.
Littleton, MA 01460

Printed in the United States of America.

ISBN 978-1-59830-380-3

Acknowledgments:
Pp. 1–14: From *A Different Mirror* by Donald Takaki. Copyright © 1993 by Little, Brown & Company. All rights reserved.
Pp. 15–38: "A Biblical Foundation" from *Just Generosity* by Ron Sider. Copyright © 1999 by Baker Books. Reprinted by permission of Baker Publishing Group.
Pp. 39–60: "Pursuing Justice" by Dennis Hollinger from *Choosing the Good: Christian Ethics in a Complex World* by Dennis P. Hollinger. Copyright © 2002 by Dennis P. Hollinger. Reprinted by permission of Baker Publishing Group.
Pp. 61–74: Reprinted from *Six Theories of Justice* by Karen Lebacqz, copyright © 1986 by Augsburg Publishing House. Used by permission of Augsburg Fortress.
Pp. 83–102: Reprinted from *Six Theories of Justice* by Karen Lebacqz, copyright © 1986 by Augsburg Publishing House. Used by permission of Augsburg Fortress.
Pp. 103–108: "Distributive Justice" by Robert Nozick. From *Anarchy, State & Utopia* by Robert Nozick. Reprinted by permission of Basic Books, a member of Perseus Books Group.
Pp. 109–130: Reprinted from *Six Theories of Justice* by Karen Lebacqz, copyright © 1986 by Augsburg Publishing House. Used by permission of Augsburg Fortress.
Pp. 131–137: *Love and Justice: Selections from the Shorter Writings of Reinhold Neibuhr* edited by D. B. Robertson. © 1957 W. L. Jenkins. Used by permission of Westminster John Knox Press.
Pp. 139–148: Reprinted from *Six Theories of Justice* by Karen Lebacqz, copyright © 1986 by Augsburg Publishing House. Used by permission of Augsburg Fortress.
Pp. 149–159: "Liberation Theology: Selected Readings of James Cone" from *Black Faith and Public Talk* edited by Dwight N. Hopkins. All rights reserved. "Risks of Faith by James H. Cone. Copyright © 1999 by James H. Cone. Reprinted by permission of Beacon Press, Boston. From *A Black Theology of Liberation* by James Cone. Reprinted by permission of Orbis Books. From *Black Theology and Black Power* by James Cone. Reprinted by permission of Orbis Books.
Pp. 161–166: Reprinted from *Six Theories of Justice* by Karen Lebacqz, copyright © 1986 by Augsburg Publishing House. Used by permission of Augsburg Fortress.
Pp. 167–172: From *Justice, Gender and the Family* by Susan Moller Okin. Copyright © 1989 by Basics Books, Inc. Reprinted by permission of Basic Books, a member of Perseus Books Group.
Pp. 173–189: From *The Price of Motherhood* by Ann Crittenden. Copyright 2001 by Ann Crittenden. Henry Holt and Company. All rights reserved.
Pp. 191–203: "Restorative Justice, Real Justice" by Erika Bai Siebels. Originally published in the March/April issue of PRISM Magazine, published by Evangelicals for Social Action. Reproduced by permission of PRISM
Pp. 205–212: "Slavery, the Constitution, and the Founding Fathers: The African American Vision" by Mary Frances Berry from *African Americans and the Living Constitution* by John Hope Franklin and Glenna Rae McNeil. Used by permission of the Smithsonian Institution Press. Copyright © 1995.
Pp. 213–231: "Weep Not, Little Ones: An Essay to Our Children About Affirmative Action" by W. H. Knight and Adrien Wing from *African Americans and the Living Constitution* by John Hope Franklin and Glenna Rae McNeil. Used by permission of the Smithsonian Institution Press. Copyright © 1995.

CONTENTS

1. A DIFFERENT MIRROR

Ronald Takaki

I had flown from San Francisco to Norfolk and was riding in a taxi to my hotel to attend a conference on multiculturalism. Hundreds of educators from across the country were meeting to discuss the need for greater cultural diversity in the curriculum. My driver and I chatted about the weather and the tourists. The sky was cloudy, and Virginia Beach was twenty minutes away. The rearview mirror reflected a white man in his forties. "How long have you been in this country?" he asked. "All my life," I replied, wincing. "I was born in the United States." With a strong southern drawl, he remarked: "I was wondering because your English is excellent!" Then, as I had many times before, I explained: "My grandfather came here from Japan in the 1880s. My family has been here, in America, for over a hundred years." He glanced at me in the mirror. Somehow I did not look "American" to him; my eyes and complexion looked foreign.

Suddenly, we both became uncomfortably conscious of a racial divide separating us. An awkward silence turned my gaze from the mirror to the passing landscape, the shore where the English and the Powhatan Indians first encountered each other. Our highway was on land that Sir Walter Raleigh had renamed "Virginia" in honor of Elizabeth I, the Virgin Queen. In the English cultural appropriation of America, the indigenous peoples themselves would become outsiders in their native land. Here, at the eastern edge of the continent, I mused, was the site of the beginning of multicultural America. Jamestown, the English settlement founded in 1607, was nearby: the first twenty Africans were brought here a year before the Pilgrims arrived at Plymouth Rock. Several hundred miles offshore was Bermuda, the "Bermoothes" where William Shakespeare's Prospero had landed and met the native Caliban in *The Tempest*. Earlier, another voyager had made an Atlantic crossing and unexpectedly bumped into some islands to the south. Thinking he had reached Asia, Christopher Columbus mistakenly identified one of the islands as "Cipango" (Japan). In the wake of the admiral, many peoples would come to America from different shores, not only from Europe but also Africa and Asia. One of them would be my grandfather. My mental wandering across terrain and time ended abruptly as we arrived at my destination. I said good-bye to my driver and went into the hotel, carrying a vivid reminder of why I was attending this conference.

Questions like the one my taxi driver asked me are always jarring, but I can understand why he could not see me as American. He had a narrow but widely shared sense of the past—a history that has viewed American as European in ancestry. "Race," Toni Morrison explained, has functioned as a "metaphor" necessary to the "construction of Americanness": in the creation of our national identity, "American" has been defined as "white."

But America has been racially diverse since our very beginning on the Virginia shore, and this reality is increasingly becoming visible and ubiquitous. Currently, one-third of the American people do not trace their origins to Europe; in California, minorities are fast becoming a majority. They already predominate in major cities across the country—New York, Chicago, Atlanta, Detroit, Philadelphia, San Francisco, and Los Angeles.

This emerging demographic diversity has raised fundamental questions about America's identity and culture. In 1990, *Time* published a cover story on "America's Changing Colors." "Someday soon," the magazine announced, "white Americans will become a minority group." How soon? By 2056, most Americans will trace their descent to "Africa, Asia, the Hispanic world, the Pacific Islands, Arabia—almost anywhere but white Europe." This dramatic change in our nation's ethnic composition is altering the way we think about ourselves. "The deeper significance of America's becoming a majority nonwhite society is what it means to the national psyche, to individuals' sense of themselves and their nation—their idea of what it is to be American."

Indeed, more than ever before, as we approach the time when whites become a minority, many of us are perplexed about our national identity and our future as one people. This uncertainty has provoked Allan Bloom to reaffirm the preeminence of Western civilization. Author of *The Closing of the American Mind*, he has emerged as a leader of an intellectual backlash against cultural diversity. In his view, students entering the university are "uncivilized," and the university has the responsibility to "civilize" them. Bloom claims he knows what their "hungers" are and "what they can digest." Eating is one of his favorite metaphors. Noting the "large black presence" in major universities, he laments the "one failure" in race relations—black students have proven to be "indigestible." They do not "melt as have *all* other groups." The problem, he contends, is that "blacks have become blacks": they have become "ethnic." This separatism has been reinforced by an academic permissiveness that has befouled the curriculum with "Black Studies" along with "Learn Another Culture." The only solution, Bloom insists, is "the good old Great Books approach."

Similarly, E. D. Hirsch worries that America is becoming a "tower of Babel," and that this multiplicity of cultures is threatening to rend our social fabric. He, too, longs for a more cohesive culture and a more homogeneous America: "If we *had* to make a choice between the *one* and the *many*, most Americans would choose the principle of unity, since we cannot function as a nation without it." The way to correct this fragmentization, Hirsch argues, is to acculturate "disadvantaged children." What do they need to know? "Only by accumulating shared symbols, and the shared information that symbols represent," Hirsch answers, "can we learn to communicate effectively with one another in our national community." Though he concedes the value of multicultural education, he quickly dismisses it by insisting that it "should not be allowed to supplant or interfere with our schools' responsibility to ensure our children's mastery of American literate culture." In *Cultural Literacy: What Every American Needs to Know,* Hirsch offers a long list of terms that excludes much of the history of minority groups.

While Bloom and Hirsch are reacting defensively to what they regard as a vexatious balkanization of America, many other educators are responding to our diversity as an opportunity to open American minds. In 1990, the Task Force on Minorities for New York emphasized the importance of a culturally diverse education. "Essentially," the *New York Times* commented, "the issue is how to deal with both dimensions of the nation's motto: 'E pluribus unum'—'Out of many, one.'"

Universities from New Hampshire to Berkeley have established American cultural diversity graduation requirements. "Every student needs to know," explained University of Wisconsin's chancellor Donna Shalala, "much more about the origins and history of the particular cultures which, as Americans, we will encounter during our lives." Even the University of Minnesota, located in a state that is 98 percent white, requires its students to take ethnic studies courses. Asked why multiculturalism is so important, Dean Fred Lukermann answered: As a national university, Minnesota has to offer a national curriculum—one that includes all of the peoples of America. He added that after graduation many students move to cities like Chicago and Los Angeles and thus need to know about racial diversity. Moreover, many educators stress, multiculturalism has an intellectual purpose. By allowing us to see events from the viewpoints of different groups, a multicultural curriculum enables us to reach toward a more comprehensive understanding of American history.

What is fueling this debate over our national identity and the content of our curriculum is America's intensifying racial crisis. The alarming signs and symptoms seem to be everywhere—the killing of Vincent Chin in Detroit, the black boycott of a Korean grocery store in Flatbush, the hysteria in Boston over the Carol Stuart murder, the battle between white sportsmen and Indians over tribal fishing rights in Wisconsin, the Jewish-black clashes in Brooklyn's Crown Heights, the black-Hispanic competition for jobs and educational resources in Dallas, which *Newsweek* described as "a conflict of the have-nots," and the Willie Horton campaign commercials, which widened the divide between the suburbs and the inner cities.

This reality of racial tension rudely woke America like a fire bell in the night on April 29, 1992. Immediately after four Los Angeles police officers were found not guilty of brutality against Rodney King, rage exploded in Los Angeles. Race relations reached a new nadir. During the nightmarish rampage, scores of people were killed, over two thousand injured, twelve thousand arrested, and almost a billion dollars' worth of property destroyed. The live televised images mesmerized America. The rioting and the murderous melee on the streets resembled the fighting in Beirut and the West Bank. The thousands of fires burning out of control and the dark smoke filling the skies brought back images of the burning oil fields of Kuwait during Desert Storm. Entire sections of Los Angeles looked like a bombed city. "Is this America?" many shocked viewers asked. "Please, can we get along here," pleaded Rodney King, calling for calm. "We all can get along. I mean, we're all stuck here for a while. Let's try to work it out."

But how should "we" be defined? Who are the people "stuck here" in America? One of the lessons of the Los Angeles explosion is the recognition of the fact that we are a multiracial society and that race can no longer be defined in the binary terms of white and black. "We" will have to include Hispanics and Asians. While blacks currently constitute 13 percent of the Los Angeles population, Hispanics represent 40 percent. The 1990 census revealed that South Central Los Angeles, which was predominantly black in 1965 when the Watts rebellion occurred, is now 45 percent Hispanic. A majority of the first 5,438 people arrested were Hispanic, while 37 percent were black. Of the fifty-eight people who died in the riot, more than a third were Hispanic, and about 40 percent of the businesses destroyed were Hispanic-owned. Most of the other shops and stores were Korean-owned. The dreams of many Korean immigrants went up in smoke during the riot: two thousand Korean-owned businesses were damaged or demolished, totaling about $400 million in losses. There is evidence indicating they were targeted. "After all," explained a black gang member, "we didn't burn our community, just *their* stores."

"I don't feel like I'm in America anymore," said Denisse Bustamente as she watched the police protecting the firefighters. "I feel like I am far away." Indeed, Americans have been witnessing ethnic strife erupting around the world—the rise of neo-Nazism and the murder of Turks in Germany, the ugly "ethnic cleansing" in Bosnia, the terrible and bloody clashes between Muslims and Hindus in India. Is the situation here different, we have been nervously wondering, or do ethnic conflicts elsewhere represent a prologue for America? What is the nature of malevolence? Is there a deep, perhaps primordial, need for group identity rooted in hatred for the other? Is ethnic pluralism possible for America? But answers have been limited. Television reports have been little more than thirty-second sound bites. Newspaper articles have been mostly superficial descriptions of racial antagonisms and the current urban malaise. What is lacking is historical context; consequently, we are left feeling bewildered.

How did we get to this point, Americans everywhere are anxiously asking. What does our diversity mean, and where is it leading us? *How* do we work it out in the post-Rodney King era?

Certainly one crucial way is for our society's various ethnic groups to develop a greater understanding of each other. For example, how can African Americans and Korean Americans work it out unless they learn about each other's cultures, histories, and also economic situations? This need to share knowledge about our ethnic diversity has acquired new importance and has given new urgency to the pursuit for a more accurate history.

More than ever before, there is a growing realization that the established scholarship has tended to define America too narrowly. For example, in his prize-winning study *The Uprooted*, Harvard historian Oscar Handlin presented—to use the book's subtitle—"the Epic Story of the Great Migrations That Made the American People." But Handlin's "epic story" excluded the "uprooted" from Africa, Asia, and Latin America—the other "Great Migrations" that also helped to make "the American People." Similarly, in *The Age of Jackson*, Arthur M. Schlesinger, Jr. left out blacks and Indians. There is not even a mention of two marker events—the Nat Turner insurrection and Indian removal, which Andrew Jackson himself would have been surprised to find omitted from a history of his era.

Still, Schlesinger and Handlin offered us a refreshing revisionism, paving the way for the study of common people rather than princes and presidents. They inspired the next generation of historians to examine groups such as the artisan laborers of Philadelphia and the Irish immigrants of Boston. "Once I thought to write a history of the immigrants in America," Handlin confided in his introduction to *The Uprooted*. "I discovered that the immigrants *were* American history." This door, once opened, led to the flowering of a more inclusive scholarship as we began to recognize that ethnic history was American history. Suddenly, there was a proliferation of seminal works such as Irving Howe's *World of Our Fathers: The Journey of the East European Jews to America*, Dee Brown's *Bury My Heart at Wounded Knee: An Indian History of the American West*, Albert Camarillo's *Chicanos in a Changing Society*, Lawrence Levine's *Black Culture and Black Consciousness*, Yuji Ichioka's *The Issei: The World of the First Generation Japanese Immigrants*, and Kerby Miller's *Emigrants and Exiles: Ireland and the Irish Exodus to North America*.

But even this new scholarship, while it has given us a more expanded understanding of the mosaic called America, does not address our needs in the post-Rodney King era. These books and others like them fragment American society, studying each group separately, in isolation from the other groups and the whole. While scrutinizing our specific pieces, we have to step back in order to see the rich and complex portrait they compose. What is needed is a fresh angle, a study of the American past from a comparative perspective.

While all of America's many groups cannot be covered in one book, the English immigrants and their descendants require attention, for they possessed inordinate power to define American culture and make public policy. What men like John Winthrop, Thomas Jefferson, and Andrew Jackson thought as well as did mattered greatly to all of us and was consequential for everyone. A broad range of groups has been selected: African Americans, Asian Americans, Chicanos, Irish, Jews, and Indians. While together they help to explain general patterns in our society, each has contributed to the making of the United States.

African Americans have been the central minority throughout our country's history. They were initially brought here on a slave ship in 1619. Actually, these first twenty Africans might not have been slaves; rather, like most of the white laborers, they were probably indentured servants. The transformation of Africans into slaves is the story of the "hidden" origins of slavery. How and when was it decided to institute a system of bonded black labor? What happened, while freighted with racial significance, was actually conditioned by class conflicts within white society. Once established, the "peculiar institution" would have consequences for centuries to come. During the nineteenth century, the political storm over slavery almost destroyed the nation. Since the Civil War and emancipation, race has continued to be largely defined in relation to African Americans—segregation, civil rights, the underclass, and affirmative action. Constituting the largest minority group in our society, they have been at the cutting edge of the Civil Rights Movement. Indeed, their struggle has been a constant reminder of America's moral vision as a country committed to the principle of liberty. Martin Luther King clearly understood this truth when he wrote from a jail cell: "We will reach the goal of freedom in Birmingham and all over the nation, because the goal of America is freedom. Abused and scorned though we may be, our destiny is tied up with America's destiny."

Asian Americans have been here for over one hundred and fifty years, before many European immigrant groups. But as "strangers" coming from a "different shore," they have been stereotyped as "heathen," exotic, and unassimilable. Seeking "Gold Mountain," the Chinese arrived first, and what happened to them influenced the reception of the Japanese, Koreans, Filipinos, and Asian Indians as well as the Southeast Asian refugees like the Vietnamese and the Hmong. The 1882 Chinese Exclusion Act was the first law that prohibited the entry of immigrants on the basis of nationality. The Chinese condemned this restriction as racist and tyrannical. "They call us 'Chink,'" complained a Chinese immigrant, cursing the "white demons." "They think we no good! America cuts us off. No more come now, too bad!" This precedent later provided a basis for the restriction of European immigrant groups such as Italians, Russians, Poles, and Greeks. The Japanese painfully discovered that their accomplishments in America did not lead to acceptance, for during World War II, unlike Italian Americans and German Americans, they were placed in internment camps. Two-thirds of them were citizens by birth. "How could I as a 6-month-old child born in this country," asked Congressman Robert Matsui years later, "be declared by my own Government to be an enemy alien?" Today, Asian Americans represent the fastest-growing ethnic group. They have also become the focus of much mass media attention as "the Model Minority" not only for blacks and Chicanos, but also for whites on welfare and even middle-class whites experiencing economic difficulties.

Chicanos represent the largest group among the Hispanic population, which is projected to outnumber African Americans. They have been in the United States for a long time, initially incorporated by the war against Mexico. The treaty had moved the border between the two countries, and the people of "occupied" Mexico suddenly found themselves "foreigners" in their "native land." As historian Albert Camarillo pointed out, the Chicano past is an integral part of America's westward expansion, also known as "manifest destiny." But while the early Chicanos were a colonized people, most of them today have immigrant roots. Many began the trek to El Norte in the early twentieth century. "As I had heard a lot about the United States," Jesus Garza recalled, "it was my dream to come here." "We came to know families from Chihuahua, Sonora, Jalisco, and Durango," stated Ernesto Galarza. "Like ourselves, our Mexican neighbors had come this far moving step by step, working and waiting, as if they were feeling their way up a ladder." Nevertheless, the Chicano experience has been unique, for most of them have lived close to their homeland—a proximity that has helped reinforce their language, identity, and culture. This migration to El Norte has continued to the present. Los Angeles has more people of Mexican origin than any other city in the world, except Mexico City. A mostly mestizo people of Indian as well as African and Spanish ancestries, Chicanos currently represent the largest minority group in the Southwest, where they have been visibly transforming culture and society.

The Irish came here in greater numbers than most immigrant groups. Their history has been tied to America's past from the very beginning. Ireland represented the earliest English frontier: the conquest of Ireland occurred before the colonization of America, and the Irish were the first group that the English called "savages." In this context, the Irish past foreshadowed the Indian future. During the nineteenth century, the Irish, like the Chinese, were victims of British colonialism. While the Chinese fled from the ravages of the Opium Wars, the Irish were pushed from their homeland by "English tyranny." Here they became construction workers and factory operatives as well as the "maids" of America. Representing a Catholic group seeking to settle in a fiercely Protestant society, the Irish immigrants were targets of American nativist hostility. They were also what historian Lawrence J. McCaffrey called "the pioneers of the American urban ghetto," "previewing" experiences that would later be shared by the Italians, Poles, and other groups from southern and eastern Europe. Furthermore, they offer contrast to the 'immigrants from Asia. The Irish came about the same time as the Chinese, but they had a distinct advantage: the Naturalization Law of 1790 had reserved citizenship for "whites" only. Their compatible complexion allowed them to assimilate by blending into American society. In making their journey successfully into the mainstream, however, these immigrants from Erin pursued an Irish "ethnic" strategy: they promoted "Irish" solidarity in order to gain political power and also to dominate the skilled blue-collar occupations, often at the expense of the Chinese and blacks.

Fleeing pogroms and religious persecution in Russia, the Jews were driven from what John Cuddihy described as the "Middle Ages into the Anglo-American world of the *goyim* 'beyond the pale.'" To them, America represented the Promised Land. This vision led Jews to struggle not only for themselves but also for other oppressed groups, especially blacks. After the 1917 East St. Louis race riot, the Yiddish *Forward* of New York compared this anti-black violence to a 1903 pogrom in Russia: "Kishinev and St. Louis—the same soil, the same people." Jews cheered when Jackie Robinson broke into the Brooklyn Dodgers in 1947. "He was adopted as the surrogate hero by many of us growing up at the time," recalled Jack Greenberg of the NAACP Legal Defense Fund. "He was the way we saw ourselves triumphing against the forces of bigotry and ignorance." Jews stood shoulder to shoulder with blacks in the Civil Rights Movement: two-thirds of the white volunteers who went south during the 1964 Freedom Summer were

Jewish. Today Jews are considered a highly successful "ethnic" group. How did they make such great socioeconomic strides? This question is often reframed by neoconservative intellectuals like Irving Kristol and Nathan Glazer to read: if Jewish immigrants were able to lift themselves from poverty into the mainstream through self-help and education without welfare and affirmative action, why can't blacks? But what this thinking overlooks is the unique history of Jewish immigrants, especially the initial advantages of many of them as literate and skilled. Moreover, it minimizes the virulence of racial prejudice rooted in American slavery.

Indians represent a critical contrast, for theirs was not an immigrant experience. The Wampanoags were on the shore as the first English strangers arrived in what would be called "New England." The encounters between Indians and whites not only shaped the course of race relations, but also influenced the very culture and identity of the general society. The architect of Indian removal, President Andrew Jackson told Congress: "Our conduct toward these people is deeply interesting to the national character." Frederick Jackson Turner understood the meaning of this observation when he identified the frontier as our transforming crucible. At first, the European newcomers had to wear Indian moccasins and shout the war cry. "Little by little," as they subdued the wilderness, the pioneers became "a new product" that was "American." But Indians have had a different view of this entire process. "The white man," Luther Standing Bear of the Sioux explained, "does not understand the Indian for the reason that he does not understand America." Continuing to be "troubled with primitive fears," he has "in his consciousness the perils of this frontier continent. . . . The man from Europe is still a foreigner and an alien. And he still hates the man who questioned his path across the continent." Indians questioned what Jackson and Turner trumpeted as "progress." For them, the frontier had a different "significance": their history was how the West was lost. But their story has also been one of resistance. As Vine Deloria declared, "Custer died for your sins."

By looking at these groups from a multicultural perspective, we can comparatively analyze their experiences in order to develop an understanding of their differences and similarities. Race, we will see, has been a social construction that has historically set apart racial minorities from European immigrant groups. Contrary to the notions of scholars like Nathan Glazer and Thomas Sowell, race in America has not been the same as ethnicity. A broad comparative focus also allows us to see how the varied experiences of different racial and ethic groups occurred within shared contexts.

During the nineteenth century, for example, the Market Revolution employed Irish immigrant laborers in New England factories as it expanded cotton fields worked by enslaved blacks across Indian lands toward Mexico. Like blacks, the Irish newcomers were stereotyped as "savages," ruled by passions rather than "civilized" virtues such as self-control and hard work. The Irish saw themselves as the "slaves" of British oppressors, and during a visit to Ireland in the 1840s, Frederick Douglass found that the "wailing notes" of the Irish ballads reminded him of the "wild notes" of slave songs. The United States' annexation of California, while incorporating Mexicans, led to trade with Asia and the migration of "strangers" from Pacific shores. In 1870, Chinese immigrant laborers were transported to Massachusetts as scabs to break an Irish immigrant strike; in response, the Irish recognized the need for inter-ethnic working-class solidarity and tried to organize a Chinese lodge of the Knights of St. Crispin. After the Civil War, Mississippi planters recruited Chinese immigrants to discipline the newly freed blacks. During the debate over an immigration exclusion bill in 1882, a senator asked: If Indians could be located on reservations, why not the Chinese?

Other instances of our connectedness abound. In 1903, Mexican and Japanese farm laborers went on strike together in California: their union officers had names like Yamaguchi and Lizarras, and strike meetings were conducted in Japanese and Spanish. The Mexican strikers declared that they were standing in solidarity with their "Japanese brothers" because the two groups had toiled together in the fields and were now fighting together for a fair wage. Speaking in impassioned Yiddish during the 1909 "uprising of twenty thousand" strikers in New York, the charismatic Clara Lemlich compared the abuse of Jewish female garment workers to the experience of blacks: "[The bosses] yell at the girls and 'call them down' even worse than I imagine the Negro slaves were in the South." During the 1920s, elite universities like Harvard worried about the increasing numbers of Jewish students, and new admissions criteria were instituted to curb their enrollment. Jewish students were scorned for their studiousness and criticized for their "clannishness." Recently, Asian American students have been the targets of similar complaints: they have been called "nerds" and told there are "too many" of them on campus.

Indians were already here, while blacks were forcibly transported to America, and Mexicans were initially enclosed by America's expanding border. The other groups came here as immigrants: for them, America represented liminality—a new world where they could pursue extravagant urges and do things they had thought beyond their capabilities. Like the land itself, they found themselves "betwixt and between all fixed points of classification." No longer fastened as fiercely to their old countries, they felt a stirring to become new people in a society still being defined and formed.

These immigrants made bold and dangerous crossings, pushed by political events and economic hardships in their homelands and pulled by America's demand for labor as well as by their own dreams for a better life. "By all means let me go to America," a young man in Japan begged his parents. He had calculated that in one year as a laborer here he could save almost a thousand yen—an amount equal to the income of a governor in Japan. "My dear Father," wrote an immigrant Irish girl living in New York, "Any man or woman without a family are fools that would not venture and come to this plentiful Country where no man or woman ever hungered." In the shtetls of Russia, the cry "To America!" roared like "wild-fire." "America was in everybody's mouth," a Jewish immigrant recalled. "Businessmen talked [about] it over their accounts; the market women made up their quarrels that they might discuss it from stall to stall; people who had relatives in the famous land went around reading their letters." Similarly, for

Mexican immigrants crossing the border in the early twentieth century, El Norte became the stuff of overblown hopes. "If only you could see how nice the United States is," they said, "that is why the Mexicans are crazy about it."

The signs of America's ethnic diversity can be discerned across the continent—Ellis Island, Angel Island, Chinatown, Harlem, South Boston, the Lower East Side, places with Spanish names like Los Angeles and San Antonio or Indian names like Massachusetts and Iowa. Much of what is familiar in America's cultural landscape actually has ethnic origins. The Bing cherry was developed by an early Chinese immigrant named Ah Bing. American Indians were cultivating corn, tomatoes, and tobacco long before the arrival of Columbus. The term *okay* was derived from the Choctaw word *oke*, meaning "it is so." There is evidence indicating that the name *Yankee* came from Indian terms for the English—from *eankke* in Cherokee and *Yankwis* in Delaware. Jazz and blues as well as rock and roll have African-American origins. The "Forty-Niners" of the Gold Rush learned mining techniques from the Mexicans; American cowboys acquired herding skills from Mexican *vaqueros* and adopted their range terms—such as *lariat* from *la reata*, *lasso* from *lazo*, and *stampede* from *estampida*. Songs like "God Bless America," "Easter Parade," and "White Christmas" were written by a Russian-Jewish immigrant named Israel Baline, more popularly known as Irving Berlin.

Furthermore, many diverse ethnic groups have contributed to the building of the American economy, forming what Walt Whitman saluted as "a vast, surging, hopeful army of workers." They worked in the South's cotton fields, New England's textile mills, Hawaii's canefields, New York's garment factories, California's orchards, Washington's salmon canneries, and Arizona's copper mines. They built the railroad, the great symbol of America's industrial triumph. Laying railroad ties, black laborers sang:

> *Down the railroad, um-huh*
> *Well, raise the iron, um-huh*
> *Raise the iron, um-huh.*

Irish railroad workers shouted as they stretched an iron ribbon across the continent:

> *Then drill, my Paddies, drill—*
> *Drill, my heroes, drill,*
> *Drill all day, no sugar in your tay*
> *Workin' on the U.P. railway.*

Japanese laborers in the Northwest chorused as their bodies fought the fickle weather:

> *A railroad worker—*
> *That's me!*
> *I am great.*

Yes, I am a railroad worker.
Complaining:
"It is too hot!"
"It is too cold!"
"It rains too often!"
"It snows too much!"
They all ran off.
I alone remained.
I am a railroad worker!

Chicano workers in the Southwest joined in as they swore at the punishing work:

Some unloaded rails
Others unloaded ties,
And others of my companions
Threw out thousands of curses.

Moreover, our diversity was tied to America's most serious crisis: the Civil War was fought over a racial issue—slavery. In his "First Inaugural Address," presented on March 4, 1861, President Abraham Lincoln declared: "One section of our country believes slavery is *right* and ought to be extended, while the other believes it is *wrong* and ought not to be extended." Southern secession, he argued, would be anarchy. Lincoln sternly warned the South that he had a solemn oath to defend and preserve the Union. Americans were one people, he explained, bound together by "the mystic chords of memory, stretching from every battlefield and patriot grave to every living heart and hearthstone all over this broad land." The struggle and sacrifices of the War for Independence had enabled Americans to create a new nation out of thirteen separate colonies. But Lincoln's appeal for unity fell on deaf ears in the South. And the war came. Two and a half years later, at Gettysburg, President Lincoln declared that "brave men" had fought and "consecrated" the ground of this battlefield in order to preserve the Union. Among the brave were black men. Shortly after this bloody battle, Lincoln acknowledged the military contributions of blacks. "There will be some black men," he wrote in a letter to an old friend, James C. Conkling, "who can remember that with silent tongue, and clenched teeth, and steady eye, and well-poised bayonet, they have helped mankind on to this great consummation. . . . " Indeed, 186,000 blacks served in the Union Army, and one-third of them were listed as missing or dead. Black men in blue, Frederick Douglass pointed out, were "on the battlefield mingling their blood with that of white men in one common effort to save the country." Now the mystic chords of memory stretched across the new battlefields of the Civil War, and black soldiers were buried in "patriot graves." They, too, had given their lives to ensure that the "government of the people, by the people, for the people shall not perish from the earth."

Like these black soldiers, the people in our study have been actors in history, not merely victims of discrimination and exploitation. They are entitled to be viewed as subjects—as men and women with minds, wills, and voices.

> *In the telling and retelling*
> *of their stories,*
> *they create communities*
> *of memory.*

They also re-vision history. "It is very natural that the history written by the victim," said a Mexican in 1874, "does not altogether chime with the story of the victor." Sometimes they are hesitant to speak, thinking they are only "little people." "I don't know why anybody wants to hear my history," an Irish maid said apologetically in 1900. "Nothing ever happened to me worth the tellin'."

But their stories are worthy. Through their stories, the people who have lived America's history can help all of us, including my taxi driver, understand that Americans originated from many shores, and that all of us are entitled to dignity. "I hope this survey do a lot of good for Chinese people," an immigrant told an interviewer from Stanford University in the 1920s. "Make American people realize that Chinese people are humans. I think very few American people really know anything about Chinese." But the remembering is also for the sake of the children. "This story is dedicated to the descendants of Lazar and Goldie Glauberman," Jewish immigrant Minnie Miller wrote in her autobiography. "My history is bound up in their history and the generations that follow should know where they came from to know better who they are." Similarly, Tomo Shoji, an elderly Nisei woman, urged Asian Americans to learn more about their roots: "We got such good, fantastic stories to tell. All our stories are different." Seeking to know how they fit into America, many young people have become listeners; they are eager to learn about the hardships and humiliations experienced by their parents and grandparents. They want to hear their stories, unwilling to remain ignorant or ashamed of their identity and past.

The telling of stories liberates. By writing about the people on Mango Street, Sandra Cisneros explained, "the ghost does not ache so much." The place no longer holds her with "both arms. She sets me free." Indeed, stories may not be as innocent or simple as they seem to be. Native American novelist Leslie Marmon Silko cautioned:

> *I will tell you something about stories . . .*
> *They aren't just entertainment.*
> *Don't be fooled.*

Indeed, the accounts given by the people in this study vibrantly re-create moments, capturing the complexities of human emotions and thoughts. They also provide the authenticity of experience. After she escaped from slavery, Harriet Jacobs wrote in her autobiography: "[My purpose] is not to tell you what I have heard but what I have seen—and what I have suffered." In their sharing of memory, the people in this study offer us an opportunity to see ourselves reflected in a mirror called history.

In his recent study of Spain and the New World, *The Buried Mirror*, Carlos Fuentes points out that mirrors have been found in the tombs of ancient Mexico, placed there to guide the dead through the underworld. He also tells us about the legend of Quetzalcoatl, the Plumed Serpent: when this god was given a mirror by the Toltec deity Tezcatlipoca, he saw a man's face in the mirror and realized his own humanity. For us, the "mirror" of history can guide the living and also help us recognize who we have been and hence are. In *A Distant Mirror*, Barbara W. Tuchman finds "phenomenal parallels" between the "calamitous 14th century" of European society and our own era. We can, she observes, have "greater fellow-feeling for a distraught age" as we painfully recognize the "similar disarray," "collapsing assumptions," and "unusual discomfort."

But what is needed in our own perplexing times is not so much a "distant" mirror, as one that is "different." While the study of the past can provide collective self-knowledge, it often reflects the scholar's particular perspective or view of the world. What happens when historians leave out many of America's peoples? What happens, to borrow the words of Adrienne Rich, "when someone with the authority of a teacher" describes our society, and "you are not in it"? Such an experience can be disorienting—"a moment of psychic disequilibrium, as if you looked into a mirror and saw nothing."

Through their narratives about their lives and circumstances, the people of America's diverse groups are able to see themselves and each other in our common past. They celebrate what Ishmael Reed has described as a society "unique" in the world because "the world is here"—a place "where the cultures of the world crisscross." Much of America's past, they point out, has been riddled with racism. At the same time, these people offer hope, affirming the struggle for equality as a central theme in our country's history. At its conception, our nation was dedicated to the proposition of equality. What has given concreteness to this powerful national principle has been our coming together in the creation of a new society. "Stuck here" together, workers of different backgrounds have attempted to get along with each other.

> *People harvesting*
> *Work together unaware*
> *Of racial problems,*

wrote a Japanese immigrant describing a lesson learned by Mexican and Asian farm laborers in California.

Finally, how do we see our prospects for "working out" America's racial crisis? Do we see it as through a glass darkly? Do the televised images of racial hatred and violence that riveted us in 1992 during the days of rage in Los Angeles frame a future of divisive race relations—what Arthur Schlesinger, Jr., has fearfully denounced as the "disuniting of America"? Or will Americans of diverse races and ethnicities be able to connect themselves to a larger narrative? Whatever happens, we can be certain that much of our society's future will be influenced by which "mirror" we choose to see ourselves. America does not belong to one race or one group, the people in this study remind us, and Americans have been constantly redefining their national identity from the moment of first contact on the Virginia shore. By sharing their stories, they invite us to see ourselves in a different mirror.

2. A BIBLICAL FOUNDATION

Ron Sider

They thrust the poor off the road; the poor of the earth all hide themselves. . . . They lie all night naked, without clothing, and have no covering in the cold. . . . (There are those who snatch the fatherless child from the breast, and take in pledge the infant of the poor.) . . . Hungry, they carry the sheaves. . . . They tread the wine presses, but suffer thirst. From out of the city the dying groan.

Job 24:4–12

They shall all sit under their own vines and under their own fig trees.

Micah 4:4 NRSV

How should Christians respond to the fact that agonizing poverty and astonishing affluence stand side by side in the United States today? This stark contrast raises tough questions. Does the growing inequality matter? Is justice satisfied as long as the laws are applied honestly, even if the outcome is poverty for some and affluence for others? Is equality the ideal, or does fairness (equity) actually demand unequal shares of the economic pie?

What kind of program to change things would fit with who persons really are? Would changing the economic structures and incentives end poverty? Or is inner spiritual transformation the key?

If something must be done, who should do it? Family? Churches and other voluntary associations? Government?

Clearly, any proposal to change the situation . . . requires answers to these questions. Just as clearly, these questions are ultimately moral and religious questions. We need more than economic analysis; we need a normative framework.

For Christians, that means searching Scripture for biblical help with these questions. Many Christians, of course, do not do that. Often unconsciously, they take their cue for economic life from secular sources, whether left or right. If we want to be biblical, however, we must submit to scriptural norms even when they contradict our inherited biases and ideological preferences.

But how can the Bible help us solve the problem of poverty today? Nowhere in Scripture do we find a systematic biblical treatise on poverty and economics. What we do find are hundreds of biblical texts scattered throughout the Bible that offer essential clues. When we combine these biblical teachings into a comprehensive summary, we discover that biblical faith offers a powerful paradigm for solving our problems.

Four questions are especially important when attempting to construct a biblical approach to helping the poor.

1. What is the relevant foundational framework for approaching the issue of poverty?
2. According to the Bible, does justice require only honest courts and fair procedures, or does it also insist on specific outcomes?
3. What is the biblical definition of equality (or equity)?
4. Who—government, family, churches—should care for the poor?

A CONCEPTUAL FRAMEWORK

Many foundational biblical truths are essential parts of the normative framework we need. The God we worship is Lord of all, including economics. The biblical understanding of the world and history, the nature of persons, the creation of wealth, the glory of work, and the reality of sin all significantly deepen our understanding of how to conquer poverty.

The Lord of Economics

The one and only God, sovereign over all, is the only absolute owner (Lev. 25:23). We are merely stewards summoned to use the wealth God allows us to enjoy for the glory of God and the good of our neighbor. We cannot worship God and mammon. Excessive preoccupation with material abundance is idolatry. God's righteous demands for justice stand in judgment on every economic system. As the Lord of history, God works now—with and through human co-workers—to create more wholesome economies that respect and nurture the dignity and worth of every human being.

The Importance of the World and History

Because it is created out of nothing (*ex nihilo*) by a loving, almighty Creator, the material world and history are finite, good, and full of meaning.

Many modern secular thinkers absolutize the historical process even while they pronounce it meaningless. (Even if life is absurd, our time here is all we have.) Some Eastern thinkers consider the world an illusion to escape. Some Christians do almost the same thing, viewing earthly life as a mere preparation for eternity. Take, for instance, the old gospel song, "This world is not my home, I'm just a-passing through."

According to the Bible, this material world is so good that the Creator of the galaxies became flesh and even promised at the second coming to restore the groaning creation to wholeness (Rom. 8:19–23). God promises to bring the glory of the nations (Rev. 21:24, 26) into the New Jerusalem and assures us that eventually the kingdoms of this world will become the kingdom of our Lord (Rev. 11: 15).

The biblical vision of the world calls human beings to revel in the goodness of the material world rather than seek to escape it. It invites persons to use the nonhuman world to create wealth and construct complex civilizations—always, of course, in a way that does not destroy the rest of creation and thereby prevent it from offering its own independent hymn of praise to the Creator. Finally, it calls persons to overcome oppression and correct injustice, knowing that the Lord Jesus will complete the victory over every evil at his return.

The Nature of Persons

Created in the image of God and fashioned as body-soul unities formed for community, persons possess inestimable dignity and value that transcend any economic process or system.

Because our bodies are a fundamental part of our created goodness, a generous sufficiency of material things is essential to human goodness. Any economic structure that prevents persons from producing and enjoying material well-being violates our God-given dignity.

Because our spiritual nature and destiny are so important that it is better to lose even the entire world than one's relationship with God, any economic system that tries to explain persons only as economic actors or that offers material abundance as the exclusive or primary way to human fulfillment contradicts the essence of human nature. Any economic structure that subordinates labor to capital thereby subordinates spiritual reality to material reality in contradiction of the biblical view of persons. Any program for comprehensive social change that deals only with the material side of persons and ignores spiritual transformation is doomed to failure. For persons invited to live forever with the living God, no material abundance, however splendid, can satisfy the human heart.

People are made both for personal freedom and communal solidarity. The God who cares so much about each person that the incarnate Creator died for the sins of the whole world and invites every person to respond in freedom to the gift of salvation demands that human economic and political systems acknowledge and protect the dignity and freedom of each individual. Any economic order that denies economic freedom to individuals or reduces them to a factor of production subordinated to mere economic goals violates their individual dignity and freedom.

Since persons are free, their choices have consequences. Obedient, diligent use of our gifts normally produces sufficiency of material things (unless powerful people oppress us). Disobedient, lazy neglect of our responsibilities normally increases the danger of poverty. As a result, completely equal economic outcomes are not compatible with human freedom.

The first few chapters of Genesis underline the fact that we are also created for community. Until Eve arrived, Adam was restless. Mutual fulfillment resulted when the two became one flesh. God punished Cain for violating community by killing his brother, Abel, but God still allowed Cain to enjoy the human community of family and city (Genesis 4). As social beings, we are physically, emotionally, and rationally interdependent. Mutual responsibility and collective decision making are essential to every form of human life. Therefore, economic and political institutions are not merely a consequence of the fall.

Because our communal nature demands attention to the common good, individual rights, whether of freedom of speech or private property, cannot be absolute. The right to private property dare not undermine the general welfare. Only God is an absolute owner. We are merely stewards of our property called to balance personal rights with the common good.

Our communal nature is grounded in God. Since persons are created in the image of the triune personal God, who is Father, Son, and Holy Spirit, "being a person means being united to other persons in mutual love." Any economic system that emphasizes the freedom of individuals without an equal concern for mutual love, cooperation, and responsibility neglects the complex balance of the biblical picture of persons. Any economic system that exaggerates the individual right of private property at the expense of mutual responsibility for the common good defies the Creator's design for human beings.

The biblical view of persons means that economic injustice is a family problem. Since we are all "God's offspring" (Acts 17:29; cf. all of vv. 24–29), we all have the same Father. Therefore, all human beings are sisters and brothers. "Exploitation is a brother or sister treating another brother or sister as a mere object." Poverty is wrong not just because it means financial hardship but also because it involves exclusion from community.

Human rights specify minimal demands for how we should treat people to whom God has given such dignity and worth. Human institutions cannot create human rights; they can only recognize and protect the inestimable value of every person that flows from the central truths of the biblical story: Every person is made in the image of God; every person is a child of the heavenly Father; every person is so loved by God that the eternal Son suffered crucifixion because God does not desire that any should perish (2 Peter 3:9); every person who accepts Christ, regardless of race, gender, or class, is justified on exactly the same basis— namely, unmerited grace offered through the cross. Since this is the way God views people, this is the way we should treat each other. Since persons are created as body-soul unities, a biblical understanding of human rights must include both freedom rights and socioeconomic rights.

Statements of human rights spell out for individuals and communities the fixed duties that implement love for our neighbors in typical situations of competing claims. Rights extend the response of love from spontaneous responses to individual needs to structured patterns of fair treatment for everyone. Vigorous commitment to human rights for all helps societies respect the immeasurable dignity and worth that the Creator has bestowed on every person.

2. A Biblical Foundation

The Creation of Wealth

The ability to create wealth is a gift from God. The one in whose image we are made creates astounding abundance and variety. Unlike God, we cannot create out of nothing; we can only retrace the divine design. But by giving us minds that can study and imitate his handiwork, God has blessed human beings with awesome power not only to reshape the earth but to produce new things that have never been.

The Creator could have directly created poetry, plays, sonatas, cities, and computers. Instead, God assigned that task to us, expecting us to cultivate the earth (Gen. 2:15), create new things, and expand human possibilities and wealth. Adam and Eve surely enjoyed a generous sufficiency. Just as surely, the Creator intended their descendants to probe and use the astoundingly intricate earth placed in their care to acquire the knowledge, power, and wealth necessary, for example, to build vast telescopes that we can use to scan the billions of galaxies about which Adam and Eve knew nothing. In a real sense, God purposely created human beings with very little so that they could imitate and glorify their Creator by producing vast knowledge and wealth. Indeed, Jesus' parable of the talents sharply rebukes those who fail to use their skills to multiply their resources. Just, responsible creation of wealth is one important way persons obey and honor the Creator.

The Glory of Work

God works (Gen. 2:1–2). God incarnate was a carpenter. St. Paul mended tents. Even before the fall, God summoned Adam to cultivate the earth and name the animals (Gen. 2:15–20). Work is not only the way we meet our basic needs. It is both the way we express our basic nature as co-workers with God and also a crucial avenue for loving our neighbors. Meaningful work by which persons express their creative ability is essential for human dignity. Any able person who fails to work disgraces and corrodes his or her very being. Any system that could but does not offer every person the opportunity for meaningful work violates and crushes the human dignity bestowed by the Creator.

The Reality of Sin

Nothing on God's good earth has escaped sin's marauding presence. Sin has twisted both individual persons and the ideas and institutions we create. Exaggerating our own importance, we regularly create economic systems—complete with sophisticated rationalizations—that oppress our neighbors. Workable economic structures must both appeal to persons' better instincts that sin has not quite managed to obliterate and also hold in check and turn to positive use the pervasive selfishness that corrupts every act. Because sin has become embedded in socioeconomic structures, justice requires structural change. And because the problem lies deeper than mere social systems and is located finally in distorted human hearts, personal spiritual conversion is also essential for long-term societal improvement.

This biblical understanding of God, the world and history, the nature of persons, wealth, work, and sin provides the best framework for designing successful programs to overcome poverty.

IS JUSTICE MORE THAN FAIR PROCEDURES?

Fair procedures are certainly at the heart of biblical justice. Scripture frequently demands honest courts unbiased toward either rich or poor (Exod. 23:3; Lev. 19:15; Deut. 10:17–18). Equally clear is the insistence on honest weights and measures for fair commercial exchange (Lev. 19:35–36; Prov. 11: 1; Amos 8:5). Without a doubt these two types of justice—which scholars sometimes call procedural justice and commutative justice—are biblical imperatives.

But is that all? According to the biblical perspective, is distributive justice (the fair distribution of wealth, resources, and power) satisfied as long as the procedures are fair, even if many people are quite poor and others are very rich? Some Christians like Calvin Beisner say yes. Economic justice is present, no matter how poor some are, as long as the laws prevent fraud, theft, and violence.

> Justice in economic relationships requires that people be permitted to exchange and use what they own—including their own time and energy and intellect as well as material objects—freely so long as in so doing they do not violate others' rights. Such things as minimum-wage laws, legally mandated racial quotas in employment, legal restrictions on import and export, laws requiring "equal pay for equal work," and all other regulations of economic activity other than those necessary to prohibit, prevent, and punish fraud, theft, and violence are therefore unjust.

Others argue that the biblical materials understand justice to include a dynamic, community-building character. Rather than having primarily a minimal, punitive, and restraining function, biblical justice also has a crucial restorative character. It identifies and corrects areas of material need.

To treat people equally, those who hold to this second view argue, justice looks for barriers that interfere with a person's access to the productive resources needed for them to acquire the basic goods of society or to be dignified, participating members of the community. Justice takes into consideration handicaps that hinder the pursuit of opportunities for wholesome life in community. The handicaps that justice considers go beyond individual physical disabilities and personal tragedies. Significant handicaps can be found in poverty or prejudice. A just society removes any discrimination that prevents equality of opportunity. Distributive justice gives special consideration to disadvantaged groups by providing basic social and economic opportunities and resources.

Biblical teaching points to the second, broader, rather than the first, narrower, exclusively procedural, understanding of justice. Four aspects of this teaching are especially important:

1. Frequently the words *love* and *justice* appear together in close relationship.
2. Biblical justice has a dynamic, restorative character.
3. The special concern for the poor running through Scripture moves beyond a concern for unbiased procedures.
4. Restoration to community—including the benefit rights that dignified participation in community require—is a central feature of biblical thinking about justice.

Love and Justice Together

In many texts we discover the words *love* and *justice* in close association. "Sow for yourselves justice, reap the fruit of steadfast love" (Hosea 10:12). Sometimes, love and justice are interchangeable: "[It is the LORD] who executes justice [*mispāt*] for the orphan and the widow, and who loves the strangers, providing them food and clothing" (Deut. 10:18 NRSV; cf. Isa. 30:18).

Justice's Dynamic, Restorative Character

The terms for *justice* are frequently associated with the words for deliverance and salvation: "God arose to establish justice [*mispāt*] to save [*hôsîa*] all the oppressed of the earth" (Ps. 76:9; cf. Isa. 63: 1). "Give justice to the weak" and. "maintain the right of the lowly" are parallel to "rescue the weak and the needy; deliver them from the hand of the wicked" (Ps. 82:3–4 NRSV).

The words for *justice* are used to describe the deliverance of the people from political and economic oppressors (Judg. 5:11), from slavery (I Sam. 12:7–8; Micah 6:4), and from captivity (Isa. 41:1–11 [cf. v. 2 for *sedeq*]; Jer. 51:10). Providing for the needy means ending their oppression, setting them back on their feet, giving them a home, and leading them to prosperity and restoration (Ps. 10: 15–18; 68:5–10). Biblical justice does not mean we should merely help victims cope with oppression; it teaches us to remove it. Biblical justice does not merely require fair procedures for the poor; it demands new opportunity!

God's Special Concern for the Poor

Hundreds of biblical verses show that God is especially attentive to the poor and needy. God is not biased. Because of unequal needs, however, equal provision of basic rights requires justice to be partial in order to be impartial. (Good firefighters do not spend equal time at every house; they are "partial" to homes on fire.) Partiality to the weak is the most striking characteristic of biblical justice. In the raging social struggles in which the poor are perennially victims of injustice, God and God's people take up the cause of the weak. Rulers and leaders have a special obligation to do justice for the weak and powerless. This partiality to the poor provides strong evidence that in biblical thought, justice is concerned with more than fair procedures.

Scripture speaks of God's special concern for the poor in at least four ways.

1. Repeatedly, the Bible says that the Sovereign of history works to lift up the poor and oppressed (Exod. 3:7–8; 6:5–7; Deut. 26:6–8). "Because the poor are despoiled, because the needy groan, I will now rise up," says the LORD (Ps. 12:5).

2. Sometimes the Lord of history tears down rich and powerful people. Mary's song is shocking: "My soul glorifies the Lord. . . . He has filled the hungry with good things but has sent the rich away empty" (Luke 1:46, 53 NIV). James is even more blunt: "Now listen, you rich people, weep and wail because of the misery that is coming upon you" (James 5:1 NIV).

Since God calls us to create wealth and is not biased against the rich, why does Scripture warn again and again that God sometimes works in history to destroy the rich? The Bible has a simple answer: The rich sometimes get rich by oppressing the poor, or they have plenty and neglect the needy. In either case, God is furious.

James warned the rich harshly because they had hoarded wealth and refused to pay their workers (5:2–6). Repeatedly, the prophets said the same thing (Ps. 10; Isa. 3:14–25; Jer. 22:13–19). "Among my people are wicked men who lie in wait like men who snare birds and like those who set traps to catch men. Like cages full of birds, their houses are full of deceit; they have become rich and powerful and have grown fat and sleek. . . . They do not defend the rights of the poor. Should I not punish them for this?" (Jer. 5:26–29 NIV). The prophets warned that God was so outraged that he would destroy the nations of Israel and Judah. Because of the way they "trample on the heads of the poor . . . and deny justice to the oppressed" (2:7 NIV), Amos predicted terrible captivity (5:11; 6:4, 7; 7:11, 17). So did Isaiah and Micah (Isa. 10: 1–3; Micah 2:2; 3:12). And it happened just as they foretold. According to both the Old and New Testaments, God destroys people and societies that get rich by oppressing the poor.

But what if we work hard and create wealth in just ways? That is good—as long as we do not forget to share. No matter how justly we have acquired our wealth, God demands that we act generously toward the poor. When we do not, God treats us in a similar way to those who oppress the poor. There is not a hint in Jesus' story of the rich man and Lazarus that the rich man exploited Lazarus to acquire wealth. He simply neglected to share. So God punished him (Luke 16:19–31; cf. Ezek. 16:49–50).

The Bible is clear. If we get rich by oppressing the poor or if we have wealth and do not reach out generously to the needy, the Lord of history moves against us. God judges societies by what they do to the people at the bottom.

3. God identifies with the poor so strongly that caring for them is almost like helping God. "He who is kind to the poor lends to the LORD" (Prov. 19:17 NIV). On the other hand, one "who oppresses the poor shows contempt for their Maker" (Prov. 14:31 NIV).

Jesus' parable of the sheep and goats is the ultimate commentary on these two proverbs. Jesus surprises those on the right with his insistence that they had fed and clothed him when he was cold and hungry. When they protested that they could not remember ever doing so, Jesus replied, "Whatever you did for one of the least of these brothers of mine, you did for me" (Matt. 2 5:40 NIV). If we believe his words, we look on the poor and neglected with entirely new eyes.

4. Finally, God demands that God's people share God's special concern for the poor. Repeatedly, the Bible calls on God's people to treat the poor in the same generous way that God has treated them (Exod. 22:21–24; Deut. 15:13–15; 2 Cor. 8:9).

The Bible, however, goes one shocking step further. God insists that if we do not imitate God's concern for the poor, we are not really God's people—no matter how frequent our worship or how orthodox our creeds. Because Israel failed to correct oppression and defend poor widows, Isaiah insisted that Israel was really the pagan people of Gomorrah (Isa. 1:10–17). God despised their fasting because they tried to worship God and oppress their workers at the same time (Isa. 58:3–7). Jeremiah 22:13–19 teaches that knowing God is *inseparable* from caring for the poor. Through Amos, the Lord shouted in fury that the very religious festivals God had ordained made him angry and sick. Why? Because the rich and powerful were mixing worship and oppression of the poor (Amos 5:21–24). Jesus was even harsher. At the last judgment, some who expect to enter heaven will learn that their failure to feed the hungry condemns them to hell (Matt. 25:31–46). If we do not care for the needy brother or sister, God's love does not abide in us (I John 3:17).

One thing is crystal clear from these biblical texts: God and God's faithful people have a great concern for the poor.

But is God biased? Earlier we saw that God is partial to the poor but not biased. God does not love the poor any more than the rich. God has an equal concern for the well-being of every single person. Most rich and powerful people, however, are genuinely biased; they care a lot more about themselves than about their poor neighbors. By contrast with the genuine bias of most people, God's lack of bias makes God appear biased. God cares equally for everyone.

How then is God partial to the poor? Because in concrete, historical situations, equal concern for everyone requires special attention to specific people. In a family, loving parents do not provide equal tutorial time to a son struggling hard to scrape by with D's and a daughter easily making A's. Precisely in order to be "impartial" and love both equally, they devote extra time to helping the needier child. In situations (e.g., apartheid) in which some people oppress others, God's lack of bias does not mean neutrality. Precisely because God loves all equally, God works against oppressors and actively sides with the oppressed.

We see this connection precisely in the texts that declare God's lack of bias: "For the LORD your God is God of gods and LORD of lords, the great, the mighty, and the terrible God, who is not partial and takes no bribe. He executes justice for the fatherless and the widow, and loves the sojourner, giving him food and clothing" (Deut. 10:17–18; cf. also Lev. 19:10–15). Justice and love are virtual synonyms in this passage. There is no suggestion that loving the sojourner is a benevolent, voluntary act different from a legal demand to do justice to the fatherless. Furthermore, there is no indication in the text that those needing food and clothing are poor because of some violation of due process such as fraud or robbery. The text simply says they are poor, and therefore, God, who is not biased, pays special attention to them.

Precisely because God is not biased, God pays special attention to the poor. Consequently, an understanding of justice that reflects this biblical teaching must be concerned with more than procedural justice. Distributive justice that insists on special attention to the poor so they have opportunity to enjoy material well-being is also crucial.

Justice as Restoration to Community

In the Bible, justice includes restoration of the things people need for digni-fied participation in their community. Since persons are created for community, Scripture portrays the good life as sharing in the essential aspects of social life. It is hardly surprising, therefore, that biblical justice includes restoration to com-munity. Justice includes helping people return to the kind of life in community that God intends for them. Leviticus 25:35–36 describes the poor as being on the verge of falling out of the community because of their economic distress. "If members of your community become poor in that their power slips *with you,* you shall make them strong . . . that they may live *with you*" (emphasis mine). The word translated as *power* here is *hand* in Hebrew. *Hand* (*yōd*) metaphorically means *power.* The solution is for those who are able to correct the situation and thereby restore the poor to community. The poor in fact are their own flesh or kin (Isa. 58:7). Poverty is a family affair.

In order to restore the weak to participation in community, the community's responsibility to its diminished members is "to make them strong" again (Lev. 25:35). This translation is a literal rendering of the Hebrew, which is the word "to be strong, " which is in the causative (Hiphil) conjugation, and therefore, means "cause him to be strong." The purpose of this empowerment is "that they may live *with you*" (v. 35, emphasis mine). According to Psalm 107, God's steadfast love leads God to care for the hungry so they are able to "establish a town to live in; they sow fields, and plant vineyards. . . . By his blessing they multiply greatly" (vv. 36–38 NRSV). Once more the hungry can be active, participating members of a community. The concern is for the whole person in community and what it takes to maintain persons in that relationship.

Community membership means the ability to share fully within one's capacity and potential in each essential aspect of community. Participation in community has multiple dimensions. It starts with physical life itself and the material resources necessary for a decent life. It also includes participation in decision making, social life, economic production, education, culture, and religion.

The basic material necessities of food and shelter are essential for communal participation. It is God "who executes justice for the oppressed; who gives food to the hungry" (Ps. 146:7 NRSV). The Lord "executes justice for the orphan and the widow, and . . . loves the strangers, providing them food and clothing" (Deut. 10: 18 NRSV). "Food and clothing" is a Hebraism for what is indispensable.

As we shall see in the next section, restoration to community involves much more than donating food and clothing to the poor. People in distress need empowerment at the point at which their participation in community has been undercut. That means restoring their productive capability. Therefore, restoration of the land, the basic productive resource in ancient Israel, is the way that Leviticus 25 commands the people to fulfill the call to "make them strong again" so "they may live with you" in the land (v. 35). As the poor return to their land, they receive a new power and dignity that restores their participation in the community.

There are also restrictions on the processes that tear people down so that their "power slips" and they cannot support themselves. Interest on loans was prohibited; food to the poor was not to be sold at profit (Lev. 25:36–37). A means of production such as a millstone (used to grind grain into flour) was not to be taken as collateral on a loan because that would be "taking a life in pledge" (Deut. 24:6 RSV). If a poor person gave an essential item of clothing as a pledge, the creditor had to return it before night came (Exod. 22:26). All these provisions are restrictions on individual economic freedom that go well beyond merely preventing fraud, theft, and violence. The law did, of course, support the rights of owners to benefit from their property, but the law placed limits on the owners' control of property and on the quest for profit. The common good of the community outweighed unrestricted economic freedom.

The fact that justice in Scripture includes benefit rights of the sort discussed above means that we must reject the claim that biblical justice is only or primarily procedural, and that, therefore, the state merely protects property, life, and equal access to the procedures of the community. That is by no means to deny that procedural justice is important. When we deny a person these protections, we cut them off from the political and civil community. Procedural justice is essential to protect people from fraud, theft, and violence.

Biblical justice, however, also includes positive rights, which are the responsibility of the community to guarantee. Biblical justice has both an economic and a legal focus. The goal of justice is not only integrity in the legal system, it also includes the restoration of the community as a place where all live together in wholeness.

The wrong to which justice responds is not merely an illegitimate process (like stealing). What is wrong is also an end result in which people are deprived of basic needs. Leviticus 19:13 condemns both stealing *and* withholding a poor person's salary for a day: "You shall not defraud your neighbor; you shall not steal; and you shall not keep for yourself the wages of a laborer until morning" (NRSV). Isaiah 5:8–10 condemns those who buy up field after field until only the rich person is left dwelling alone in his big, beautiful house. Significantly, however, the prophet here does not denounce the acquisition of the land as illegal. Through legal foreclosing of mortgages or through debt bondage, the property could be taken legally. Isaiah nevertheless condemns the rulers for permitting this injustice to the weak. He appeals to social justice above the technicalities of current law. Restoration to community is central to justice.

From the biblical perspective, justice demands both fair courts and fair economic structures. It includes both freedom rights and benefit rights. Precisely because of its equal concern for wholeness for everyone, it pays special attention to the needs of the weak and marginalized.

None of the above claims, however, offers a norm that describes the actual content of distributive justice. The next three sections seek to develop such a norm.

EQUITY AS ADEQUATE ACCESS TO PRODUCTIVE RESOURCES

Equality has been one of the most powerful slogans of our century. But what does it mean? Does it mean equality before the law? One person, one vote? Equality of opportunity in education? Identical income shares? Or absolute identity as described in the satirical novel *Facial Justice*?

As we saw earlier, equality of economic results is not compatible with human freedom and responsibility. Free choices have consequences; therefore, when immoral decisions reduce someone's earning power, we should, other things being equal, consider the result just. Even absolute equality of opportunity is impossible unless we prevent parents from passing on any of their knowledge or other capital to their children. (Proverbs 13:22 explicitly endorses such inheritance.)

So what definition of equality—or better, equity—do the biblical materials suggest?

Capital in an Agricultural Society

The biblical material concerning Israel and the land offers important clues about what a biblical understanding of equity would look like. The contrast between early Israel and surrounding societies was striking. In Egypt, most of the land belonged to the pharaoh or the temples. In most other Near Eastern contexts, a feudal system of landholding prevailed. The king granted large tracts of land, worked by landless laborers, to a small number of elite royal vassals. Only at the theological level did this feudal system exist in early Israel. Yahweh the King owned all the land and made important demands on those to whom he gave it to use. Under Yahweh, however, each family had their own land. Israel's ideal was decentralized family "ownership," understood as stewardship under Yahweh's absolute ownership.

Land was the basic capital in early Israel's agricultural economy, and the law said the land was to be divided in such a way that each extended family had the resources to produce the things needed for a decent life.

Joshua 18 and Numbers 26 contain the two most important accounts of the division of the land and represent Israel's social ideal with regard to the land.

Originally, the land was divided among the tribes, clans, and families so that a relatively similar amount of land was available to all the family units. The larger tribes received a larger portion and the smaller tribes a smaller portion (Num. 26:54). By lot the land was further subdivided among the protective associations of families (*mispāhâ*), and then the extended families (*bêth-'av*) (Joshua 18–19). The criterion of the division according to Ezekiel's vision of a future time of justice, was equality. In this redistribution of the land, it was to be divided "equally" (literally, "each according to his brother" [Ezek. 47:14]). The concern, however, was not the implementation of an abstract ideal of equality but the empowerment of all the people.

The picture of land ownership in the time of the judges suggests some approximation of equality of land ownership—at least up to the point at which every family had enough to enjoy a decent, dignified life in the community if they acted responsibly.

We should not understand "necessities" as the minimum necessary to keep from starving. In the nonhierarchical, relatively egalitarian society of small farmers depicted in the Book of Judges, families possessed resources to earn a living that would have been considered reasonable and acceptable, not embarrassingly minimal. That is not to suggest that every family had exactly the same income. It does mean, however, that every family had an equality of economic opportunity up to the point that they had the resources to earn a living that would enable them not only to meet minimal needs of food, clothing, and housing but also to be respected participants in the community. Possessing their own land enabled each extended family to acquire the necessities for a decent life through responsible work.

Two astonishing biblical texts—Leviticus 25 and Deuteronomy 15—show how important this basic equality of opportunity was to God. The Jubilee text in Leviticus demanded that land return to its original owners every fifty years, and Deuteronomy 15 called for the release of debts every seven years.

The Year of Jubilee

Leviticus 25 is one of the most radical texts in all of Scripture, at least to people committed either to communism or to unrestricted capitalism. Every fifty years, God said, land was to return to its original owners. Physical handicaps, death of a breadwinner, or lack of natural ability may lead some families to become poorer than others. But God did not want such disadvantages to lead to ever increasing extremes of wealth and poverty with the result that the poor eventually lacked the basic resources to earn a decent livelihood. God therefore gave his people a law to guarantee that no family would permanently lose its land. Every fifty years, land returned to its original owners so that every family had enough productive resources to function as dignified, participating members of the community (Lev. 25:10–24). Private property was not abolished. Regularly, however, the means of producing wealth were to be equalized—up to the point of every family having the resources to earn a decent living.

What is the theological basis for this startling command? Yahweh's ownership of everything: "The land shall not be sold in perpetuity, for the land is mine; for you are strangers and sojourners with me" (Lev. 25:23). God, the landowner, permits his people to sojourn on his good earth, cultivate it, eat its produce, and enjoy its beauty. But we are only stewards.

Before and after the Year of Jubilee, land could be "bought" or "sold." Actually, the buyer purchased a specific number of harvests, not the land itself (Lev. 25:16). And woe to the person who tried to get more than a just price for the intervening harvests from the date of purchase to the next Jubilee! "If the years are many you shall increase the price, and if the years are few you shall diminish the price, for it is the number of the crops that he is selling to you. You shall not wrong one another, but you shall fear your God; for I am the LORD your God" (Lev. 25:16–17).

Yahweh is Lord of all, even of economics. There is no hint here of a sacred law of supply and demand that operates independently of biblical ethics and the lordship of Yahweh. The people of God should submit to God, and God demands economic justice among his people.

The assumption in this text that people must suffer the consequences of wrong choices is also striking. An entire generation or more could suffer the loss of ancestral land. Every fifty years, however, the basic source of wealth returned to its original owners so that each family had the opportunity to provide for its basic needs.

Leviticus 25:25–28 implies that this equality of opportunity was of higher value than that of absolute property rights. If a person became poor and sold his land to a more prosperous neighbor but then recovered enough to buy back his land before the Jubilee, the new owner was obligated to return it. The original owner's right to have his ancestral land to earn his own way took precedence over the right of the second owner to maximize profits.

This passage prescribes justice in a way that haphazard handouts by wealthy philanthropists never will. The Year of Jubilee was an institutionalized structure that affected all Israelites automatically. It was the poor family's right to recover their inherited land at the Jubilee. Returning the land was not a charitable courtesy that the wealthy might extend if they pleased.

Interestingly, the principles of Jubilee challenge both unrestricted capitalism and communism in a fundamental way. Only God is an absolute owner. No one else has absolute property rights. The right of each family to have the means to earn a living takes priority over a purchaser's property rights or an unrestricted market economy. At the same time, Jubilee affirms not only the right but the importance of private property managed by families who understand that they are stewards responsible to God. This text does not point us in the direction of the communist model in which the state owns all the land. God wants each family to have the resources to produce its own livelihood. Why? To strengthen the family (this is a very important pro-family text), to give people the freedom to participate in shaping history, and to prevent the centralization of power—and totalitarianism, which almost always accompanies centralized ownership of land or capital by either the state or small elites.

It is not clear from the historical books how much the people of Israel implemented the Jubilee. Regardless of its antiquity or possible lack of implementation, however, Leviticus 25—and the social ideal it expresses—remains a part of God's authoritative Word.

The teaching of the prophets about the land underlines the principles of Leviticus 25. In the tenth to the eighth centuries B.C., major centralization of landholding occurred. Poorer farmers lost their land, becoming landless laborers or slaves. The prophets regularly denounced the bribery, political assassinations, and economic oppression that destroyed the earlier decentralized economy described above. Elijah condemned Ahab's seizure of Naboth's vineyard (1 Kings 21). Isaiah attacked rich landowners for adding field to field until they dwelt alone in the countryside because the smaller farmers had been destroyed (Isa. 5:8–9).

The prophets, however, did not merely condemn. They also expressed a powerful hope for a future day of justice when all would have their own land again. In the "latter days" (the future day of justice and wholeness), "they shall all sit under their own vines and under their own fig trees" (Micah 4:4 NRSV; cf. also Zech. 3:10). No longer will the leaders oppress the people; instead they will guarantee that all people will again enjoy their ancestral land (Ezek. 45:1–9, especially vv. 8–9).

In the original division of the land, the Jubilee provisions for maintaining that decentralized ownership, the prophets' denunciation of oppressors who seized the land of the poor, and the eschatological vision of a new day when once again all will delight in the fruits of their own land and labor we see a social ideal in which families are to have the economic means to earn their own way. A basic equality of economic opportunity up to the point that all can at least provide for their own basic needs through responsible work is the norm. Failure to act responsibly has economic consequences, so there is no assumption of equality. Central, however, is the demand that each family have the necessary capital (land) so that responsible stewardship will result in an economically decent life. A friend of mine likes to summarize this biblical principle as follows: "According to the Bible, private property is so good that everybody ought to have some."

The Sabbatical Year

God's law also provided for liberation of soil, slaves, and debtors every seven years. Again the concern was justice for the poor and disadvantaged (as well as the well-being of the land). A central goal was to protect people against processes that would result in the loss of their productive resources and to restore productive resources after a time of loss.

Every seven years the land was to lie fallow (Exod. 23: 10–11; Lev. 25:2–7). The purpose, apparently, was both ecological and humanitarian. Not planting any crops every seventh year helped to preserve the fertility of the soil. It also was God's way of showing his concern for the poor: "For six years you shall sow your land and gather in its yield; but the seventh year you shall let it rest and lie fallow, that the poor of your people may eat" (Exod. 23:10–11). In the seventh year the poor were free to gather for themselves whatever grew spontaneously in the fields and vineyards.

The sabbatical provision on loans (Deut. 15:1–6) called for cancellation of debts every seventh year. Yahweh even added a footnote for those with a sharp eye for loopholes: It is sinful to refuse a loan to a poor person just because it is the sixth year and financial loss might occur in twelve months.

> Be careful that you do not entertain a mean thought, thinking, "The seventh year, the year of remission, is near," and therefore view your needy neighbor with hostility and give nothing; your neighbor might cry to the LORD against you, and you would incur guilt. Give liberally and be ungrudging when you do so, for on this account the LORD your God will bless you in all your work and in all that you undertake.
>
> Deuteronomy 15:9–10 NRSV

If followed, this provision would have protected small landowners from the exorbitant interest of moneylenders and thereby helped prevent them from losing their productive resources.

Hebrew slaves also received their freedom in the sabbatical year (Deut. 15:12–18). Poverty sometimes forced Israelites to sell themselves as slaves to more prosperous neighbors (Lev. 25:39–40). But this inequality and lack of property, God decreed, was not to be permanent. At the end of six years Hebrew slaves were to be set free, and masters were to share the proceeds of their joint labors with departing male slaves: "And when you let him go free from you, you shall not let him go empty-handed; you shall furnish him liberally out of your flock, out of your threshing floor, and out of your wine press; as the LORD your God has blessed you, you shall give to him" (Deut. 15:13–14; see also Exod. 21:2–6). As a consequence, the freed slave would again have some productive resources so he could earn his own way.

As in the case of the Year of Jubilee, this passage involves structured justice rather than mere charity. The sabbatical release of debts was an institutionalized mechanism to prevent economic divisions in which a few people possessed all the capital while others had no productive resources.

The sabbatical year, unfortunately, was practiced only sporadically. Some texts suggest that failure to obey this law was one reason for the Babylonian exile (Lev. 26:34–36; 2 Chron. 36:20–21). Disobedience, however, does not negate God's demand. Institutionalized structures to prevent poverty are central to God's will for his people.

The central normative principle that emerges from the biblical material concerning the land and the sabbatical release of debts is this: Justice demands that every person or family has access to productive resources (land, money, knowledge) so they have the opportunity to earn a generous sufficiency of material necessities and be dignified participating members of their community. This norm offers significant guidance for ways to shape the economy so that people normally have the opportunity to earn their own way.

Inequality and Power

Equality of income is not the biblical norm for equity. Biblical faith, however, demands something that goes well beyond what America—or any other society today—offers: namely, equality of opportunity up to the point that every person or family has the productive resources necessary to earn their own way and be dignified participants in their community. But meeting that goal would not preclude major differences in income and wealth between rich and poor.

Does that mean that biblical norms do not care about differences between rich and poor? Up to a point, the answer is, differences *are* morally acceptable, in fact, even morally necessary. In a moral universe, bad economic choices rightly produce negative economic consequences. That means differences in income and wealth. Furthermore, Scripture explicitly commends situations in which children inherit from righteous parents (Prov. 13:22). Hence, additional inequality.

Does that mean that biblical people should be indifferent to great extremes between rich and poor? Not at all. Precisely because of what Scripture tells us about sin and power, biblical people must always oppose great extremes of power. In a fallen world, powerful people will almost always take advantage of weak neighbors. And money, especially in a market economy, is power. Therefore, great extremes of poverty and wealth threaten justice and democracy.

The special attention that Scripture gives to the plight of the widow, the orphan, the poor, and the resident alien reflects the awareness in Scripture that when persons lack basic power, evil frequently follows. Thus, in the center of Job's declaration of the injustices to these groups is the statement: "The powerful possess the land" (Job 22:8 NRSV; cf. Job 35:9; Eccles. 4:1). In the real world since the fall, sinful actions against others pervert the intention of the Creator. Sinful persons and evil forces often prevent weak persons from being co-workers with God to shape their lives and world the way the Creator intended. This fallen use of power to oppose the Creator's intentions for the lives of others is exploitative power. Exploitative power allows lust to work its will. "Alas for those who devise wickedness and evil deeds on their beds! When the morning dawns, they perform it, because it is in their power. They covet . . . they oppress" (Micah 2:1–2 NRSV). Unequal power leads to exploitation.

The biblical understanding of human nature warns us about the potential for evil afforded by sharp differences in power among individuals and groups in society. John Calvin described a "rough equality" in the Mosaic law. In commenting on the canceling of debts in the sabbatical year, he wrote,

> In as much as God had given them the use of the franchise, the best way to preserve their liberty was by maintaining a condition of rough equality

[mediocrem statum], lest a few persons of immense wealth oppress the general body. Since, therefore, the rich if they had been permitted constantly to increase their wealth, would have tyrannized over the rest, God put a restraint on immoderate power by means of this law.

A Christian political philosophy and economic theory accordingly must be based on a realism about sinful human nature. Because great imbalances of power almost inevitably lead to injustice, Christians must oppose great extremes of wealth and poverty.

To be sure, that norm is general. It does not tell us explicitly whether a ratio of 10 to 1 between the top and bottom 20 percent is dangerous and immoral. But the general warning against great extremes plus the clear demand that everyone have access to adequate productive resources does offer significant guidance. Certainly, whenever—as at present—the bottom 20 percent lack adequate productive resources and are losing ground, *and at the same time* the top 20 percent are rapidly expanding their share of total income, the ratio is seriously askew. In such times, biblical people should demand change.

But what should be done for those—whether the able-bodied who experience an emergency or dependents such as orphans, widows, and the disabled—who for shorter or longer periods simply cannot provide basic necessities through their own efforts alone?

GENEROUS CARE FOR THOSE WHO CANNOT CARE FOR THEMSELVES

Again the biblical material is helpful. Both in the Old Testament and the New Testament, we discover explicit teaching on the community's obligation to support those who cannot support themselves.

The Pentateuch provides at least five important provisions designed to help those who could not help themselves:

1. The third year tithe was to go to poor widows, orphans, and sojourners, as well as the Levites (Deut. 14:28–29; 26:12).
2. Laws on gleaning stipulated that the corners of the grain fields and the sheaves and grapes that dropped were to be left for the poor, especially widows, orphans, and sojourners (Lev. 19:9–10; Deut. 24:19–21).
3. Every seventh year, fields were to remain fallow and the poor were allowed to reap the natural growth (Exod. 23: 10–11; Lev. 25:1–7).
4. A zero-interest loan was to be available to the poor, and if the balance was not repaid by the sabbatical year, it was forgiven (Exod. 22:25; Lev. 25:35–38; Deut. 15: 1–11).
5. Israelites who became slaves to repay debts went free in the seventh year (Exod. 21:1–11; Lev. 25:47–53; Deut. 15:12–18). And when the freed slaves left, God commanded, their temporary "master" was obligated to provide

liberally, giving the former slaves cattle, grain, and wine (Deut. 15:14) so they could again earn their own way.

In his masterful essay on this topic, John Mason argues that the primary assistance to the able-bodied person was probably the no-interest loan. This would maintain the family unit, avoid stigmatizing people unnecessarily, and require work so that long-term dependency did not result.

Dependent poor such as widows and orphans received direct "transfer payments" through the third-year tithe. But other provisions such as those on gleaning required the poor to work for the "free" produce they gleaned. The widow Ruth, for example, labored in the fields to feed herself and her mother-in-law (Ruth 2:1–23).

It is important to note the ways in which the provisions for helping the needy point to what we now call "civil society." Not only did Ruth and the poor folk have to glean in the fields, wealthy landowners had the responsibility to leave the corners of the fields and the grapes that dropped. And in the story of Ruth, Boaz as the next of kin took responsibility for her well-being (chapters 3, 4). Laws such as these emphasize the role of the family and neighbors in meeting the needs of the poor.

The texts seem to assume a level of assistance best described as "sufficiency for need," "with a fairly liberal interpretation of need." Deuteronomy 15:8 specifies that the poor brother receive a loan large enough to net his need. Frequently, God commanded those with resources to treat their poor fellow Israelites with the same liberality that God showed them at the Exodus, in the wilderness, and in giving them their own land (Exod. 22:21; Lev. 25:38; Deut. 24:18, 22). God wanted those who could not care for themselves to receive a liberal sufficiency for need offered in a way that encouraged work and responsibility, strengthened the family, and helped the poor return to self-sufficiency.

Were those "welfare provisions" part of the law to be enforced by the community? Or were they merely suggestions for voluntary charity? The third-year tithe was gathered in a central location (Deut. 14:28) and then shared with the needy. Community leaders would have to act together to carry out such a centralized operation. In the Talmud, there is evidence that the proper community leaders had the right to demand contributions. Nehemiah 5 deals explicitly with violations of the provisions concerning loans to the poor. The political leader would call an assembly, bring "charges against the nobles," and command that the situation be corrected (Neh. 5:7; cf. vv. 1–13). Old Testament texts often speak of the "rights" or "cause" of the poor. Since these terms have clear legal significance, they support the view that the provisions we have explored for assisting the poor would have been legally enforceable. "The clear fact is that the provisions for the impoverished were part of the Mosaic legislation, as much as other laws such as those dealing with murder and theft. Since nothing in the text allows us to consider them as different, they must be presumed to have been legally enforceable."

The sociopolitical situation was dramatically different in the New Testament. The early church was a tiny religious minority with few political rights in a vast pagan Roman empire. But within the church, the standard was the same. Acts 2:43–47 and 4:32–37 record dramatic economic sharing in order to respond to those who could not care for themselves. The norm? "Distribution was made to each as any had need" (Acts 4:35). As a result, "there was not a needy person among them" (v. 34).

The great evangelist Paul spent much of his time over several years collecting an international offering for the impoverished Christians in Jerusalem (2 Corinthians 8–9). For his work, he found a norm (2 Cor. 8:1 3–15)—equality of basic necessities—articulated in the Exodus story of the manna in which every person ended up with "as much as each of them needed" (Exod. 16:18 NRSV).

Throughout Scripture we see the same standard. When people cannot care for themselves, their community must provide a liberal sufficiency so that their needs are met.

A ROLE FOR GOVERNMENT?

Thus far we have seen that the biblical paradigm calls for an economic order in which all who are able to work enjoy access to appropriate productive resources so they can be creative co-workers with God, create wealth to bless their family and neighbors, and be dignified participating members of their community. For those who cannot care for themselves, the biblical framework demands generous assistance so that everyone has a liberal sufficiency of basic necessities.

Institutions including the family, the church, the schools, and business have crucial obligations. Certainly government does not have sole responsibility. But what role should government play?

At different points in the biblical text it is clear that the family has the first obligation to help needy members. In the text on the Jubilee in Leviticus 25, the first responsibility to help the poor person forced by poverty to sell land is the next of kin in the extended family (Lev. 25:25, 35). But the poor person's help does not end with the family. Even if there are no family members to help, the poor person has the legal right to get his land back at the next Jubilee (25:28). Similarly, I Timothy 5:16 insists that a Christian widow's relatives should be her first means of support. Only when the family cannot help should the church step in. Any policy or political philosophy that immediately seeks governmental solutions for problems that could be solved just as well or better at the level of the family violates the biblical framework that stresses the central societal role of the family.

But is there a biblical basis for those who seek to exclude government almost completely from the area of the economy? Not at all. The state is not some evil to be endured like an appendectomy. According to Romans 13, the state is a gift from God designed for our good. Hence, John Calvin denounced those who regarded magistrates "only as a kind of necessary evil." Calvin called civil authority "the most honorable of all callings in the whole life" of mortal human beings; its function among human beings is "no less than that of bread, water, sun, and air. "

The earlier discussion of the economic components of justice is central for a biblical view of the role of government: "The LORD . . . has made you king to execute justice and righteousness" (I Kings 10:9 NRSV; cf. Jer. 22:15–16). And these two key words—*justice* and *righteousness*—as we have seen, refer not only to fair legal systems but also to just economic structures. Again and again the biblical texts call on the king to promote justice and righteousness.

The positive role of government in advancing economic justice is seen in the biblical materials that describe the ideal monarch. Both the royal psalms and the messianic prophecies shed light on this ideal ruler.

Psalm 72, one of the royal psalms, gives the following purpose for the ruler: "May he defend the cause of the poor of the people, give deliverance to the needy, and crush the oppressor" (v. 4 NRSV). And this task is identified as the work of justice (vv. 1–3, 7). In this passage, justice includes using power to deliver the needy and oppressed.

According to Psalm 72, there are oppressors of the poor separate from the state who need to be crushed. State power, despite its dangers, is necessary for society because of the evil power of such exploiting groups. "On the side of their oppressors there was power," Ecclesiastes 4:1 NRSV declares. Without governmental force to counter such oppressive power there is no one to comfort (Eccles. 4:1). Whether it is the monarch or the village elders (Amos 5:12, 15), governmental power should deliver the economically weak and guarantee the "rights of the poor" (Jer. 22:15–16; also Ps. 45:4–5; 101:8; Jer. 21:12).

Sin makes government intervention in the economy necessary. When selfish, powerful people deprive others of their rightful access to productive resources, the state rightly steps in with intervening power to correct the injustice. When other individuals and institutions in the community do not or cannot provide basic necessities for the needy, government rightly helps.

Prophecies about the coming messianic ruler also contribute to the picture of the ideal ruler. "With righteousness he shall judge the poor, and decide with equity for the meek of the earth; he shall strike the earth with the rod of his mouth, and with the breath of his lips he shall kill the wicked" (Isa. 11:4 NRSV). This ideal ruler will act like a shepherd in taking responsibility for the needs of the people. "He shall feed them and be their shepherd" (Ezek. 34:23 NRSV). Ezekiel 34:4 denounces the failure of the shepherds (i.e., the rulers) of Israel to "feed" the people. Then in verses 15–16, the same phrases are repeated to describe God's promise of justice:

"And I will make them lie down," says the LORD God. "I will seek the lost, and I will bring back the strayed, and I will bind up the injured, and I will strengthen the weak, but the fat and the strong I will destroy. I will feed them with justice" (NRSV).

This promise will be fulfilled by the coming Davidic ruler (vv. 23–24). Similarly in Isaiah 32:1–8, the promised just and wise monarch is contrasted to the fool who leaves the hungry unsatisfied (v. 6).

This teaching on the role of government applies not just to Israel but to government everywhere. The ideal monarch was to be a channel of God's justice (Ps. 72:1), and God's justice extends to the whole world (e.g., Ps. 9:7–9). All legitimate rulers are instituted by God and are God's servants for human good (Rom. 13:1, 4). In this passage, Paul states a positive reason for government (government acts "for your good" [v. 4] before he specifies its negative function ("to execute wrath on the wrongdoer" [v. 4]). Romans 13 is structurally similar to Psalm 72:1 in viewing the ruler as a channel of God's authority. All people everywhere can pray with the Israelites: "Give the king your justice, O God" (Ps. 72:1 NRSV).

Daniel 4:27 shows that the ideal of the monarch as the protector of the weak has universal application. God summons the Babylonian monarch no less than the Israelite king to bring "justice and . . . mercy to the oppressed." Similarly in Proverbs 31:9, King Lemuel (generally considered to be a northern Arabian monarch) is to "defend the rights of the poor and needy" (NRSV). "The general obligation of the Israelite king to see that persons otherwise not adequately protected or provided for should enjoy fair treatment in judicial proceedings and should receive the daily necessities of life is evidently understood as the duty of all kings."

The teaching on the ideal, just monarch of Israel, whether in royal psalms or messianic prophecies, cannot be restricted to some future messianic reign. God demanded that the kings of Israel provide in their own time what the messianic ruler would eventually bring more completely: namely, justice that delivers the needy from oppression. God's concern in the present and in the future within Israel and outside of Israel is that there be a community in which the weak are strengthened and protected from their foes.

Government is an aspect of community and is inherent in human life as an expression of our created social nature. Governmental action to empower the poor is one way we promote the common good and implement the truth that economic justice is a family affair.

Frequently, of course, the state contributes to social cohesion by encouraging and enabling other institutions in the community—whether family, church, nongovernmental social agencies, and unions—to carry out their responsibilities to care for the economically dependent. Sometimes, however, the depth of social need exceeds the capacity of nongovernmental institutions. When indirect approaches are not effective in restraining economic injustice, providing economic opportunity to all, or in providing care for those who cannot care for themselves, the state rightly acts to demand patterns of justice and provide vital services.

CONCLUSION

Does the biblical material offer a norm for distributive justice today? Some would argue that the biblical material only applies to God's covenant community. But that is to ignore the fact that the biblical writers did not hesitate to apply revealed standards to persons and societies outside Israel. Amos announced divine punishment on the surrounding nations for their evil and injustice (Amos 1–2). Isaiah condemned Assyria for its pride and injustice (Isa. 10:12–19). The Book of Daniel shows that God removed pagan kings such as Nebuchadnezzar in the same way he destroyed Israel's rulers when they failed to show mercy to the oppressed (Dan. 4:27). God obliterated Sodom and Gomorrah no less than Israel and Judah because they neglected to aid the poor and feed the hungry (Ezek. 16:49). The Lord of history applies the same standards of social justice to all nations.

That does not mean, however, that we should try to apply the specific mechanisms of the Jubilee and the sabbatical release to late-twentieth-century global market economies. It is the basic paradigm that is normative for us today. Land, for example, has a very different function in an industrial economy. Appropriate application of these texts requires that we ask how their specific mechanisms functioned in Israelite culture and then determine what specific measures would fulfill a similar function in our very different society. Since land in Israelite society represented productive power, we must identify the forms of productive power in modern societies. In an industrial society the primary productive power is machinery, and in an information society it is knowledge. Faithful application of these biblical texts in such societies means finding mechanisms that offer everyone the opportunity to share in the ownership of these productive resources. If we start with the Jubilee's call for everyone to enjoy access to productive power, we must criticize all socioeconomic arrangements in which productive power is owned or controlled by only one class or group (whether bourgeoisie, aristocracy, or workers), or by a state or party oligarchy. Indeed, we saw that the prophets protested the development of an economic system in which land ownership was shifted to a small group within society. Today we must develop appropriate intervening processes in society to restore access to productive resources to everyone.

The traditional criterion of distributive justice that comes closest to the biblical paradigm is distribution according to needs. That is not to ignore the important truth that bad choices rightly have negative economic consequences. Nor is it to forget that the able-bodied have an obligation to work to earn their way. But it does mean that a theory of distributive justice grounded in Scripture places much more emphasis on structural arrangements that guarantee basic needs for life in community than do other views. Other views of distributive justice place primary emphasis on birth, or might, or ability, or contract, or achievement.

To be sure, these other criteria of distributive justice are not all irrelevant, Indeed, some of them are at least assumed in the biblical approach. Achievement (e.g., ability in the market, so stressed in Western culture) has a legitimate role. It must be subordinate, however, to the central criterion of distribution according to needs for the sake of inclusion in community.

The biblical material provides at least three norms pertaining to distribution of resources to meet basic needs:

1. Normally, all people who can work should have access to the productive resources so that, if they act responsibly, they can produce or purchase an abundant sufficiency of all that is needed to enjoy a dignified, healthy life in community.
2. The difference in wealth between the rich and the poor dare not become so great that great inequalities of wealth and therefore power lead to oppression.
3. Those who cannot care for themselves should receive from their community a liberal sufficiency of the necessities of life provided in ways that preserve dignity, encourage responsibility, and strengthen the family.

Those three norms are modest in comparison with some ideals presented in the name of equality. At the same time they demand fundamental change in our nation.

If God's Word is true, then the United States today stands in blatant defiance of God's norms for society. Anyone who seeks to be biblical must demand an end to the scandal of poverty in the richest nation on earth. If the Bible teaches that private property is so good that everybody ought to have some, then biblical people will lead the way in offering new opportunity to the bottom 20 percent.

3. Pursuing Justice

Dennis Hollinger

Dennis Hollinger *is the vice provost, college pastor, and professor of Christian ethics at Messiah College.*

Mickey Mantle was a baseball superstar. During the 1950s and 1960s, Mantle was known for his unusual combination of speed and power, as he led the New York Yankees to twelve American League pennants and seven World Series championships. Three times he was the league's most valuable player, and many considered him the greatest all-around player in baseball history. "With a telegenic, boyish grin, an aw-shucks Oklahoma drawl and a big No. 7 across his muscular back, he became everyone's idea of what a great baseball player should look and sound like."[1]

But there was a dark side to Mantle's life, for off the field he was known for his high living, carousing, and consumption of alcohol. Mantle was an alcoholic and in 1995 received a liver transplant as a result of cirrhosis and hepatitis C. But unbeknown to the transplant physicians, cancer was present in other parts of his body, and in August of that same year he died. At a news conference several weeks before his death, Mantle expressed remorse for his years of abusing his body, declaring to young people that he was not a true role model. On his deathbed Mantle is reported to have had a spiritual conversion to Christ through the influence of his former teammate, Bobby Richardson.

Though sports fans mourned the passing of Mantle, his reception of a new liver just before his death set off a wave of controversy regarding organ transplants. The quickness with which Mantle received his liver caused some to ask whether celebrities were receiving preferential treatment. Would he have received the organ so soon had he not been Mickey Mantle? Moreover, should the former baseball great have been a recipient given his decades of careless living and drinking? Should lifestyle be a factor in deciding who gets the medical goods when there are not enough to go around?

The Southwest Organ Bank officials and Mantle's doctors denied that Mantle's celebrity status was a factor in his quick reception of an organ. The chief of transplant surgery at the hospital said Mantle received priority "because he was sicker than anybody else."[2] One's position on the waiting list is determined by the degree of sickness and length of time on the waiting list, combined with other factors of compatibility. But given the fact that in 2001 there were 77,000 people waiting for transplants and in 2000 fewer than 23,000 transplants were performed,[3] many continue to wonder whether the Mantle transplant was just.

Justice is an issue in all societies, and it is a central theme in Christian ethics. It emerges in regard to organ transplants, race and ethnic group relations, economics, environmental issues, business transactions, and gender issues. At the heart of justice is the question, What is due a person? in relationship to certain actions performed or by virtue of being a member of a particular group, including the human race. While justice according to the ancient philosophers and medieval theologians was a virtue (along with wisdom, fortitude, and temperance), today justice is also viewed as a principle or even a social vision to guide humans and societies in ordering their relationships. The topic of justice is included in part 4 because it involves social relationships and the way we seek to carry out the Christian worldview in relation to the larger communities and societies in which we live.

There are actually several spheres of justice, but essentially they can be broken down into two main categories: retributive and distributive. Retributive justice focuses on what is due a person when that person has perpetrated wrong. The issue involves the sorts of punishments and liabilities that are just in light of the suffering or damage that person has caused. A perennial issue has been whether capital punishment is a just or unjust retribution for murder. Recently, another debate has emerged in retributive justice: whether it is just for judges to order "deadbeat dads" to abstain from procreating or face imprisonment. Some have even proposed mandatory sterilization as a punishment for failure to take care of one's children.

Distributive justice is positive in nature, focusing on the kinds of rewards, rights, opportunities, services, and treatments due a person because of who that person is, what he or she has done, or even the group to which he or she belongs. Distributive justice "concerns a wide variety of goods and services distributed (such as money, health care, honors, educational opportunities, and protection from threats to life . . .) by a wide variety of agents (such as . . . [family], employers in a business, civil government, and even God . . .) to an equally wide variety of recipients (such as children . . . , employees, citizens, and businesses)."[4] Distributive justice involves some of the toughest justice issues as we attempt in a complex society to decide what is owed people in given circumstances and by whom it is owed. The Mickey Mantle transplant fits in the sphere of distributive justice. How do we decide a just way of allocating resources when there are not enough for everyone?

This chapter focuses on distributive justice as we seek to grasp what the Christian worldview can contribute to the complex issues we face as individuals, institutions, and societies. A number of significant theological and philosophical issues attend to this matter, and ultimately, we must decide on a definition of justice. From the outset, we must recognize that debates concerning justice have often been skewed by the vested interests of particular groups, ideological commitments, and the general "rightsism" ethos so prevalent in our time. This chapter will attempt to clarify what is at stake in the justice debates and the way justice fits within the larger framework of Christian understandings and normative commitments.

THE BIBLICAL TEACHINGS ON JUSTICE

The Bible contains much teaching on justice. As the foundation for human justice, God is portrayed as just in both character and action:

> God . . . who is not partial and takes no bribe, who executes justice for the orphan and the widow, and who loves the strangers, providing them food and clothing.
>
> Deuteronomy 10: 17–18

> The LORD works vindication
> and justice for all who are oppressed.
>
> Psalm 103:6

> The LORD maintains the cause of the needy,
> and executes justice for the poor.
>
> Psalm 140:12

> For I the LORD love justice.
>
> Isaiah 61:8

> I am the LORD; I act with steadfast love, justice, and righteousness in the earth, for in these things I delight.
>
> Jeremiah 9:24

> Here is my servant, whom I have chosen. . . . I will put my Spirit upon him, and he will proclaim justice to the Gentiles . . . He brings justice to victory.
>
> Matthew 12:18, 20

> And will not God grant justice to the chosen ones who cry to him day and night?
>
> Luke 18:7

> If our injustice serves to confirm the justice of God, what should we say?
>
> Romans 3:5

> He scatters abroad, he gives to the poor; his righteousness [justice] endures forever. He . . . will . . . increase the harvest of your righteousness [justice].
>
> 2 Corinthians 9:9–10

Because God, the foundation of Christian ethics, is just, God's people are called to just actions and character:

Justice, and only justice, you shall pursue, so that you may live and occupy the land that the LORD your God is giving you.

Deuteronomy 16:20

Maintain justice, and do what is right.

Isaiah 56:1

Let justice roll down like waters,
and righteousness like an ever-flowing stream.

Amos 5:24

What does the Lord require of you
but to do justice, and to love kindness,
and to walk humbly with your God.

Micah 6:8

Blessed are those who hunger and thirst for righteousness [justice], for they will be filled.

Matthew 5:6

Woe to you, scribes and Pharisees, hypocrites! For you tithe mint, dill, and cummin, and have neglected the weightier matters of the law: justice and mercy and faith.

Matthew 23:23

. . . Who through faith conquered kingdoms, administered justice.

Hebrews 11:33

The above texts are, of course, only a sampling of the many biblical references to justice, and beyond those references are many allusions to actions that correspond to justice, without mention of the term.

An examination of the Hebrew and Greek words used for justice reveals that they are sometimes translated "judgment" and "righteousness." The main Hebrew words are *mishpat* (justice, judgment) and *tsedaqah* (righteousness, justice). The primary Greek words are *dikaiosune* (justice, righteousness), *krima* (judgment, justice), and *krisis* (judgment, decision, justice).

When we probe the meaning and usage of these words throughout Scripture, we find that they are used in different ways, with the same word carrying various meanings in different contexts. For example, at times justice refers to God's retributive justice or judgment, which is closely linked to God's holiness. At other times God's righteousness/justice (*tsedaqah, dikaiosune*) is what meets the demands of God's holiness and retributive justice, thereby procuring human salvation through Christ's death on the cross. Thus, the apostle Paul states that through Christ's atoning death God shows his righteousness "to prove at the present time that he himself is righteous [*dikaiosune*] and that he justifies the one who has faith in Jesus" (Rom. 3:26). Through God's saving work in Christ, recipients of divine grace are now declared righteous or just, in the sense that Christ's own righteousness/justice becomes our own before our maker (Rom. 4:24; Gal. 3:6). But this righteousness is not merely a forensic declaration; it is also a way of life to be pursued by those who by faith have experienced God's justifying work of grace through Christ.

The striking feature of many biblical texts is the way righteousness and justice, in terms of human character and actions, go hand in hand and are intimately related. What are we to make of this? Righteousness (as both God's declaration through justification and the resulting outworking in our moral lives) can never be far removed from justice. Thus, to be a righteous person because of the work of Christ is also to be a just person. While we tend to think of righteousness primarily in terms of character or personal actions, its link to justice demonstrates that it invariably has a social dimension, a reality sometimes obscured by particular translations of the Bible. How do we discern whether the Hebrew and Greek words should be translated "righteousness" or "justice"? "A rule of thumb is that when one sees *righteousness* or *judgment* in the context of social responsibility or oppression, one can assume that *justice* would be a better translation."[5] And yet human justice in the social arena is ultimately rooted in God's own justice, made possible through his own righteousness, which then overflows to us. If God's work of righteousness does not result in both personal righteousness and social justice, then we can say with James that faith without works is dead (James 2:17, 26).

Though the Bible contains much teaching on justice, it is not always clear as to what justice actually entails. In other words, what is due human beings from the biblical perspective? To answer that question we need to move beyond the mere statements of the biblical texts to see them in their contexts and in relationship to the entire biblical narrative. That is, we need to develop a theology of justice (we will return to this in a later section). From a cursory overview of the texts themselves, however, several things stand out about the content of justice. First, justice is associated with fairness and integrity, as in fair trials (Lev. 19:15; Deut. 16:18–20) and just weights or measures (Lev. 19:35–36). Second, justice is right living in all areas of life (Isa. 1:16–17; 26:7). In the biblical understanding, one cannot be just in relation to social issues and lack personal character, or have personal character and lack social justice. This follows not only from texts that combine the two but also from the interchangeability of the various words translated "justice" and "righteousness." Third, as evidenced in many of the texts cited earlier, justice is clearly associated with a special concern for the oppressed, the poor, and those who lack the means of self-sufficiency. This stands in contrast to many historic conceptions of justice. As Nicholas Wolterstorff notes, "By contrast, when Plato in *The Republic* spoke of the just society, widows, orphans, aliens and the impoverished were nowhere in view. The fundamental contour of justice was identified by Plato with a certain kind of 'law and order.'"[6]

As we attempt to work out the biblical concept of justice amid the complexities of life, we are faced with some immediate questions: What is the relationship between justice and love? What is the relationship between justice and freedom?

Which understanding of justice (i.e., what is due people) best reflects the Christian worldview? From whom or what is justice owed? How we seek to relate Christian ethics to the cultures and societies in which we live is related to these questions.

LOVE AND JUSTICE

People often speak of justice and love as if they go hand in hand and are virtually the same. The Bible sometimes proclaims them in the same breath, as when Micah says that the Lord requires justice and mercy (6:8), or Hosea admonishes, "Sow for yourselves righteousness [or justice, *tsedaqah*]; reap steadfast love" (10:12). But an examination of the issues relative to these two moral norms reveals that things are not so simple. For example, the opening narrative about Mickey Mantle shows that love will not solve the moral quandary surrounding organ transplants. Or take the example of racial justice. Love alone did not end slavery or procure the necessary civil rights laws to facilitate justice in the United States. In fact, during the slavery era, some owners no doubt showed a kind of love to their slaves, treating them with compassion and mercy, but such love never got to the fundamental issue of what was owed the slaves as human beings created in the image of God. Justice, as a moral concept, was needed to bring an end to slavery, for love alone (at least thought of in terms of personal mercy and compassion) was insufficient.

What is the relationship between love and justice? Theologians and ethicists have long debated this issue, and there are several views. Emil Brunner, the twentieth-century neoorthodox theologian from Switzerland, argued that love and justice are two different things. Love, which ultimately is comprehended only by faith, is most visibly revealed in Jesus Christ. Love, according to Brunner, is always personal in nature, as it seeks to respond to a particular person in his or her uniqueness. But "justice is a totally different thing. When we are just, and deal justly, we render to the other what is his due. Justice makes no free gift; it gives precisely what is due to the other, no more and no less. Its basis is strictly realistic, sober and rational."[7] While love always regards a person in light of his or her particular context and needs, justice is always in a sense blind.

Brunner saw justice related to the world of systems and institutions, a realm in which love cannot sufficiently operate. A person of love, acting in institutions, must turn his or her love into justice or run the risk of ruining institutional life. "Love which is not just in the world of institutions is sentimentality. And sentimentality, feeling for feeling's sake, is the poison, the solvent that destroys all just institutions."[8] Thus, within the world of institutions, we must essentially change our mode of operation from love to justice in order that people receive their due. Love can certainly do more than justice within the personal realm, but Brunner believed that justice is always the precondition of love, and love can never render justice void. In essence then, for Brunner, love is the operating virtue in personal relationships patterned after the *agape* love of Christ. Justice, known by reason, is the operating virtue in the institutions of society. Both are needed, each in its own sphere.

Some who follow Brunner's lead of separating justice and love emphasize that because the state cannot love, it has no role in meeting economic welfare needs. Responding to the needs of humans in their economic deprivation is a responsibility of individuals and is motivated by love. Because the state is the sphere of justice and not love, it cannot respond to specific human need; it can only establish just or fair procedures in economics and carry out retributive justice.[9]

There is, of course, a sense in which Brunner's separation of love and justice for differing spheres of life is correct. Frequently, love is more personal in nature, and justice more related to institutions. We can love people, but it is quite difficult to love institutional patterns and processes. But the problem with this view is twofold. First, it does not accord with Scripture, in which love and justice are interrelated and closely held together. Second, separating love and justice too far allows institutional life and the state to boil justice down to a few basic rights. This form of justice misses its full biblical understanding. When love, as virtue and principle, is removed from the person effecting justice, that person will likely lack the sensitivities needed to render justice.

Another view of love and justice is seen in the thinking of Reinhold Niebuhr. For Niebuhr, love and justice are not only distinct, as in Brunner's view, but are also often in tension with each other. Niebuhr, as a social realist, believed that the ethics of Jesus (with its emphasis on love and the kingdom of God) could never be a guide in the rough and tumble of societal life. It could not be a guide amid the competing claims and interests of institutions, societies, and nations. In fact, in such spheres love could actually do harm. In those spheres, only justice is applicable, and its demands are at times in tension with *agape* love. Moreover, the justice that is applicable in societal spheres is not ideal justice but a balance of power among the competing interests. As Niebuhr once described it:

> The New Testament never guarantees the historical success of the "strategy" of the cross [love]. . . . Since this possibility does not exist, it is not even right to insist that every action of the Christian must conform to *agape*, rather than to the norms of relative justice. . . . For as soon as the life and interest of others than the agent are involved in an action or policy, the sacrifice of those interests ceases to be "self-sacrifice." It may actually become an unjust betrayal of their interests.[10]

The sinfulness of humanity and the inability of social life to transcend the forces of history send love and justice in opposite directions, according to Niebuhr. Love is an "impossible possibility" that hovers over all we do and judges even the best intentions. It is never achievable. Justice is all we can hope for within the confines of historic contingency, and it will by necessity be a justice that seeks to balance the competing powers, though always with an eye toward increasing power for the victims of injustice. Justice for Niebuhr was a relative justice, a tolerable harmony between the competing claims of a sinful world. This means that "society must strive for justice even if it is forced to use means, such as self-assertion, resistance, coercion and even resentment, which cannot gain the moral sanction of the most sensitive moral spirit."[11]

Niebuhr was perhaps correct that tension can exist between love and justice in the midst of a fallen world. But are the Christian conceptions of justice and love defined primarily by the contingencies and complexities of history or by the transcendent beckoning of a God beyond us? The tension between individual and social morality is significant, but pulling them apart too far allows "morally upright" people too much latitude in the administration of justice. Niebuhr allowed "industrial groups, societies and governments a disturbing amount of license"[12] in the name of justice.

How then should we think about love and justice? Richard Higginson has wisely suggested that love and justice mutually supplement each other. Love needs justice, and justice needs love. While love tends to be personal and justice institutional, separating them into distinct spheres (Brunner) or setting them in tension (Niebuhr) is not only contrary to biblical teaching but also fails to appreciate their mutual reinforcement in the midst of historic situations. As Higginson notes, love must provide a supplement to the verdict of justice:

> Where justice makes life hard for someone, love remains attentive to the individual's needs, and seeks to mitigate the harshness of the verdict. If justice does dictate that long-term considerations take priority over short-term ones, love does its utmost to make those immediate consequences bearable. If society was ever to adopt a stricter abortion law, then it is vital that compassion be awakened for many thousands of unhappy women who will be expected to go through pregnancies against their will.[13]

At the same time, justice must be a supplement to love, for "awe-inspiring though love is as an ethical principle, it requires direction and in some cases correction from the principle of justice."[14] As Higginson sees it, justice has the ability to look beyond the immediate needs calling for love to the long-term commitments. Similarly, "Love tends to respond to the most eye-catching and desperate types of need, whereas justice demands that one spreads one's gaze rather more widely." Thus, "A just ordering of medical resources is sensitive to the whole gamut of human need,"[15] not merely the glaring needs that catch us emotionally. Justice also directs love by exposing the structural dimensions of social or ethical issues, thus requiring not just charity but actual changes in the way things operate.

The mutual supplementing of love and justice is evident in issues of race relations. Justice calls for policies and procedures that ensure races and ethnic groups equal access to jobs, education, and power in society. Justice is sensitive to past wrongs and seeks to overcome them, addressing issues of institutional racism. But such justice may not improve actual relations among the various races or ethnic groups. Love calls for personal engagement among the groups so that prejudices are overcome and reconciliation occurs. Stopping at racial reconciliation will not complete the divine task in racial relations, for justice ensures that policies, laws, and structures render to people their due, simply because they are made in the image of God. But to stop at just policies, laws, and structures will not achieve God's vision for humanity either, for God desires that in our differences we learn empathy, understanding, and mercy. Justice and love must walk together. When they do, they nurture each other and guard against the excesses of a single principle or virtue pursued alone.

FREEDOM AND JUSTICE

Often freedom and justice are seen as going hand in hand or even as the same thing. In this common assumption, to pursue justice is to pursue freedom and vice versa. Freedom was particularly the cry of the Enlightenment philosophers as they sought to build societies free from tyranny, oppression, and external obstacles to human aspirations and desire. Life, liberty, and the pursuit of happiness (or wealth in the original version) was the mantra, often built on the assumption of human autonomy. Thus, a just society was a free society.

John Stuart Mill was a utilitarian who believed that justice was determined by maximizing good for the greatest number of people. But he believed that the most fundamental principle of society and the key to its justice was freedom. Mill wrote, "The only freedom which deserves the name is that of pursuing our own good in our own way, so long as we do not attempt to deprive others of theirs, or impede their efforts to obtain it."[16] For Mill and many other proponents of the supremacy of freedom, a good and just society is a free society.

But justice and freedom in real life do not always reside together so easily. The reality is that justice in some manner always limits freedom. This, of course, is obvious within the sphere of retributive justice, but it is also true concerning distributive justice. To grant someone his or her due invariably places limits on someone else's freedom to act as he or she sees fit. Conversely, a pursuit of freedom alone will never result in justice, though some argue for such.[17]

Take the example of abuses stemming from the work conditions during the burgeoning Industrial Revolution. As industrialism spread and market economies flourished, economic prosperity emerged, but often at the expense of many workers. Women and children were initially used in the coal mines because of their short stature, often for long periods of time and to the detriment of their health. There were virtually no safety regulations in factories, and it was quite common for workers to lose fingers and limbs or to be maimed for life. Employees had no rights, pay was poor, conditions were unhealthy, and six days of work for twelve hours a day took its toll on men, women, and children. The cries for justice, first heard in England, came from Christians such as Lord Shaftesbury, who led the way in championing labor laws to procure justice and dignity in the workplace.[18] The pleas for justice were countered by cries for freedom. Many of the industrialists argued that workers were free to come and go as they pleased; they did not have to work in the factories. Moreover, factory owners believed that because they owned the factories, they should have the freedom to run them as they saw fit. If freedom in the workplace was not honored, they would go out of business. Freedom was essential to the economic market.

Justice in these situations clearly meant a limitation on entrepreneurs' freedom. Laws that limited working hours, required safety devices on the machines, and stipulated ventilation in the factories limited the freedom of some for the justice of others. Of course, debates have ensued since those days as to the limits of both labor and management claims, but the point is that freedom for some is curtailed for the sake of justice.

A similar example can be seen with regard to ecological justice. Many have argued that justice is about how we treat not only humans but also the environment, which in turn affects human beings. There is a biblical mandate for caring for the earth and its resources, but it is clear that demands of justice with regard to the environment place limits on the pursuits of humans. Some today argue that economic freedom and the need to meet human needs call for limits to environmental justice, while others argue that economic freedom and prosperity must be limited for the sake of environmental justice and ultimately human health. Environmentalist debates invariably come down to debates about freedom versus justice.

As Christians, what are we to make of the tension between the two? True Christian freedom is found in relationship with God through Christ and the way of life that follows: "If you continue in my word, you are truly my disciples; and you will know the truth, and the truth will make you free" (John 8:31). But political freedom can also be argued from several biblical and theological sources: human creation in the image of God, the story and paradigm of the exodus, and the existence of the church as a distinct entity apart from the government's jurisdiction.

Perhaps the kind of society that best reflects the Christian worldview is one that maintains a tension between justice, freedom, and order.[19] A society that has a singular focus on justice will lack freedom and overly accentuate order, as witnessed by Marxist or communist governments of the twentieth century. A society with a singular focus on freedom will lack justice and order, tending toward anarchy. And a society that focuses solely on order will lack justice and freedom, tending toward totalitarianism. Holding the three together will not solve all public policy debates and certainly will not inevitably lead to one specific political ideology. But it does provide a framework for Christians seeking to apply their moral commitment to a complex, fallen world. It is, moreover, a framework that Christians can appeal to in a pluralistic world in which people do not share the Christian worldview assumptions.

WHAT IS DUE? DEFINITIONS OF JUSTICE

Most of the debates about justice today ultimately boil down to the definitions employed: What do we actually owe people in given situations of life? The varying definitions lead to divergent views regarding a host of issues. Essentially, there are three primary theories or paradigms for defining distributive justice: merit, equality, and need.[20]

Meritorious Justice

Justice understood as merit focuses on what is owed a person by virtue of his or her actions, efforts, and impact. In this version, there is impartiality in rewarding human effort, with a minimal focus on actual outcomes. Justice is best achieved by establishing fair procedures within a given sphere of activity and then rewarding people according to what they merit. As long as just mechanisms are in place, merit is deemed the best way to reward people, even though the rewards for merit will often vary significantly even for similar kinds of activities. Generally this view has espoused a minimal role for government in distributive justice. Merit is not understood in terms of a person's role or position in life but in terms of what that person actually performs within his or her role or position.

If this definition of justice is used to decide who gets an organ transplant, an immediate answer will not be found. The question will remain, What form of merit? Ability to pay, one's efforts to procure an organ, or one's contribution to society and the immediate community? Many who espouse this definition would argue that it is not an approach for issues such as scarce medical resources, in which merit is difficult to define, but it is a good approach for areas such as economics and education.

A number of Christian scholars have argued for this view of distributive justice on the grounds that the Bible calls for a limited state and thus precludes federal actions to ensure egalitarian outcomes or appeals to human need as the basis for public policy. Ronald Nash believes that unbridled "statism" is the result of egalitarian or need-based theories of justice. He argues that "the widespread tendency to connect moral and economic merit ought to be avoided. Because many people are offended by the fact that someone who is less deserving in a moral sense is worth more economically, they believe steps should be taken to alter the situation through statist action."[21] What justice calls for, says Nash, are just procedures that ensure that there is no way of knowing ahead of time what the results will be. Nash does not use the term merit justice, but that is clearly the sentiment of his theory once just procedures are in place. Merit is clearly evidenced in his assertion that "while each person should be given an equal chance to enjoy the best possible life, it is sometimes necessary to give extra attention to the especially gifted. Since the gifted are often people who lead society, aiding them helps all within society. At the very least, society should place no obstacle in the path of the more gifted."[22] Similarly, Calvin Beisner argues for a minimalist, procedural justice that prevents fraud, theft, and violence. The Christian conception of justice in economics "requires that people be permitted to exchange and use what they own . . . freely so long as in so doing they do not violate others' rights."[23] Beisner believes, therefore, that minimum wage laws, racial quotas for employment, laws requiring equal pay for equal work, and legal restrictions on imports and exports are all unjust.

Both Beisner and Nash seem to reflect the philosophical influence of Robert Nozick. Writing from a purely rational framework, Nozick argues for a minimal state with a few basic rights: the right to freely choose our course of action in life, the right to own property, and the right against injury by others. Following Kant, he believes that we should treat people as ends, not merely as means, and grant them natural rights that are inherent within their nature. The state's only responsibility is to protect those basic rights and ensure fair mechanisms for pursuing them. Nozick's basic principle is that whatever happens from a just situation by just procedures is just. He believes that "past circumstances or actions of people can create . . . differential deserts to things,"[24] and it is clearly unjust for the state to reverse those outcomes. The minimal state allows people the freedom to pursue their own goals, limited only by harm to others. "Treating us with respect by respecting our rights, it allows us . . . to choose our life and to realize our ends . . . aided by the voluntary cooperation of other individuals possessing the same dignity."[25] While Nozick says he rejects any formula of "to each according to . . . ," including merit, once his procedures are in place, his theory is closest to the merit view.

What are Christians to make of the merit view of justice? Clearly, there are spheres of life in which what people are owed ought to reflect their effort and expertise. Most people agree that grades in the academic arena ought to reflect merit—the effort and quality of work from the student. Moreover, it also seems just that in economic exchanges merit should be significant in what is owed. If two people—doing the same job—reflect differences in energy, expertise, and output, they should be rewarded according to merit. Indeed, when people in the marketplace are not rewarded for the amount and quality of their work, not only are they demoralized but society itself also suffers. Furthermore, there are biblical grounds for merit. Second Thessalonians 3:10 states, "Anyone unwilling to work should not eat," and Jesus said, "Laborers deserve their food" (Matt. 10:10; cf. Luke 10:7). In the parable of the talents told by Jesus in Matthew 25:14–30, there is reward for those who wisely invested and demerit for the one who wasted his resource.

But is the merit understanding of justice sufficient for all circumstances of life? Do we want to settle the organ transplant issue on the basis of some form of merit? Many believe that if people received organs based on their creative efforts to get an organ or their ability to pay, only the wealthy and powerful would ever receive transplants. There seems to be something about the nature of organ transplants, with human life in the balance, that calls for a different approach. Even the idea that Mickey Mantle should not have received a liver on the basis of his lifestyle (a demerit) seems problematic in practice. Do we really want finite, sinful creatures to decide who lives and who dies on the basis of issues related to lifestyle? Certainly, lifestyle might be weighed as a medical factor, but that is different from making it a decisive element of justice. Wisely, the transplant system in the United States has not employed the merit definition of justice.

But what about economic life, the realm most talked about by the defenders of this definition? Do we really want merit alone to determine how mentally handicapped people are compensated economically? Are they owed a meager existence because their mental capacity precludes them from ever meriting economic rewards? If we allow merit alone to determine all of economic life, we will find it difficult to meet the biblical challenge to care for the least of our brothers and sisters. Of course, one can argue that caring for them is the work of compassion or love, to be meted out by individuals and the church. But in a complex, fallen world, in which injustices abound and many are outside the reach of compassionate communities, we are still left with the question as to whether government has a role in procuring justice for the economically disenfranchised.

Merit clearly must be part of the picture in regard to justice, but taken alone it can never achieve God's designs arid standards of justice.

Egalitarian Justice

Egalitarian justice encompasses two forms: equal outcomes and equal access. In the first form, justice is defined by the actual outcome of reaching some type of equality. Since all humans in their very being are of equal value, they ought to be compensated in the various spheres of life in basically the same way. Various forms of socialism have tended toward the equal outcome definition, and some feminists have pursued this course as well. The most obvious problem is that in history this egalitarian utopianism has not worked. Such a system treats people unfairly in order to produce equal outcomes (thereby nullifying both merit and need), and it tends toward an all-encompassing political structure to achieve them.

The more popular form of egalitarianism has been the equal access approach, whereby all people are ensured equal access to jobs, rights, housing, and pay. This does not mean that all people will get the jobs they want or entrance into the schools they desire, but no personal or external factors will prevent people from fairly competing for the rights and goods available in a given society. Within this definition, "Justice can be understood to mean similar treatment for similar cases. . . . All those who are in a comparable situation should be treated equally."[26] Egalitarian justice generally calls for a more activistic government than does merit justice to ensure that people have equal access to the rights, goods, and privileges within society and that they are treated similarly in similar situations.

If we employ this definition of justice to decide who gets the organs when there are not enough to go around, we will emphasize a procedure that ensures that all people have an equal opportunity to receive an organ. Clearly, there will not be equal outcomes, which this definition never ensures, but each person will have the same opportunity to receive an organ. In its pure form, this approach does not consider need or merit.

The name most often associated with egalitarian justice is John Rawls, the moral and political philosopher who taught for many years at Harvard and authored *A Theory of Justice*, deemed by some to be one of the most pivotal works on the topic. For Rawls, justice is the first virtue of social institutions, as it relates to the fitting allocation of duties, rights, and benefits to people who participate freely and equally in political society. Justice is particularly relevant in those social situations in which there may be disagreements over entitlements or a scarcity of resources. The heart of justice in these situations is fairness, achieved by a "veil of ignorance" that precludes certain kinds of knowledge that could make the distribution unfair.

Within this general framework, Rawls sets forth two primary principles to determine justice.[27] The first is the principle of equal liberty in which "each person is to have an equal right to the most extensive total system of equal basic liberties compatible with a similar system of liberty for all."[28] Given the reality that society is never a "zero sum game," there will not be equal outcomes, but theoretically equality would be the outcome if society started from that reality. Because there will be differences of outcome in the competition for scarce resources and in the disagreements over rights, Rawls proposes a second principle for achieving justice: maximize the minimum. Rawls states, "Social and economic inequalities, for example inequalities of wealth and authority, are just only if they result in compensating benefits for everyone, and in particular for the least advantaged members of society."[29] In the allocation of rights and goods, the only social and economic inequalities in the distribution must be aimed at advantaging the least advantaged. Rawls's two principles are focused primarily on the macro-level in society, not the micro-level. That is, they "are geared toward the basic structure of society, not toward every act of every level where justice is a concern."[30]

How should we assess egalitarian justice? The theme of equality has been central to modern democracies. It has given people hope that no matter what their background, color, or status in society, they will have in principle an equal access to its rights, goods, and liberties. While this, of course, is never fully achieved, it nonetheless grants to all human beings a vision of fairness and a confidence that in principle the social system will not treat them according to external characteristics such as race, gender, ethnicity, or religion. Egalitarian justice has been the foundation of basic human rights.

While equality as we speak of it today is primarily a child of the Enlightenment, there are biblical and theological foundations for the concept. Creation in the image of God means that every human being bears an equal dignity and value before God that ought to be honored by society. That is the ultimate foundation for any concept of human rights, sense of fairness, or vision of equality. The Old Testament law mandated equality in the judicial procedures: "You shall not render an unjust judgment; you shall not be partial to the poor or defer to the great: with justice you shall judge your neighbor" (Lev. 19:15). Jesus echoed an egalitarian note when he said that the Father in heaven "makes his sun rise on the evil and on the good, and sends rain on the righteous and on the unrighteous" (Matt. 5:45).

But the egalitarian definition of justice also faces some challenges. A practical problem is determining what equal access or fairness looks like in real life. A few years ago a rather humorous but nonetheless serious issue emerged in the state legislature of Virginia—the debate over "potty parity." As the news reported it, "A legislator decided to go against the flow when he noticed how much more time women spent in restrooms than men, so he penned a 'potty parity' resolution to help relieve the situation."[31] The legislator contended that the state plumbing code, which called for a 50-50 ratio of space for men's and women's restrooms, was essentially discriminatory. The equal space code did not take into consideration the fact that urinals occupy less space than toilet stalls, and hence, men's restrooms have more facilities. Moreover, elderly people take longer in restrooms, and there are more elderly women than men. Beyond that, women often have children with them. The result, contended the legislator, is that women's restrooms should be larger than men's. This story makes the point well: Equality does not take into consideration the contextual factors or specific needs concerning an issue.

Some have critiqued equality on the grounds that it will not redress past injustices. That is, if unjust procedures and actions have existed in the past, there may need to be some form of redress, or equal access can never become a reality.[32] Others have argued that equality too easily negates the role of merit, the effort and quality of individuals in their pursuit of the goods and privileges of society. For example, Rawls's second principle seems to assume an equal effort by the least advantaged of society. There are, of course, many reasons for being disadvantaged in a society, but surely one of them has to do with effort. Still others have been concerned with the way in which egalitarian justice seems to proliferate the state's entrance into domains of life in which it should not play a role. Obviously, at this point, one's understanding of the nature and role of the state plays a significant role in one's definition of justice.

Need Justice

In need justice, what individuals are owed is based primarily on their concrete needs in a given sphere. The defenders of this approach believe that at times equality must be laid aside to respond to the specific needs of individuals or groups of people within society. Frequently, adherents focus on redressing past injustices that the principle of equality is not able to reverse. They believe that the merit approach too easily allows for rewards that are inevitably tied up with status and privilege in society, and they generally call for an activistic government to address the concrete needs of individuals and groups who have not shared adequately in society's rights and resources. The approach is captured by Marx's famous statement, "From each according to his ability, to each according to his need."[33]

If we take this approach in determining who gets an organ for transplant, we will focus on the greatest need at the moment. Decisions will not be made based on who merits the organ or on an egalitarian principle such as a lottery method. If taken alone, this definition calls for the sickest person at the moment to receive the scarce medical resource.

To some extent we have already been introduced to this definition of justice in John Rawls's second principle, acting for the benefit of the least advantaged in society. While Rawls's approach is fundamentally egalitarian in nature, he employs a kind of need justice in giving special attention to those who are at the bottom of economic society.

From a Christian perspective, this definition of justice has been clearly articulated by Stephen Mott and Ronald Sider. Mott believes that justice must be attentive to the unique needs of those to whom God has shown special care, the poor and disenfranchised. He believes that equality alone will not address the needs of those who cannot compete successfully in the world. Thus, "The equal provision of basic rights requires unequal response to unequal needs. Justice must be partial in order to be impartial."[34] Mott argues that biblical justice is dominated by the idea of redress, which means attempts must be made to correct the inequalities of the past and hence to allow for more equitable justice to take over. "The goal of redress is to return people to a normal level of advantage and satisfaction in the community, particularly with respect to the capacity to earn a living." He sees the Year of Jubilee in Leviticus 25 as a clear indication that God desires redress, meaning justice as response to need, especially needs created by past injustices. Thus, Mott contends, "When the number of sufferers becomes too large, private charity cannot cope with the ills of society; love then requires structural measures to achieve social justice."[35]

Sider joins Mott in heralding need as the essential biblical understanding of justice. In an article written together, they rehearse the numerous biblical texts that speak of God lifting up the poor and oppressed, tearing down the rich and powerful, and inviting his people to share in that divine action. They note, "Hundreds of biblical verses show that God is especially attentive to the poor and needy. God is not biased. But because of unequal needs, however, equal provision of basic rights requires justice to be partial in order to be impartial. . . . Partiality to the weak is the most striking characteristic of biblical justice."[36]

It is quite clear that this view has generated some of the strongest heat in the debates about justice, in part because of its affinity to Marx's dictum quoted earlier: "From each according to his ability, to each according to his need." But this view does not necessarily entail a Marxist understanding of reality or economics. The view has appeal in its contention that love and justice must be held closely together; what love begins, justice must complete. Unlike the merit and egalitarian understandings, this approach wants "blindfolded" fairness, along with a clear vision of human and historical realities. It argues that the other understandings of justice are not as attuned to what is happening in the world.

In Scripture, justice and human need are often held together. The texts listed near the beginning of this chapter reveal God's special concern for the weak and least in society and the call for God's people to respond. Some might contend that these texts do not call for government but the covenant people to respond. But clearly we cannot get around the biblical teaching that "the LORD maintains the cause of the needy, and executes justice for the poor" (Ps. 140:12). As Mary put it in the Magnificat, "He has brought down the powerful from their thrones, and lifted up the lowly; he has filled the hungry with good things, and sent the rich away empty" (Luke 1:52–53).

While need justice has strong biblical and emotional appeal (i.e., compassion), it also faces some challenges. One of the major challenges is in discerning the need of a person or group. It is easy to respond to a visible and immediate need and not touch the deeper, long-term need. For example, slowly American society is awakening to the reality that welfare or aid to the poor does not really address the most fundamental needs of the poor: the need for dignity, self-worth, opportunity, and skills, whereby they could enter into the economic realm with new possibilities. A system that focuses purely on the need of the moment does not address these more fundamental human needs, which are at the heart of a Christian understanding of reality. Work in the biblical framework is a creation mandate and a significant means not only of livelihood but of self-worth and camaraderie with others. Clearly, many government programs that attempt to be compassionate and achieve justice have frequently worked against these more fundamental needs. Thus, a just government is one that allows work to flourish and people to participate in the economic arena. At the same time, we must recognize that there will always be some who are not able to participate adequately in the economic realm because of physical, emotional, or contextual limitations. Need justice must come into play in these situations, though in a way that does not demean these individuals or severely limit economic opportunity within society.

There is a second danger associated with need justice: Human need can move one to sentimentality and away from the dimension of justice as fairness. As we have seen, justice in the biblical sense is not only a response to human need but a pursuit of fairness in treatment. Historically, justice has often been signified by a blindfold, which symbolizes its transcendence of historical realities that at times can easily distort vision and perspective.

For example, people are often moved by feelings of compassion at the sight of human need, but in reality the most visible form of compassion is sometimes not the ethical or just course of action. There are times when a person might, for the sake of justice, have to let someone go from a job because that person has not performed the work or is a detriment to the functioning of others. Such an act may seem cold and compassionless, but at the same time it is the most just action for the other workers, for the company as a whole, and perhaps even for the worker.

Similarly, if we look to need justice alone regarding the issue of abortion, we may get caught up in the singular appeal of compassion for the mother's plight or the "need" to use embryonic stem cells for research. In such situations, human need and appeals to compassion overlook justice and what is owed those human lives that are most vulnerable to the designs and "needs" of others. Need justice, by itself, can easily turn into sentimentality.

Need justice is one dimension of just actions and a just society, but taken alone it is inadequate. It does not sufficiently allow for merit, in places where merit should count, and it does not give adequate due to fairness and equality.

An Evaluation of Definitions

It is evident that there is theological and biblical support for all three definitions of justice. As a result, it may be helpful to recognize that the different definitions of justice apply to different activities and spheres of reality. As William

Werpehowski puts it, "Specification of justice requires specification of criteria appropriate to the nature of the relationship in question."[37] In some spheres of life, the various definitions need to be held together in a creative tension.

In the economic realm, merit must play a significant role to do justice to one's effort, expertise, and responsibility and to maintain productivity for the entire society. Without productivity human need is not met, and justice is not rendered. At the same time, people need equal opportunity when applying for jobs or seeking advancement. Simultaneously, there must be provisions for those who are poor and those who find it difficult to enter into the economic rewards of society. This does not entail a particular commitment to political ideology, for justice in principle transcends ideology. Ethically sensitive Christians must be committed to such areas of justice regardless of their political persuasion.

Other realms of life require differing scenarios of justice. Currently, the United States transplant system uses a combination of need (i.e., sickest patients) and egalitarian considerations. The complex system is not without its problems, but in principle a combination of these two definitions seems to best fit that sphere of life.

When it comes to political rights, housing, and educational opportunities, an egalitarian justice seems to be most appropriate. We should not allow one group a disproportionate amount of political power for the sake of securing that group's interests. Such an approach clearly stereotypes a given group in society as having only one set of perspectives or interests and hence destroys the dignity of each individual.

Obviously, defining justice is no easy matter. Attempting to discern the appropriate definition or combination of definitions for the various spheres of human activity is a challenge that calls for clear thinking and analysis that moves beyond ideological commitments.

FROM WHOM OR WHAT IS JUSTICE OWED?

One more issue often divides people today in discussions about justice. Who or what is responsible for justice? The state, citizens, the Christian church, or Christian individuals? Most Christians would argue that the Bible means what it says when it speaks of God's compassion for the poor and the need for a commitment to justice on their behalf. But some people do not think this is primarily the role of the state. Others believe that when the Bible speaks of social justice the primary mediator is government. In these debates, the issue is not always different definitions of justice or even variant interpretations of biblical texts. Sometimes the debate hinges on differing understandings about the nature and role of the state.

The central question here is whether the state has the responsibility to ensure justice or whether justice is the domain of individuals and the church. If both have a role, which spheres of justice reside with the government and which spheres reside with individuals and the church? Most Christians agree that the Bible is clear on the issue of retributive justice—the punishment meted out for breaking the law, harming others, and violating other people's rights. As Romans 13 indicates, this sphere of justice is not In the hands of individuals or the church but the state. The larger debates involve distributive justice, particularly in the realm of economic life. While it seems clear that government ought to have laws that protect basic rights, property, and ensure equal opportunity for all, it is not immediately clear how far government should go in seeking distributive justice economically.

When we look to Scripture and theological paradigms, we do not find immediate answers to these issues, but we can garner some basic understandings that give us perspective and general direction. First, it is certainly clear that justice is a responsibility of individuals. While it always has a social dimension, justice ought to be deeply entrenched in a Christian's personal character and a firmly held principle for making judgments in a complex world. The fact that the Bible uses the same words for righteousness and justice and holds the two together in various texts implies that individual believers are responsible for justice in all the spheres of life into which God places them.

Second, Christians should maintain some caution regarding the extent to which the state regulates and carries out distributive justice. If the state holds justice, freedom, and order together, it will invariably be limited in its efforts at achieving justice. A society focused exclusively on distributive justice will not be a free society; a society fixated on freedom will not be ordered or just. Christian ambivalence about the state can also be argued from biblical teaching in which the state is described as both servant and beast. In Romans 13, the state is a servant for good and is to be obeyed and not rendered inoperative by the Christian church (cf. 1 Peter 2:13–17). Revelation 13, however, portrays the state as a beast and an enemy of the church. In similar fashion, Jesus refers to Herod, a government official, in derogatory fashion as a fox (Luke 13:32), and in Acts, the early apostles engage in civil disobedience by not heeding the government's policy forbidding evangelism. They proclaim in the court, "We must obey God rather than any human authority" (5:29). Similar ambivalence about government is also found in the Old Testament. Queen Esther comes to the halls of power in Persia for "such a time as this" (Esther 4:14), but at the same time there is grave concern about Israel having a king like the governments of surrounding nations (1 Samuel 8).

Thus, biblical and theological understandings of the state preclude us from giving a carte blanche to human governments, even if we see the state as ordained by God from creation and not merely a result of the fall.[38] Christians should be predisposed to question a state that becomes so expansive that it limits both individual initiative and the significant role that other mediating institutions (i.e., family, church, voluntary organizations) can play in society.

Third, there is biblical support for the role of government in distributive justice, amid caution about government and instruction concerning the role that individuals and mediating institutions should play. In a petition for the king of Israel, the psalmist prays, "Give the king your justice, O God, and your righteousness to a king's son. May he judge your people with righteousness, and your poor with justice. . . . May he defend the cause of the poor . . . give deliverance to the needy" (Ps. 72:1–2, 4). Similar passages calling for governmental action are Psalm 45:4, Jeremiah 21:12, and Amos 5:12, 15. One might object to this view, stating that Israel's government at the time was more akin to the church today than to secular, human governments. In one sense that is true, for Israel was called to be God's people, just as the church is today. Nonetheless, Israel, unlike the church, was also a nation and with its own sinful proclivities was given mandates for justice, not only of a retributive nature. Moreover, throughout the Old Testament, not only Hebrew kings were called to justice; even the pagan kings were expected to rule with justice (Prov. 8:15–18; 31:8–9; Dan. 4:27).

Thus, while individuals and churches must play a role in distributive justice, and while Christians must be cautious regarding an all-encompassing state, the state has a significant role to play in effecting justice in society. At the same time, we need to realize that in the personal-rights-oriented society of today, many negate personal responsibility when it comes to issues of justice. Perhaps one of the most neglected arenas is the role that family breakdown plays in poverty. The impact of divorce on families is staggering in terms of poverty, and most children born outside marriage live in households that are extremely poor.[39] Justice can never be too far removed from the choices people make and the lifestyles people live. To make justice the domain of government alone is to negate personal responsibility and to expect too much of this necessary but fallen institution.

CONCLUSION

Justice is always a concern in human societies. And justice is a major theme of the Bible. As this chapter has shown, however, justice is a complex issue. The biblical understandings of justice relative to merit, equality, need, love, and freedom do not render a clear picture of exactly how justice should be accomplished in society. The government certainly has a role in distributive justice, but it should not negate or overwhelm the unique role that individuals and mediating institutions can and should play. Moreover, Christians have reason to be concerned about an expansive state that dominates and controls spheres of life that are not intended for the impersonal, bureaucratic rule of government agencies.

Clearly, then, Christians and all peoples will continue to debate what justice should look like in society and how it should be effected. What Christians cannot evade is the biblical mandate to "let justice roll down like waters, and righteousness like an ever-flowing stream" (Amos 5:24).

NOTES

1. Bart Barnes, "Mick Mantle, Legend of Baseball, Dies at 63," *Washington Post,* 14 August 1995.
2. "Mantle Illness Impacts Organ Donor Program," Associated Press, 14 August 1995.

3. "Critical Data: U.S. Facts About Transplantation," from the United Network of Organ Sharing, www.unog.org. The 77,000 is for July 2001, and the number of organ transplants (22,854) is for the year 2000.

4. Peter Richardson, "Justice," in *Baker's Dictionary of Christian Ethics,* ed. Car. F. H. Henry (Grand Rapids: Baker, 1973), 361.

5. Stephen Mott, *Biblical Ethics and Social Change* (New York: Oxford University Press, 1982), 59.

6. Nicholas Wolterstorff, "Justice and Peace," in *New Dictionary of Christian Ethics and Pastoral Theology,* ed. David J. Atkinson, David F. Field, Arthur Holmes, and Oliver O'Donovan (Downers Grove, Ill.: InterVarsity Press, 1995), 18.

7. Emil Brunner, *Justice and the Social Order* (London: Lutterworth Press, 1945), 115.

8. Ibid., 117.

9. In some of the earlier writings of Carl Henry, we find this view. See, for example, Carl Henry, *Aspects of Christian Social Ethics* (Grand Rapids: Eerdmans, 1964), 146–71.

10. Reinhold Niebuhr, *The Nature and Destiny of Man,* vol. 2, *Human Destiny* (New York: Scribners, 1964), 87–88.

11. Reinhold Niebuhr, *Moral Man and Immoral Society* (New York: Scribners, 1932), 237.

12. Richard Higginson, *Dilemmas: A Christian Approach to Moral Decision Making* (Louisville: Westminster/John Knox Press, 1988), 110.

13. Ibid., 183.

14. Ibid., 178.

15. Ibid., 180–81.

16. John Stuart Mill, *On Liberty* (New York: F. S. Crofts, 1947), 95.

17. See, for example, Robert Nozick, *Anarchy, State, and Utopia* (New York: Basic Books, 1974).

18. Earle Cairns, *Saints and Society: The Social Impact of Eighteenth-Century Revivals and Its Contemporary Relevance* (Chicago: Moody Press, 1960).

19. Dennis Hollinger, "The Purpose of the State: A Theological Perspective," in *Politics and Public Policy: A Christian Response,* ed. Tim Demy and Gary Stewart (Grand Rapids: Kregel, 2000).

20. There have been other definitions offered and other typologies proposed. For a range of definitions and proponents, see Karen Lebacqz, *Six Theories of Justice: Perspectives from Philosophical and Theological Ethics* (Minneapolis: Augsburg Press, 1986).

21. Ronald Nash, *Social Justice and the Christian Church* (Milford, Mich.: Mott Media, 1983), 57.

22. Ibid., 37.

23. E. Calvin Beisner, *Prosperity and Poverty: The Compassionate Use of Resources in a World of Scarcity* (Westchester, Ill.: Crossway, 1988), 54.

24. Nozick, *Anarchy, State, and Utopia,* 155.

25. Ibid., 334.

26. Higginson, *Dilemmas,* 173.

27. For a helpful overview of Rawls's framework and principles of justice, see Lebacqz, *Six Theories*, 33–50.

28. John Rawls, *A Theory of Justice* (Cambridge: Harvard University Press, 1971), 302.

29. Ibid., 15.

30. Lebacqz, *Six Theories*, 40.

31. "Legislator Isn't Kidding About 'Potty Parity,'" *Elkhart Truth*, 9 May 1988, p. A1.

32. For a Christian defense of this perspective and the need for redress, see Mott, *Biblical Ethics and Social Change*, 65–72.

33. Karl Marx, *Critique of the Gotha Programme* (Peking: Foreign Language Press, 1972), 18.

34. Mott, *Biblical Ethics and Social Change*, 66.

35. Ibid., 68.

36. Stephen Mott and Ronald Sider, "Economic Justice: A Biblical Paradigm," in *Toward a Just and Caring Society: Christian Responses to Poverty in America*, ed. David P. Gushee (Grand Rapids: Baker, 1999), 27.

37. William Werpehowski, "Justice," in *The Westminster Dictionary of Christian Ethics*, ed. John MacQuaire (Philadelphia: Westminster Press, 1986), 331.

38. There has been considerable debate about this issue, whether God ordained the state from creation or whether it was a providential concession resulting from sin's entrance into the world with the fall.

39. For an excellent treatment of the role marriage and family play in poverty, see David P. Gushee, "Rebuilding Marriage and the Family," in *Toward a Just and Caring Society*, 499–530. Gushee combs through the literature showing the relationship between poverty and both marital dissolution and childbirth outside of marriage.

4. INTRODUCTION TO
SIX THEORIES OF JUSTICE

Karen Lebacqz

The following chapters contain excerpts from the book, Six Theories of Justice, *by Dr. Karen Lebacqz who is professor emeritus of Christian ethics at the Pacific School of Religion.*

There may be no more urgent cry today than that of "justice"—and no more frequent accusation than that of "injustice." But what is meant when these terms are used?

OF ELEPHANTS AND JUSTICE

Alasdair MacIntyre suggests that modern moral utterance must be understood as a series of "fragmented survivals" from the past: remnants of former ethical systems survive, but without the social cohesion needed to give them force.[1] Cries of justice and accusations of injustice appear as such fragments.

Justice is thus a bit like the proverbial elephant examined by blindfolded explorers. Each feels a different part—the foot, the ears, the tusks—and consequently each describes the beast differently—gnarled and tough, thin and supple, smooth and hard. The elephant itself—justice—is not encompassed by any of the individual descriptions. At times they seem incompatible. And yet, each contributes something to its definition.

This book is about justice. Six approaches to justice will be our blindfolded explorers. If MacIntyre's charge is true, then it is to be expected that these fragments will not be easily reconciled. There will be no single way of defining justice and no single theory of justice that satisfies all.

Indeed, the exploration is complicated at the outset because there is precious little agreement as to how the arena of justice is to be characterized and defined.[2] Do we seek for our elephant among mammals or reptiles? The theories to be examined here are roughly in the arena of "distributive justice." But one of our theorists explicitly rejects distributive justice in favor of the more narrow range of "commutative" justice (justice in exchange). And another approach adds to distributive justice a notion of "social justice" with a distinctive flavor.

Thus the views to be examined here are not theories of "distributive justice" in a narrow sense. They are simply theories of justice. Included in their concerns are questions about allocation of goods, powers, and opportunities, about access to decision-making processes, about fundamental respect among people, and about the basic structures of society. They attend to distributive justice in a broad sense: the issue is not simply, Who gets how much of the pie? but also, What kind of pie is it to be? and, Who is to decide?[3]

SIX FRAGMENTS ON JUSTICE

This book explores only six of those "fragmented survivals" of moral systems regarding justice—six ways of "making *mishpat* the measure" (Isa. 28:17). There are many other blindfolded explorers who might have served as well. The choice of six approaches to justice out of all possible contenders is not an easy task, and I make no claim that the six offered here are the only ones worthy of pursuit.

These six were chosen as representatives of different schools of thought. Though three of the fragments are forms of liberalism and three are forms of Christian theology, each offers a distinctive approach to justice. They were chosen also for accessibility: in all cases but one, the reader may supplement this text with a single accompanying document. But, above all, they were chosen in the conviction that each raises fundamental issues for other theories of justice. Each offers a perennial challenge to other contenders.

A Utilitarian Challenge

We begin with a utilitarian challenge. There are few unabashed utilitarians today. Since the theory of utilitarianism was first given definitive shape a century ago, it has been battered and batted around until it bears the scars of age. Yet, forms of utilitarianism linger in the "cost-benefit analyses" so popular in government circles. And the perennial question, *Does* the end justify the means? haunts contemporary proponents of justice. The significance of utilitarianism is perhaps best attested by the fact that it provides the foil for the other two contemporary philosophical theories that will be considered in this volume.

John Stuart Mill's *Utilitarianism* will represent the utilitarian approach to justice here. Mill's exposition lacks the systematic development and meticulous exposition of some later utilitarians, such as Henry Sidgwick or G. E. Moore; but his approach is more readily accessible than some others. And it is generally to Mill that contemporary theorists return when they wish to joust with utilitarianism. Thus Mill's understanding of justice gives us the original challenge and sets the stage for developing a theory of justice.

A Contract Response

One jouster responding to that challenge is John Rawls. No one disputes the importance of Rawls' massive effort, *A Theory of Justice*. This work has dominated philosophical reflections on justice for the last decade. There simply is no way to talk about justice today without attending to Rawls' response to the utilitarian challenge. Rawls draws on a contract model to offer a Kantian alternative to utilitarianism. He offers a defense of the liberal democratic state that takes "welfare" needs seriously.

An Entitlement Alternative

But Rawls' view is not the only response to utilitarianism. Robert Nozick's entitlement view of justice gives voice to the concerns of many liberals today. Where Rawls' contract theory would permit government involvement to bring about distributive justice, Nozick sets out to show that there is no moral ground for a distributive justice that demands structures of government beyond the minimal state. His *Anarchy, State and Utopia* has become—rightly or wrongly— the theory undergirding contemporary proponents of private enterprise and minimal government. It offers a clear alternative to both the utilitarian theory and to Rawls.

A Catholic Response

For all their differences, these three philosophical theories operate within a common "liberal" tradition. They share significant assumptions regarding the role and place of the individual as the bearer of moral value and the use of reason as the grounds for any theory of justice. Although Mill argued that utilitarianism was an expression of the golden rule, and many find Rawls' concern for the disadvantaged compatible with Christian sympathies, none of these philosophical theories depends directly on a religious base for its concept of justice. What happens, then, when we turn to the Christian tradition to see what views of justice it offers?

Here we begin with Catholic tradition. In the last hundred years that tradition has developed a multifaceted approach to social justice. Any number of papal encyclicals or other ecclesial documents might have been taken as an example of this approach in its development. The *Pastoral Letter on Catholic Social Teaching and the U.S. Economy* of the National Conference of Catholic Bishops is chosen because of its contemporary interest and its efforts to synthesize and incorporate the long tradition. And it offers a stark contrast to Nozick, arguing for a corporate rather than individualistic understanding of human beings and hence for a broader understanding of social justice.

A Protestant Alternative

Catholic tradition always has its critics from the Protestant side. One who dominated the scene of American Protestantism during much of this century was Reinhold Niebuhr. His stress on sin and his "dialectical" approach to justice and love offers a clear alternative to the Catholic approach.[4] Yet the choice of Niebuhr raises a problem regarding accessibility of accompanying texts. His short volume entitled *An Interpretation of Christian Ethics* gives much of the core of his early theory.[5] Yet Niebuhr later refused to defend this work.[6] Thus, the reader may wish to consult instead *Moral Man and Immoral Society, The Nature and Destiny of Man,* or *Love and Justice: Selections from the Shorter Writings of Reinhold Niebuhr* (ed. D. B. Robertson).

A Liberation Challenge

Finally, a new challenge is being raised today—a challenge to Protestants and Catholics as well as to liberal philosophers. Liberation theology is emerging around the world in places where oppressed peoples are doing their own theological reflection.[7] To represent liberation theology, I have chosen Jose Porfirio Miranda's analysis of justice in *Marx and the Bible.* The stage can be set for his analysis by a brief look at the works of Gustavo Gutierrez, widely acknowledged as a "founder" of liberation theology and one of its most important proponents.

Both Miranda and Gutierrez work out of a Latin American and Catholic context. However, not all liberation theology is Latin American and not all liberation theology is Catholic. It is a diverse and rapidly growing theological approach. Miranda's focus on economic justice accords well with the Latin American context for liberation theology and with our general concerns for distributive justice. In other contexts, however, other questions would loom larger in the liberation perspective.[8]

Thus, Miranda does not speak for all liberation theologians any more than Mill speaks for all utilitarians, Rawls for all contract theorists, Nozick for all Kantians, the National Conference of Catholic Bishops for all Catholics, or Reinhold Niebuhr for all Protestants. Each figure is chosen partly as the representative of a school of thought, but partly also because of the distinctive contribution of that person to the school.

These six fragments are offered in the conviction that each speaks to something so fundamental that, no matter what its defects, it leaves a permanent legacy. Each of these theories has left, or promises to stamp, a lingering mark on our understanding of justice. They may be only fragments, but they are world-shaping fragments.

OF BLINDFOLDED EXPLORATION

All theory is part of an ongoing dialog. Each of these theories has been controversial. Accompanying the exposition of each theory, therefore, is a sampling of critical commentary. No doubt the theorists or supporters from their schools would wish to rebut many of the criticisms reported here. Space precludes a full-fledged debate about each theory, and I have resisted the temptation to offer my own assessments at every point. Even the most recent of the theories presented here will be revised and surpassed by subsequent reflection by the time this book is in print. Readers are encouraged to explore original sources and to judge for themselves the strengths and weaknesses of each approach.

A few preliminary cautions are in order, however. First, of the six approaches represented here, only one author set out explicitly to write a "theory" of justice. The others had other tasks in mind, and whatever "theory" of justice is culled from their work will remain always a bit foreign to their central purposes. The views presented here are perhaps better understood as "windows" on justice rather than as theories per se. A window provides a frame and gives a view. It offers perspective. However, it also requires viewing through a glass and entails the inevitable distortions of that glass.

Indeed, the fragments offered here will reflect the distortions of their social locations. One is from the previous century, one from nearly half a century ago, and the remainder are recent. Most did their work with direct reference to the United States, but two did not. Catholic thought—so often deemed to proceed by papal decree—is represented by a group document. Liberationists, on the other hand, who claim a certain group identity, are nonetheless represented largely by a single thinker. Regrettably, none of our major explorers is a woman.[9] They are a strange group, our blindfolded explorers.

In spite of this fact, I have made no attempt to probe their social locations or personal histories. This is not because I think social location makes no difference to theory. Indeed, it makes all the difference: much of any theory may be attributed to the cultural and personal background of the author. For that very reason, however, the exploration of theory itself will often reveal the author's social location.

Further, theory has a life and an integrity of its own. Thus, the task here is to get "inside" each theory, to the best of our ability, and then to listen to its critics. We have before us six descriptions of an elephant—six proposals for "making *mishpat* the measure." Perhaps we will find that they are not compatible. Perhaps we will find that they are. Can they speak to each other?

With all the interest in justice today, there has been precious little effort to put philosophical and theological theories in dialog. Indeed, theological approaches to justice have not received the systematic exposition and exploration of their philosophical counterparts. This volume is but a small step toward a needed exchange in which the gifts, the assumptions, and the limitations of different views can be explored. Perhaps we shall never define the elephant accurately. But we can at least put the descriptions in juxtaposition. Perhaps as we do so, we will get some sense of the nature of the beast.

NOTES

1. Alasdair MacIntyre, *After Virtue* (Notre Dame: University of Notre Dame Press, 1981), p. 104.
2. Joel Feinberg has proposed that traditional classifications of justice—distributive, retributive, and commutative—are not particularly helpful. See "Noncomparative Justice," in J. Feinberg and Hyman Gross, *Justice: Selected Readings* (Belmont, Calif.: Wadsworth, 1977), p. 55. His proposal reflects the ambiguities to be encountered in this volume.

3. Explicitly excluded from our study is the arena of retributive justice. Yet, even here, John Stuart Mill does not separate the distributive from the retributive aspects of justice.

4. Another tempting alternative is Emil Brunner's *Justice and the Social Order* (London: Lutterworth, 1945), which presents a more classic two-kingdoms approach than does Niebuhr. The choice of Niebuhr instead of Brunner is justified by Niebuhr's importance to the formation of Protestant thought in the United States.

5. See Paul Ramsey, "Love and Law," in *Reinhold Niebuhr: His Religious, Social, and Political Thought*, ed. C. W. Kegley and R. W. Bretall (New York: Macmillan, 1956), p. 95. I concur with John Bennett's claims that the essential structure of Niebuhr's thought was formed in the 1930s and 1940s; that period, therefore, represents Niebuhr's thought here. See John C. Bennett, "Reinhold Niebuhr's Social Ethics," in Kegley and Bretall, p. 47.

6. Reinhold Niebuhr, "Reply to Interpretation and Criticism," ibid., p. 434.

7. Liberation theology is often the result of groups of people working together for liberation. Thus, as Gustavo Gutierrez puts it, "it makes little difference whose name appears on articles and books." See *The Power of the Poor in History* (Maryknoll, N.Y.: Orbis, 1983), p. 204.

8. Liberation theology is emerging in Asia, Africa, and North America as well as in Latin America. Obviously, the liberation concerns of a Korean farmer will not be the same as those of a black industrial worker in North America. Women add some distinctive concerns as well. I regret that none of the six theories represented here is a feminist theory. I chose Latin American liberation theology, not out of a conviction that it is the only, nor even the most important context for liberation theology, but out of appreciation for Miranda's contributions to an understanding of justice.

9. This does not mean, however, that no women are represented here. John Stuart Mill often attributed his inspiration to his wife. Much contemporary liberation theology is done by women.

5. THE UTILITARIAN CHALLENGE: JOHN STUART MILL

Karen Lebacqz

Classical utilitarianism took root in the latter half of the 19th century and the early part of the 20th. It is associated with such names as Jeremy Bentham, James Mill, John Stuart Mill, Henry Sidgwick, and G. E. Moore. It influenced generations of thinkers, and its legacy is still apparent in "cost-benefit analyses" and defenses of market economies.

We turn to the classical approach as defended by John Stuart Mill in *Utilitarianism*. Mill's exposition is of sufficient clarity and persuasiveness to set the stage for the theories of justice that dominate the landscape today.[1]

Utility

The basic idea of utilitarianism is simple: the right thing to do is what produces the most good. Since this is in fact the way many people approach ethical decisions, it is easy to see why the theory has had such appeal. But it deserves more detailed scrutiny.

A summary statement of the utilitarian principle is provided by Mill:

> "Utility" or the "greatest happiness principle" holds that actions are right in proportion as they tend to promote happiness; wrong as they tend to produce the reverse of happiness. By happiness is intended pleasure and the absence of pain. . . .[2]

Into this short statement are packed two crucial assumptions that lay the groundwork for a discussion of justice from a utilitarian perspective.

First, the goal of life is happiness. Both Mill and Jeremy Bentham before him argue this.[3] How do we know this? Bentham offers little "proof" of the assumption that happiness is the goal of life. He rests on the claim that "by the natural constitution of the human frame" we embrace these ends, and he asserts that fundamental principles are not susceptible to direct proof.[4] Mill agrees that "questions of ultimate ends are not amenable to direct proof," but he offers as argument the fact that people universally *do* desire happiness.[5] Thus, the end or goal of human life is taken to be happiness, and we know this because people do desire happiness and because doing so appears to be "natural" to us.

But what is happiness? Bentham defined it in terms of pleasure and the absence of pain. Mill expands on this by arguing explicitly for a recognition of different *kinds* of pleasure and pain. The pleasures of the intellect for Mill are not simply circumstantially more "useful" than those of the flesh, but are intrinsically superior.[6] Hence, a distinction arose among utilitarians between those who consider "happiness" to consist primarily in pleasure and pain and those who add other goals or ends (truth, beauty). The two schools are called "hedonistic" and "ideal" utilitarianism, respectively.[7]

Second, the "rightness" of acts is determined by their contributions to happiness. This makes utilitarianism a form of teleology: the end (*telos*) determines what is right. The "right" is determined by calculating the amount of good to be produced. Thus, the "good" is prior to the "right" and the right is dependent upon it.[8] As Mill puts it, actions are right in proportion as they "tend" to promote happiness.

But this formulation raises a question: must the results of *each action* be calculated to determine its overall "utility" and therefore to decide whether it is right? At first glance this appears to be Bentham's view. In his attempt to render a scientific basis for morality, Bentham offered a method for taking "an exact account" of the tendency of any act:

> Proceed as follows. Begin with any one person of those whose interests seem most immediately to be affected by it: and take an account, 1. Of the value of each distinguishable *pleasure*. . . . 2. Of the value of *pain*. . . . 5. Sum up all the values of all the *pleasures* on the one side, and those of all the *pains* on the other. . . . 6. Take an account of the *number* of persons whose interests appear to be concerned; and repeat the above process with respect to each. . . . Take the *balance*. . . .[9]

Such a description makes it appear that every act must be subjected to a lengthy and time-consuming calculus. In the literature on utilitarianism, this approach of judging the "utility" of each act is called "extreme" or "act-" utilitarianism.

However, Bentham made it clear that he did not expect such a procedure to be "strictly pursued previously to every moral judgment."[10] Mill moves even a step further, proposing that history teaches us the "tendencies of actions" and that these historical lessons give rise to "corollaries from the principle of utility."[11] One does *not*, therefore, "endeavor to test each individual action directly by the first principle" of utility.[12] Rather, the individual act is right if it conforms to a "secondary principle" which has been shown to have utility overall. Taking note of this argument by Mill, Urmson proposes that Mill is best classified as a "restricted" or "rule-" utilitarian.[13] Most commentators have followed Urmson's lead, and the distinction between act- and rule-utilitarianism has become an arena for much debate and discussion.

In sum, the basic idea of utilitarianism is that actions are determined to be right or wrong depending on whether they promote "happiness" or good. This idea has striking implications when we turn to considerations of justice.

Utility and Justice

Traditional notions of justice appear to be flouted by a theory that claims the "right" act is whatever maximizes the good. Individual rights or claims would be overridden by consideration of the "happiness" of others. For example, if the bloodshed of a threatened race riot could be averted by framing and lynching an innocent person, it seems that the utilitarian would have to say it is "right" to do so. So long as the "greater good" required it, all individual rights and claims would be ignored. Because of such apparent implications of utilitarian theory, issues of justice have consistently been a stumbling block for utilitarians.

Both Bentham and Mill recognized this. Indeed, Bentham's overriding concern was to render the penal system more fair and to avoid injustice in the retributive sphere.[14] We focus here on Mill's discussion of the relation between utility and distributive justice.

Mill acknowledges the strength of the feelings people have about justice and the indignation felt at instances of injustice such as undue punishment. This very strength of feeling makes it difficult for people to see justice as a part of utility.[15] Mill therefore sets about to determine whether justice is sui generis or whether it is a part of utility. He concludes that it is not a separate principle arising independently, but is a part of utility: "I dispute the pretensions of any theory which sets up an imaginary standard of justice not grounded on utility."[16] In so doing, Mill follows closely in the footsteps of David Hume, whose defense of the utilitarian basis of justice is worth reviewing.

No one doubts that justice is useful to society, asserts Hume. The question is whether public utility is the *sole* origin of justice.[17] Hume attempts to show that it is by demonstrating that rules of justice do not arise in circumstances where they would not be useful. In situations of extreme deprivation, in circumstances characterized primarily by benevolence, in places where there is such an overabundance that all needs can be met without dispute—in such cases rules of justice would not be "useful" and therefore do not arise. The "use" and "tendency" of the virtue of justice, therefore, are "to procure happiness and security, by preserving order in society."[18] Thus, any rules of justice will depend on the particular state or condition in which people find themselves. All such rules "owe their origin and existence to that *utility,* which results to the public from their strict and regular observance."[19]

Hume does not offer a direct definition of justice. However, from his discussion it can be seen that justice has to do with "separating" and respecting claims about private property.[20] It is where people have conflicting claims over possession in circumstances of moderate scarcity that issues of distributive justice arise. This notion of justice as dealing with *conflicting claims regarding possessions* in *circumstances of scarcity* becomes a pervasive theme throughout modern discussions.

Mill takes over Hume's basic contention that justice does not arise from a "simple, original instinct in the human breast" but arises solely out of its necessity to the support of society.[21] "Justice," he asserts, "is a name for certain moral requirements which, regarded collectively, stand higher in the scale of social utility, and are therefore of more paramount obligation, than any others."[22]

Mill's path to this conclusion has three parts. First, he enumerates instances of "injustice" and searches for a common thread among them. Second, he attempts to discern why there is a particularly strong *feeling* about justice and whether this feeling is grounded in utility. Third, he reviews several controversial cases to show that appeals to "justice" will not resolve the controversy and that only calculations of utility will do so.

Mill finds six common circumstances generally agreed to be "unjust": (1) depriving people of things to which they have a *legal* right; (2) depriving them of things to which they have a *moral* right; (3) people not obtaining what they *deserve*—good to those who do right, and evil to those who do wrong; (4) *breaking faith* with people; (5) being *partial*, i.e., showing favor where favor does not apply; and (6) treating people *unequally*.[23]

These circumstances of injustice seem quite diverse. What is it that unifies them? The notion of legal restraint seems to run through them all, but Mill notes that this notion applies to all of morality: "duty is a thing which may be exacted from a person."[24] What, then, distinguishes justice from other kinds of duty or other aspects of morality?

To answer this question, Mill adopts Kant's distinction between duties of perfect obligation and duties of imperfect obligation. Duties of perfect obligation generate *rights* on the part of the recipient: if I have a duty not to harm you, you have a right not to be harmed by me. Duties of imperfect obligation, on the other hand, do not give rise to corresponding rights: I have a duty to do good, but you have no "right" that I do good for you. Mill suggests that all those duties of perfect obligation that give rise to rights are the arena of justice: "Justice implies something which it is not only right to do, and wrong not to do, but which some individual person can claim from us as his moral right."[25] What distinguishes justice, then, is the notion of rights or claims. Here, Mill echoes Hume, though he does not restrict claims to the arena of property.

Whence, then, comes the special *feeling* that attaches to justice—or that is evoked by instances of injustice? According to Mill, the "sentiment of justice" is "the animal desire to repel or retaliate a hurt or damage" to oneself or to others.[26] In itself, there is nothing moral in this feeling. However, when it is subordinated to "the social sympathies" so that the desire for vengeance becomes a desire that those who infringe rules of justice should be punished, then it becomes a moral feeling. In short, behind justice lies our interest in security, "the most vital of all interests."[27] The rules of justice are therefore supported by the utility of preserving security. When one asks *why* society should defend my rights, the answer lies in the general interest in security. Justice is therefore grounded in utility.

Moreover, Mill suggests that the most intense feelings are raised around certain types of injustice, to wit, "acts of wrongful aggression or wrongful exercise of power over someone" and then acts of "wrongfully withholding from him something which is his due."[28] Such wrongful withholding includes the withholding of good. Thus such common standards of justice as "good for good and evil for evil" are easily encompassed into the utilitarian perspective. And if each is to get what is deserved, then a concept of equal treatment follows: "it necessarily follows that society should treat all equally well who have deserved equally well of *it*. . . . This is the highest abstract standard of social and distributive justice."[29] Strong feelings and commonly accepted standards of justice are therefore explained by the utilitarian view.

Indeed, the utilitarian view will not only explain accepted standards, but will help adjudicate among them. Mill offers three examples of social conflict where the requirements of "justice" are under dispute and generally accepted standards cannot settle the claims. One of these is the question whether remuneration should be based on contribution or on effort. Appealing to "justice" will not solve the issue, for some think justice requires reward for contribution and others think it requires reward for effort. How then do we decide what justice really requires? "From these confusions there is no other mode of extrication than the utilitarian."[30] Justice is ultimately dependent on utility, because conflicts in the common rules of justice can be adjudicated only by reference to utility.

Hence, Mill concludes:

> Justice is a name for certain classes of moral rules which concern the essentials of human well-being more nearly, and are therefore of more absolute obligation, than any other rules for the guidance of life; and the notion which we have found to be of the essence of the idea of justice—that of a right residing in an individual—implies and testifies to this more binding obligation.[31]

REVIEW

In sum, Mill's approach to justice rests on an analysis of the common sense and moral sensitivities of his day. He begins with those things considered unjust in his own society, and he presumes a universal verity for those considerations. His focus is on actions, not on systems or structures per se. His examples are largely at the microlevel; no clear distinctions are made between interpersonal injustices and larger social injustices. He accepts an understanding of justice as dealing with personal claims or rights and attempts to undergird those claims with a utilitarian argument.

Hence, for Mill, there can be no theory of justice separate from the demands of utility. *Justice* is the term given to those rules that protect claims considered essential to the well-being of society—claims to have promises kept, to be treated equally, etc. But those claims are subject to the dictates of a utilitarian calculus; they can be overridden when the "greater good" demands it. Similarly, any conflicts among the rules of justice that protect those claims are also subject to the dictates of a utilitarian calculus and can be overridden. Justice depends on utility and does not contradict utility.

The essential features of justice on the utilitarian scheme are these: It acknowledges the existence of individual *rights* which are to be supported by society. It permits—indeed, for Mill, it requires—*rules* determined to be for the good of society to ensure compliance with certain stringent obligations and to protect individual rights. It can incorporate notions of *equal treatment* and of *desert*. But, most important, justice is not sui generis but is dependent on social *utility* for its foundation. Hence, all rules of justice, including equality, can bow to the demands of utility: "each person maintains that equality is the dictate of justice, except where he thinks that expediency requires inequality."[32] Whatever does the greatest overall good will be "just."

NOTES

1. John Stuart Mill, *Utilitarianism* (New York: Bobbs-Merrill, 1957).
2. Ibid., p. 10.
3. For Jeremy Bentham's argument, see *An Introduction to the Principles of Morals and Legislation*, ed. J. H. Bums and H. L. A. Hart (London: Methuen, 1982), pp. 11–12.
4. Ibid., p. 13.
5. Mill, *Utilitarianism*, pp. 7 and 48.
6. Ibid., p. 12.
7. See David Lyons, *Forms and Limits of Utilitarianism* (Oxford: Clarendon, 1965), p. 9. W. D. Ross in *The Right and the Good* (Oxford: Clarendon, 1930), p. 17, argues that "ideal" utilitarianism is logically the more basic of the two.
8. Teleology is contrasted with deontology, in which the right is prior to the good. The theory of John Rawls, to be considered in the next chapter, is a form of deontology.
9. Bentham, *An Introduction*, pp. 39–40.
10. Ibid., p. 40.
11. Mill, *Utilitarianism*, pp. 30–31.
12. Ibid., p. 31.
13. J. O. Urmson, "The Interpretation of the Moral Philosophy of J. S. Mill," in *Contemporary Utilitarianism*.
14. Bentham, *An Introduction*. p. 1.
15. Mill, *Utilitarianism*. p. 53.
16. Ibid., p. 73.
17. David Hume, "Of Justice" (section 3 of *An Enquiry Concerning the Principles of Morals*, first published in 1751), reprinted in J. Feinberg and H. Gross, *Justice: Selected Readings* (Belmont, Calif: Wadsworth, 1977), p. 75.
18. Ibid., p. 76. Note that Hume deals with justice, not as a set of principles for distribution, but as a *virtue:* "the cautious, jealous virtue of justice" (p. 75).
19. Ibid., p. 77. Rawls argues that Hume is not a true utilitarian, since what he calls "utility" really amounts to a form of common good rather than a strict utilitarian calculus in which the good of some compensates for losses to others (A *Theory of Justice*, pp. 32–33).
20. Hume, "Of Justice," p. 78, declares that it is "requisite, for the peace and interest of society, that men's possessions should be separated." Elsewhere he speaks of establishing rules for property "which are, on the whole, most *useful* and *beneficial*" (ibid., p. 79).

21. Ibid., pp. 81–82.
22. Mill, *Utilitarianism.* p. 78.
23. Ibid., pp. 54–57.
24. Ibid., p. 60.
25. Ibid., p. 62.
26. Ibid., p. 65.
27. Ibid., p. 67.
28. Ibid., p. 74.
29. Ibid., p. 76.
30. Ibid., p. 72. Mill does not show *how* the utilitarian formula helps to solve the problem any better than the various appeals to "justice." He merely *asserts* that this is the case.
31. Ibid., p. 73.
32. Ibid., p. 57.

6. UTILITARIANISM

John Stuart Mill

*Utilitarianism is a theory of morality rooted in the thought of **Jeremy Bentham** (1748–1832) and **John Stuart Mill** (1806–1873). From a utilitarian perspective, an economic distribution or social policy is just if it produces, on balance, more pleasure, happiness, or utility than alternative economic distributions or social policies. One can also think about utilitarian approaches to justice from the standpoint of minimizing pain, unhappiness, or disutility, but generally speaking utilitarianism is focused on maximizing some social good among all persons (or even sentient animals) who are impacted by a particular policy or economic distribution.*

One of the foundational building blocks of utilitarian theories of justice is the concept of utility. Jeremy Bentham originally defined the concept in relation to the experience of pain or pleasure. The experience of pleasure increased utility; pain decreased it. Because Bentham believed that "pushpin is as good as poetry," all forms of human pleasure were ultimately of equal worth (pushpin was a game, similar to checkers, that was played by the lower classes of England). In fact, Bentham allowed that the pain and pleasure experienced by sentient animals could be taken into account as one evaluated the justice of certain policies or distributions. Accordingly, some modern-day philosophers, like Peter Singer, have made some compelling arguments for "animal rights" based on utilitarian thought.

John Stuart Mill brought considerable respectability to utilitarian thought in his work Utilitarianism *(1863), an excerpt of which appears below. In that essay, Mill rescued Bentham's crudely defined concept of utility by distinguishing between lower and higher pleasures. However, in making this distinction, the concept of utility became roughly synonymous with "desirable" outcomes (which, by definition, depended more upon the subjective perceptions of individuals instead of an objective quality that could be aggregated and measured). Mill also offered a strong defense of utilitarian ideas in relation to the more traditional categories of justice. He argued that we revere fundamental notions of justice because they produce, on balance, more utility or happiness for the society as a whole.*

Today, one of the strongest manifestations of utilitarian thinking comes in the form of contemporary cost-benefit analysis. This reflects the significant impact that utilitarianism has had on the discipline of economics, where utility has been understood in terms of "real income and wealth" or as a quality manifest in the "revealed preferences" of consumers in the marketplace. Since cost-benefit analysis is the primary tool used by corporations and governmental agencies in evaluating the desirability of different policies (and has even extended its influence into law), one could argue that utilitarianism is still the dominant moral orientation of policy makers within the United States. —VW

WHAT UTILITARIANISM IS

The creed which accepts as the foundation of morals, Utility, or the Greatest Happiness Principle, holds that actions are right in proportion as they tend to promote happiness, wrong as they tend to produce the reverse of happiness. By happiness is intended pleasure, and the absence of pain; by unhappiness, pain, and the privation of pleasure. . .

Now, such a theory of life excites in many minds, and among them in some of the most estimable in feeling and purpose, inveterate dislike. To suppose that life has (as they express it) no higher end than pleasure—no better and nobler object of desire and pursuit they designate as utterly mean and groveling; as a doctrine worthy only of swine, to whom the followers of Epicurus were, at a very early period, contemptuously likened; and modern holders of the doctrine are occasionally made the subject of equally polite comparisons by its German, French, and English assailants.

When thus attacked, the Epicureans have always answered, that it is not they, but their accusers, who represent human nature in a degrading light; since the accusation supposes human beings to be capable of no pleasures except those of which swine are capable. . .

The comparison of the Epicurean life to that of beasts is felt as degrading, precisely because a beast's pleasures do not satisfy a human being's conceptions of happiness. Human beings have faculties more elevated than the animal appetites, and when once made conscious of them, do not regard anything as happiness which does not include their gratification. . . It is quite compatible with the principle of utility to recognize the fact, that some kinds of pleasure are more desirable and more valuable than others. It would be absurd that while, in estimating all other things, quality is considered as well as quantity, the estimation of pleasures should be supposed to depend on quantity alone.

If I am asked, what I mean by difference of quality in pleasures, or what makes one pleasure more valuable than another, merely as a pleasure, except its being greater in amount, the re is but one possible answer. Of two pleasures, if there be one to which all or almost all who have experience of both give a decided preference, irrespective of any feeling of moral obligation to prefer it, that is the more desirable pleasure. If one of the two is, by those who are competently acquainted with both, placed so far above the other that they prefer it, even though knowing it to be attended with a greater amount of discontent, and would not resign it for any quantity of the other pleasure which their nature is capable of, we are justified in ascribing to the preferred enjoyment a superiority in quality, so far outweighing quantity as to render it, in comparison, of small account.

Now it is an unquestionable fact that those who are equally acquainted with, and equally capable of appreciating and enjoying, both, do give a most marked preference to the manner of existence which employs their higher faculties. Few human creatures would consent to be changed into any of the lower animals, for a promise of the fullest allowance of a beast's pleasures; no intelligent human being would consent to be a fool, no instructed person would be an ignoramus, no person of feeling and conscience would be selfish and base, even though they should be persuaded that the fool, the dunce, or the rascal is better satisfied with his lot than they are with theirs. They would not resign what they possess more than he for the most complete satisfaction of all the desires which they have in common with him. If they ever fancy they would, it is only in cases of unhappiness so extreme, that to escape from it they would exchange their lot for almost any other, however undesirable in their own eyes. A being of higher faculties requires more to make him happy, is capable probably of more acute suffering, and certainly accessible to it at more points, than one of an inferior type; but in spite of these liabilities, he can never really wish to sink into what he feels to be a lower grade of existence. . .

It is indisputable that the being whose capacities of enjoyment are low, has the greatest chance of having them fully satisfied; and a highly endowed being will always feel that any happiness which he can look for, as the world is constituted, is imperfect. . . It is better to be a human being dissatisfied than a pig satisfied; better to be Socrates dissatisfied than a fool satisfied. And if the fool, or the pig, are a different opinion, it is because they only know their own side of the question. The other party to the comparison knows both sides.

It may be objected, that many who are capable of the higher pleasures, occasionally, under the influence of temptation, postpone them to the lower. But this is quite compatible with a full appreciation of the intrinsic superiority of the higher. Men often, from infirmity of character, make their election for the nearer good, though they know it to be the less valuable; and this no less when the choice is between two bodily pleasures, than when it is between bodily and mental. They pursue sensual indulgences to the injury of health, though perfectly aware that health is the greater good. . .

I must again repeat, what the assailants of utilitarianism seldom have the justice to acknowledge, that the happiness which forms the utilitarian standard of what is right in conduct, is not the agent's own happiness, but that of all concerned. As between his own happiness and that of others, utilitarianism requires him to be as strictly impartial as a disinterested and benevolent spectator. In the golden rule of Jesus of Nazareth, we read the complete spirit of the ethics of utility. To do as you would be done by, and to love your neighbor as yourself, constitute the ideal perfection of utilitarian morality. As the means of making the nearest approach to this ideal, utility would enjoin, first, that laws and social arrangements should place the happiness, or (as speaking practically it may be called) the interest, of every individual, as nearly as possible in harmony with the interest of the whole; and secondly, that education and opinion, which have so vast a power over human character, should so use that power as to establish in the mind of every individual an indissoluble association between his own happiness and the good of the whole; especially between his own happiness and the practice of such modes of conduct, negative and positive, as regard for the universal happiness prescribes; so that not only he may be unable to conceive the possibility of happiness to himself, consistently with conduct opposed to the` general good, but also that a direct impulse to promote the general good may be in every individual one of the habitual motives of action, and the sentiments connected therewith may fill a large and prominent place in every human being's sentient existence. . .

ON THE CONNECTION BETWEEN JUSTICE AND UTILITY

In all ages of speculation, one of the strongest obstacles to the reception of the doctrine that Utility or Happiness is the criterion of right and wrong, has been drawn from the idea of justice. . .

It is necessary to attempt to ascertain what is the distinguishing character of justice, or of injustice: what is the quality, or whether there is any quality, attributed in common to all modes of conduct designated as unjust (for justice, like many other moral attributes, is best defined by its opposite). . .

To find the common attributes of a variety of objects, it is necessary to begin by surveying the objects themselves in the concrete. Let us therefore advert successively to the various modes of action, and arrangements of human affairs, which are classed, by universal or widely spread opinion, as Just or as Unjust. . .

In the first place, it is mostly considered unjust to deprive any one of his personal liberty, his property, or any other thing which belongs to him by law. Here, therefore, is one instance of the application of the terms just and unjust in a perfectly definite sense, namely, that it is just to respect, unjust to violate, the *legal rights* of any one. But this judgment admits of several exceptions, arising from the other forms in which the notions of justice and injustice present themselves. For example, the person who suffers the deprivation may (as the phrase is) have *forfeited* the rights which he is so deprived of. . .

Secondly, the legal rights of which he is deprived, may be rights which *ought* not to have belonged to him; in other words, the law which confers on him these rights, may be a bad law. When it is so, or when (which is the same thing for our purpose) it is supposed to be so, opinions will differ as to the justice or injustice of infringing it. Some maintain that no law, however bad, ought to be disobeyed by an individual citizen; that his opposition to it, if shown at all, should only be shown in endeavoring to get it altered by competent authority. This opinion . . . is defended, by those who hold it, on grounds of expediency; principally on that of the importance, to the common interest of mankind, of maintaining inviolate the sentiment of submission to law. Other persons, again, hold the directly contrary opinion, that any law, judged to be bad, may blamelessly be disobeyed, even though it be not judged to be unjust, but only inexpedient; while others would confine the license of disobedience to the case of unjust laws. . . Among these diversities of opinion, it seems to be universally admitted that there may be unjust laws, and that law, consequently, is not the ultimate criterion of justice, but may give to one person a benefit, or impose on another an evil, which justice condemns. When, however, a law is thought to be unjust, it seems always to be regarded as being so in the same way in which a breach of law is unjust, namely, by infringing somebody's right; which, as it cannot in this case be a legal right, receives a different appellation, and is called a moral right. We may say, therefore, that a second case of injustice consists in taking or withholding from any person that to which he has a moral right.

Thirdly, it is universally considered just that each person should obtain that (whether good or evil) which he *deserves*; and unjust that he should obtain a good, or be made to undergo an evil, which he does not deserve. This is, perhaps, the clearest and most emphatic form in which the idea of justice is conceived by the general mind. As it involves the notion of desert, the question arises, what constitutes desert? Speaking in a general way, a person is understood to deserve good if he does right, evil if he does wrong; and in a more particular sense, to deserve good from those to whom he does or has done good, and evil from those to whom he does or has done evil. . .

Fourthly, it is confessedly unjust to *break faith* with any one: to violate an engagement, either express or implied, or disappoint expectations raised by our conduct, at least if we have raised those expectations knowingly and voluntarily. Like the other obligations of justice already spoken of, this one is not regarded as absolute, but as capable of being overruled by a stronger obligation of justice on the other side; or by such conduct on the part of the person concerned as is deemed to absolve us from our obligation to him, and to constitute a *forfeiture* of the benefit which he has been led to expect.

Fifthly, it is, by universal admission, inconsistent with justice to be partial; to show favor or preference to one person over another, in matters to which favor and preference do not properly apply. Impartiality, however, does not seem to be regarded as a duty in itself, but rather as instrumental to some other duty; for it is admitted that favor and preference are not always censurable, and indeed the cases in which they are condemned are rather the exception than the rule. A person would be more likely to be blamed than applauded for giving his family or friends no superiority in good offices over strangers, when he could do so without violating any other duty; and no one thinks it unjust to seek one person in preference to another as a friend, connection, or companion. . . Impartiality where rights are concerned is of course obligatory, but this is involved in the more general obligation of giving to every one his right. A tribunal, for example, must be impartial, because it is bound to award, without regard to any other consideration, a disputed object to the one of two parties who has the right to it. Impartiality, in short, as an obligation of justice, may be said to mean, being exclusively influenced by the considerations which it is supposed ought to influence the particular case in hand; and resisting the solicitation of any motives which prompt to conduct different from what those considerations would dictate.

Nearly allied to the idea of impartiality is that of *equality*; which often enters as a component part both into the conception of justice and into the practice of it, and, in the eyes of many persons, constitutes its essence. But in this, still more than in any other case, the notion of justice varies in different persons, and always conforms in its variations to their notion of utility. Each person maintains that equality is the dictate of justice, except where he thinks that expediency requires inequality. The justice of giving equal protection to the right of all, is maintained by those who support the most outrageous inequality in the rights themselves. Even in slave countries it is theoretically admitted that the rights of the slave, such as they are, ought to be as sacred as those of the master; and that a tribunal which fails to enforce them with equal strictness is wanting in justice; while, at the same time, institutions which leave to the slave scarcely any rights to enforce, are not deemed unjust, because they are not deemed inexpedient. Those who think that utility requires distinction of rank, do not consider it unjust that riches and social privileges should be unequally dispensed; but those who think this inequality inexpedient, think it unjust also. . .

Some Communists consider it unjust that the produce of the labor of the community should be shared on any other principle than that of exact equality; others think it just that those should receive most whose wants are greatest; while others hold that those who work harder, or who produce more, or whose services are more valuable to the community, may justly claim a larger quota in the division of the produce. And the sense of natural justice may be plausibly appealed to in behalf of every one of these opinions. . .

The two essential ingredients in the sentiment of justice are, the desire to punish a person who has done harm, and the knowledge or belief that there is some definite individual or individuals to whom harm has been done.

Now it appears to me, that the desire to punish a person who has done harm to some individual is a spontaneous outgrowth from two sentiments, both in the highest degree natural, and which either are or resemble instincts; the impulse of self-defence, and the feeling of sympathy.

It is natural to resent, and to repel or retaliate, any harm done or attempted against ourselves, or against those with whom we sympathise. The origin of this sentiment it is not necessary here to discuss. Whether it be an instinct or a result of intelligence, it is, we know, common to all animal nature; for every animal tries to hurt those who have hurt, or who it thinks are about to hurt, itself or its young. Human beings, on this point, only differ from other animals in two particulars. First, in being capable of sympathising, not solely with their offspring, or, like some of the more noble animals, with some superior animal who is kind to them, but with all human, and even with all sentient, beings. Secondly, in having a more developed intelligence, which gives a wider range to the whole of their sentiments, whether self-regarding or sympathetic. By virtue of his superior intelligence, even apart from his superior range of sympathy, a human being is capable of apprehending a community of interest between himself and the human society of which he forms a part, such that any conduct which threatens the security of the society generally, is threatening to his own, and calls forth his instinct (if instinct it be) of self-defence. The same superiority of intelligence joined to the power of sympathising with human beings generally, enables him to attach himself to the collective idea of his tribe, his country, or mankind, in such a manner that any act hurtful to them, raises his instinct of sympathy, and urges him to resistance...

This sentiment, in itself, has nothing moral in it; what is moral is, the exclusive subordination of it to the social sympathies, so as to wait on and obey their call. For the natural feeling would make us resent indiscriminately whatever any one does that is disagreeable to us; but when moralised by the social feeling, it only acts in the directions conformable to the general good: just persons resenting a hurt to society, though not otherwise a hurt to themselves, and not resenting a hurt to themselves, however painful, unless it be of the kind which society has a common interest with them in the repression of...There is involved, in addition, the conception of some definite person who suffers by the infringement; whose rights are violated by it...

When we call anything a person's right, we mean that he has a valid claim on society to protect him in the possession of it, either by the force of law, or by that of education and opinion... To have a right, then, is, I conceive, to have something which society ought to defend me in the possession of. If the objector goes on to ask, why it ought? I can give him no other reason than general utility... The interest involved is that of security, to every one's feelings the most vital of all interests. All other earthly benefits are needed by one person, not needed by another; and many of them can, if necessary, be cheerfully foregone, or replaced by something else; but security no human being can possibly do without on it we depend for all our immunity from evil, and for the whole value of all and every good, beyond the passing moment; since nothing but the gratification of the instant could be of any worth to us, if we could be deprived of anything the next instant by whoever was momentarily stronger than ourselves. Now this most indispensable of all necessaries, after physical nutriment, cannot be had, unless the machinery for providing it is kept unintermittedly in active play...

We are continually informed that Utility is an uncertain standard, which every different person interprets differently, and that there is no safety but in the immutable, ineffaceable, and unmistakable dictates of justice, which carry their evidence in themselves, and are independent of the fluctuations of opinion. One would suppose from this that on questions of justice there could be no controversy; that if we take that for our rule, its application to any given case could leave us in as little doubt as a mathematical demonstration. So far is this from being the fact, that there is as much difference of opinion, and as much discussion, about what is just, as about what is useful to society. Not only have different nations and individuals different notions of justice, but in the mind of one and the same individual, justice is not some one rule, principle, or maxim, but many, which do not always coincide in their dictates, and in choosing between which, he is guided either by some extraneous standard, or by his own personal predilections...

Is, then, the difference between the Just and the Expedient a merely imaginary distinction? Have mankind been under a delusion in thinking that justice is a more sacred thing than policy, and that the latter ought only to be listened to after the former has been satisfied? By no means. The exposition we have given of the nature and origin of the sentiment, recognises a real distinction; and no one of those who profess the most sublime contempt for the consequences of actions as an element in their morality, attaches more importance to the distinction than I do. While I dispute the pretensions of any theory which sets up an imaginary standard of justice not grounded on utility, I account the justice which is grounded on utility to be the chief part, and incomparably the most sacred and binding part, of all morality. justice is a name for certain classes of moral rules, which concern the essentials of human well-being more nearly, and are therefore of more absolute obligation, than any other rules for the guidance of life; and the notion which we have found to be of the essence of the idea of justice, that of a right residing in an individual implies and testifies to this more binding obligation...

Justice remains the appropriate name for certain social utilities which are vastly more important, and therefore more absolute and imperative, than any others are as a class (though not more so than others may be in particular cases); and which, therefore, ought to be, as well as naturally are, guarded by a sentiment not only different in degree, but also in kind; distinguished from the milder feeling which attaches to the mere idea of promoting human pleasure or convenience, at once by the more definite nature of its commands, and by the sterner character of its sanctions.

7. A CONTRACT RESPONSE: JOHN RAWLS

Karen Lebacqz

Whatever its shortcomings, classical utilitarianism sets an important agenda for other theories of justice. The strengths of utilitarianism in the arena of justice are two: (1) it provides—in theory at least—a concrete method for making difficult decisions; and (2) it recognizes the importance of happiness or the general good as part of a theory of justice. Yet we also saw that utilitarianism presents problems for justice: it appears not to honor individual persons, and it has implications that are often "counterintuitive, sometimes manifestly abhorrent."[1]

The task that John Rawls sets himself in *A Theory of Justice* is to propose an alternative theory of justice that avoids the weaknesses of utilitarianism while demonstrating similar strengths.[2] He hopes to construct a theory that takes persons seriously and does not risk their well-being or rights for the sake of others' good, but which also offers a concrete method for making the most fundamental decisions about distributive justice. The result is "justice as fairness."

Method

"Justice as fairness" has its roots in two places: the social contract theories of Locke and Rousseau, and the deontology of Kant. The basic idea is astonishingly simple, though its working out in theory is very complex. Rawls' aim is to use the concept of a social contract to give a procedural interpretation to Kant's notion of autonomous choice as the basis for ethical principles. Principles for justice (and moral philosophy in general) are to be the outcome of rational choice.[3]

In essence, the approach is this: imagine a group of people who are going to choose principles for assessing the justice of basic structures of society. Clearly, if the principles are to be just, they must be chosen in a situation that is itself fair. That is, no one must be allowed to dominate the choice, nor to use to unfair advantage such contingencies as natural endowments or social position. Hence, principles of justice will be the result of fair choice—"justice as fairness."[4]

How, then, do we make the circumstances of choice—the "original position" from which the parties choose—fair? Rawls proposes that the representative persons in the original position choose from behind a "veil of ignorance."[5] The veil of ignorance and other stipulations of the original position become the lynchpins of the system: "the idea of the initial situation is central to the whole theory and other basic notions are defined in terms of it."[6]

The veil of ignorance means that the parties choosing principles lack certain kinds of knowledge that might make the bargaining process unfair.[7] They do not know what position they hold in society, nor what their own particular goals or life plans might be. They do not know what society they belong to, nor what generation they are. Such particular kinds of knowledge always make it possible for persons to skew principles in their own favor. This would clearly not be fair, and so there must be an adequate veil of ignorance to remove such possibilities.

What the parties do know are two things. First, their society will be subject to the "circumstances of justice."[8] This means that it is characterized by conflict as well as by cooperation, but that cooperation is possible and beneficial.[9] Along lines suggested earlier by Hume, Rawls proposes that circumstances of justice obtain "whenever mutually disinterested persons put forward conflicting claims to the division of social advantages under conditions of moderate scarcity."[10] Questions of justice arise in situations of scarcity and conflict of interest.

Second, they must know something about economic theory, something about social organization, and something about human psychology.[11] In short, they must know enough about human society to be able to make some predictions about the likelihood that principles chosen can be strictly adhered to without undue stress or "strains of commitment."[12]

Moreover, the parties are mutually disinterested.[13] That is, they take no *particular* interest in each other's aims and purposes, whatever those might be. They are also rational, knowing that they want more of the primary goods of life if possible.[14] And they are not "envious"—that is, they prefer to gain in primary goods even if others gain more than they do.[15]

In short, we have a circumstance in which people do not know their specific life plans, but know only that they are likely to want more of those basic goods that help to support any life plan. They enter the bargain with a view to furthering their own interests in obtaining such goods, but without the kind of envy that would make them refuse gain for themselves accompanied by greater gain for others. They are ignorant of the kinds of things that would give them an unfair advantage in any bargaining position. Under these stipulations, the hypothetical "contract" can proceed.

They are then offered a choice of a range of principles for the distribution of rights and duties and of the benefits and burdens of social cooperation. These principles will govern the basic structure of society—the network of institutions that determines to a large extent what their life chances will be. It should be noted here that they also choose for a "well-ordered society," that is, for a society in which they can expect that the concept of justice chosen is public and that people comply strictly with its requirements.[16] Which principles will they choose?

Principles of Justice

Rawls argues that under such conditions, the parties choosing in the original position would choose two principles of justice. First, they would be concerned to secure their equal liberty, and they would establish a principle to that effect:

> Each person is to have an equal right to the most extensive total system of equal basic liberties compatible with a similar system of liberty for all.[17]

That is, they would separate out basic human liberties and secure them against any unequal division.

Indeed, Rawls argues that except under very stringent circumstances, the parties in the original position would never want to permit any compromising of basic liberties for the sake of other social or economic benefits. Thus, not only is equal liberty the first principle, but it stands in serial ("lexical") order, so that liberty can be restricted only for the sake of liberty and not for the sake of economic or other social gains.[18]

Next comes the question whether they would permit any inequalities in income, wealth, power, and so on. Here, it might seem as though the obvious answer is no. That is, people choosing principles from an initial situation of equal ignorance and not knowing what their position in society will be might choose to ensure that goods are always divided equally. Indeed, if society were a "zero sum game" in which the size of the store of goods to be distributed could never be increased, this is precisely what Rawls says they would do.[19]

However, human society is not a "zero sum game." Through the efforts of social cooperation it is possible to increase the quantity of goods to be distributed. For example, suppose there is a shoe factory with five workers, each currently earning $10,000 per year.[20] One of these workers has a particularly arduous task, and it is because of the time required for that task that a bottleneck occurs and production is held at current levels. Now it might be possible to induce this person to work faster by paying $13,000 per year (or to attract to the job a more skilled person than could be attracted by $10,000). If the increased productivity releases the bottleneck overall, so that the net income of the company is now $60,000, then there is a "utility surplus" of $7,000 (net income less salaries). This surplus could be divided among the other workers, bringing their salaries up to $11,750. Incomes are no longer equal, but everyone is better off.

Given that human society works this way and that the parties in the original position would know such general facts about society, surely they would choose the unequal incomes represented by the increased salaries here. This was, of course, precisely the challenge raised by utilitarianism: justice in its full sense seems to require some accounting for the *amount* of good as well as for its allocation.

However, utilitarianism might stipulate that justice is done even if one person loses in the transition, so long as "the greater good for the greater number" or the "greater net good" was done. Suppose the rearrangement of the shoe factory will put one person's salary at $9,000 while others move to $12,333 and one moves to $13,000. Under the utilitarian scheme, this represents the greater net good and the greater good for the greater number. But one person is worse off.

Why would persons in the original position choose a principle that might make them *worse* off than they were before? Rawls argues that the parties in the original position would not choose the utilitarian principle. Since they are concerned to protect their own interests, they would not risk lesser income only for the benefit of others. Rather, they would choose a principle such as the following:

> Social and economic inequalities, for example inequalities of wealth and authority, are just only if they result in compensating benefits for everyone, and in particular for the least advantaged members of society.[21]

Called the "difference principle," this principle becomes the core of Rawls' substantive theory of justice. It permits some inequalities in distribution, but only those that protect or improve the position of the least advantaged in society.

Choice of the difference principle over a principle such as maximizing average utility rests on one of the more controversial aspects of Rawls' theory: his adoption of the strategy of "maximin." In brief, this strategy stipulates that the parties in the original position would choose in such a way as to "maximize the minimum."[22]

The choice of "maximin" as a strategy can be understood this way: Suppose I am in this original bargain. I do not know who I will be in society, nor what kind of a society I may encounter when the veil of ignorance is lifted. With no way of calculating my chances of being the least advantaged, it is reasonable for me to act protectively to preserve the position of the least advantaged member of society, since that person might be me. Thus, I will permit inequalities only if they work to the benefit of the least advantaged. Hence, I will try to avoid the worst results and "maximize the minimum." Thus, I am concerned not merely that any inequalities result in compensating benefits for everyone, but especially that they result in benefits for the "least advantaged." The strategy of maximin is thus "the vital bridge linking the rules of justice with the conditions described by the original position."[23]

Moreover, those in the original position would want to be sure that any inequalities of position and power are not locked in for all time, but are subject to fair competition and open to all persons to try for them. Though they would be willing to permit social inequalities that work' to their advantage, they will stipulate that such inequalities be attached to positions open to all on a liberal principle of "fair equality of opportunity."[24] Finally, since they are not sure to which generation they belong, they will require that one generation not squander resources but enact a "just savings principle" toward the good of future generations.

Thus, the final formulation of Rawls' second principle of justice for institutions is as follows:

> Social and economic inequalities are to be arranged so that they are both:
> (a) to the greatest benefit of the least advantaged, consistent with the just savings principle, and
> (b) attached to offices and positions open to all under conditions of fair equality of opportunity.[25]

Added to the principle of equal liberty, we now have the two principles that form the core of Rawls' theory of justice for the basic structures of society.

These two principles are a "special case" of a general concept of justice. The general concept is that social values "are to be distributed equally unless an unequal distribution of any, or all, of these values is to everyone's advantage."[26] In contrast to the utilitarian "greatest good" criterion, Rawls' conception requires that *each person* benefit from any social inequalities.[27] The requirement that *each* person benefit becomes the requirement that the *least advantaged* benefit under the stipulations of maximin in the original position.

The full theory, therefore, takes the form of a fundamental affirmation of liberty and a limited acceptance of certain inequalities, judged from the perspective of their impact on the position of the least advantaged. These principles are those that would be chosen by autonomous individuals situated in a "fair" setting. They are thus, in Rawls' view, "categorical imperatives" expressing the autonomy of "free and equal rational beings."[28] Most importantly, perhaps, the principles that would be chosen are *not* those of classical utilitarianism or its numerous revisions.

Justification

If Rawls is right, then the two principles cited above are the principles that would be chosen by those in the original position as principles for distributing rights and duties, burdens and benefits. But are these principles *just*? Does the fact that they are chosen mean that they are right? To ask this question is to ask about the justification for the principles.

The answer to the question may be given in several ways. First, "justice as fairness" yields "pure procedural justice." In pure procedural justice there is no standard for deciding what is "just" apart from the procedure itself.[29] "Justice" applies not to the outcome, but to the system. Rawls develops this concept in discussing the place of "equal opportunity" as a principle of justice. However, it may also apply to "justice as fairness" as a theory: whatever is chosen by the parties in the original position is just simply by virtue of being the outcome of the decision procedure. Thus, if the parties do in fact choose Rawls' two principles, then these are the principles that provide justice.

Much depends, therefore, on the original position and the strictures established around the choice procedure. Here Rawls proposes two constraints to assess the fairness of the procedure. The first is that the premises introduced into the original position should be as "weak" as possible and should be widely accepted.[30] Only those things that are generally agreed to constitute "fair" or "minimal" assumptions should be necessary in the original position. Hence, for example, we cannot propose that everyone share a particular goal or life plan, for this would require some strong assumptions about the human good; however, we can propose that each party will have his or her own life plan, and will seek certain primary goods as means necessary to that life plan. Thus, "the conditions embodied in the description of the original position are ones that we do in fact accept."[31]

The second constraint or qualification is a method of assessment called "reflective equilibrium."[32] This method involves testing the description of the original position by seeing whether it yields principles that really do match our considered convictions about justice. Do the principles that arise seem to us to require what is fair when we deliberate about it? If not, then we can either change our considered convictions (pruning or stretching them as the principles might require) or we can alter the stipulations about the original position until it yields new principles that give us a better match. With this "back and forth" method of testing, "eventually we shall find a description of the initial situation that both expresses reasonable conditions and yields principles which match our considered judgments duly pruned and adjusted."[33]

The second and third parts of *A Theory of Justice* are devoted largely to testing out the implications of the principles: do they yield social institutions that match our considered convictions about justice? Do they offer a vision of a well-ordered and fair society? Rawls argues that the principles, worked out in social institutions, would help us to discard those ordinary precepts of justice that are not helpful on a fundamental level, and would confirm other common suppositions about justice. Perhaps most important here is his rejection of any concept of distribution in accord with virtue; all legitimate expectations are shown to be based on social institutions, not on such factors as the contingencies of birth or advantages of upbringing.[34]

The final test of the theory depends on the coherence of all these elements together: the original position, the arguments for the principles chosen, the kinds of institutional arrangements which they might engender, and the fit between these arrangements and our considered convictions of justice.

REVIEW

"Justice as fairness" provides a clear contrast to the utilitarian view. Principles of justice are derived not by assessing the utility of actions (or of tendencies of actions) but by rational choice in a fair setting. Those principles are geared toward the basic structure of society, not toward every act or every level where justice is a concern. Rawls deals on the macrolevel rather than the microlevel. *A Theory of Justice* offers a complex and subtle theory, based on a striking insight about the potential for using the social contract as a basis for a theory of justice.

Most important, where Mill's utilitarian approach leaves the individual vulnerable to the demands of the greater good of others, Rawls' principles clearly protect those who are least advantaged. No "trade-offs" are allowed between their liberty or well-being and the well-being of others. Basic liberties must be distributed equally and cannot be sacrificed for the sake of economic gain. While income and social status, power and privilege, may be distributed unequally, such unequal distribution is allowed only where it renders the least advantaged better off than they would otherwise be.

NOTES

1. Robert Paul Wolff, *Understanding Rawls: A Reconstruction and Critique of* A Theory of Justice (Princeton: Princeton University Press, 1977), p. 11.
2. John Rawls, *A Theory of Justice* (Cambridge, Mass.: Harvard University Press, 1971).
3. Ibid., p. 11.
4. Ibid., p. 12.
5. Ibid.
6. Ibid., p. 516.
7. Ibid., pp. 136f.
8. Ibid., p. 137.
9. Ibid., pp. 126–127.
10. Ibid., p. 128.
11. Ibid., pp. 137f.
12. Ibid., p. 176.
13. Ibid., pp. 144f.
14. Ibid., p. 143.
15. Ibid., pp. 143, 148–149.
16. Ibid., p. 8.
17. Ibid., p. 302.
18. Ibid.
19. Ibid., p. 539.
20. The figures have been changed here, but I am indebted to Wolff for the basic example (*Understanding Rawls,* pp. 30f.).
21. Rawls, *A Theory of Justice,* p. 15.
22. See ibid., pp. 152–156.
23. Benjamin R. Barber, "Justifying Justice: Problems of Psychology, Politics, and Measurement in Rawls," in *Reading Rawls,* ed. Norman Daniels (New York: Basic Books, n.d.), p. 297.
24. Rawls, *A Theory of Justice,* p. 83.
25. Ibid., p. 302.
26. Ibid., p. 62.
27. Social cooperation requires reciprocal advantages, claims Rawls (ibid., p. 33). He suggests that the utilitarian approach requires too much identification with the plight of others (p. 198).
28. Rawls, *A Theory of Justice,* p. 253.
29. Ibid., pp. 85–89.
30. Ibid., p. 18.
31. Ibid., p. 21.
32. See ibid., pp. 48f.
33. Ibid., p. 20.
34. Ibid., p. 310.

8. A THEORY OF JUSTICE

John Rawls

John Rawls (1921–2003), a political philosopher who taught at Harvard University for many years, is credited by many for having developed the most significant theoretical account of justice of the twentieth century, so significant that a colleague at Harvard, Robert Nozick, himself famous for developing a well-known theory of justice, remarked that "political philosophers must now either work within [Rawls's theory] or explain why not."

Rawls's immediate target was utilitarianism. His A Theory of Justice *(1971) was aimed particularly at discrediting utilitarianism by suggesting that an empirical principle such as utility cannot be a foundation for justice. On the contrary, said Rawls, certain individual rights, founded in justice, are so fundamental that they cannot be overridden even in the name of the common good.*

However, Rawls went beyond a critique of utilitarianism. The strength of his contribution lies in his apparent ability to provide not only a defense, but also a new foundation for a strong egalitarian interpretation of American democracy, one that attempts to reconcile liberty and equality with particular concern for the least advantaged. Rawls's work went a long way towards developing the philosophical justification for developing the welfare state of the 1960s and '70s.

This excerpt from A Theory of Justice *includes the heart of Rawls's justification of this foundation: his account of the "original position," a hypothetical device in which free, rational persons contract with each other on neutral grounds, allowing them to establish principles of justice that will be fair to all. Other works by John Rawls include* Political Liberalism *(1993), where he considers how justice might best be considered given America's evident religious pluralism, and* Law of Peoples *(2000), where he considers whether his theories concerning justice might have international implications. —PB*

The Subject of Justice

Many different kinds of things are said to be just and unjust: not only laws, institutions, and social systems, but also particular actions of many kinds, including decisions, judgments, and imputations. We also call the attitudes and dispositions of persons, and persons themselves, just and unjust. Our topic, however, is that of social justice. For us the primary subject of justice is the basic structure of society, or more exactly, the way in which the major social institutions distribute fundamental rights and duties and determine the division of advantages from social cooperation. By major institutions I understand the political constitution and the principal economic and social arrangements. Thus the legal protection of freedom of thought and liberty of conscience, competitive markets, private property in the means of production, and the monogamous family are examples of major social institutions. Taken together as one scheme, the major institutions define men's rights and duties and influence their life prospects, what they can expect to be and how well they can hope to do. The basic structure is the primary subject of justice because its effects are so profound and present from the start. The intuitive notion here is that this structure contains various social positions and that men born into different positions have different expectations of life determined, in part, by the political system as well as by economic and social circumstances. In this way the institutions of society favor certain starting places over others. These are especially deep inequalities. Not only are they pervasive, but they affect men's initial chances in life; yet they cannot possibly be justified by an appeal to the notions of merit or desert. It is these inequalities, presumably inevitable in the basic structure of any society, to which the principles of social justice must in the first instance apply. These principles, then, regulate the choice of a political constitution and elements of the economic and social system. The justice of a social scheme depends essentially on how fundamental rights and duties are assigned and on the economic opportunities and social conditions in the various sectors of society. . .

The Main Idea of the Theory of Justice

My aim is to present a conception of justice which generalizes and carries to a higher level of abstraction the familiar theory of the social contract as found, say, in Locke, Rousseau, and Kant. In order to do this we are not to think of the original contract as one to enter a particular society or to set up a particular form of government. Rather, the guiding idea is that the principles of justice for the basic structure of society are the object of the original agreement. They are the principles that free and rational persons concerned to further their own interests would accept in an initial position of equality as defining the fundamental terms of their association. These principles are to regulate all further agreements; they specify the kinds of social cooperation that can be entered into and the forms of government that can be established. This way of regarding the principles of justice I shall call justice as fairness.

Thus we are to imagine that those who engage in social cooperation choose together, in one joint act, the principles which are to assign basic rights and duties and to determine the division of social benefits. Men are to decide in advance how they are to regulate their claims against one another and what is to be the foundation charter of their society. Just as each person must decide by rational reflection what constitutes his good, that is, the system of ends which it is rational for him to pursue, so a group of persons must decide once and for all what is to count among them as just and unjust. The choice which rational men would make in this hypothetical situation of equal liberty, assuming for the present that this choice problem has a solution, determines the principles of justice.

In justice as fairness the original position of equality corresponds to the state of nature in the traditional theory of the social contract. This original position is not, of course, thought of as an actual historical state of affairs, much less as a primitive condition of culture. It is understood as a purely hypothetical situation characterized so as to lead to a certain conception of justice. Among the essential features of this situation is that no one knows his place in society, his class position or social status, nor does any one know his fortune in the distribution of natural assets and abilities, his intelligence, strength, and the like. I shall even assume that the parties do not know their conceptions of the good or their special psychological propensities. The principles of justice are chosen behind a veil of ignorance. This ensures that no one is advantaged or disadvantaged in the choice of principles by the outcome of natural chance or the contingency of social circumstances. Since all are similarly situated and no one is able to design principles to favor his particular condition, the principles of justice are the result of a fair agreement or bargain. . .

One feature of justice as fairness is to think of the parties in the initial situation as rational and mutually disinterested. This does not mean that the parties are egoists, that is, individuals with only certain kinds of interests, say in wealth, prestige, and domination. But they are conceived as not taking an interest in one another's interests. . .

Once the principles of justice are thought of as arising from an original agreement in a situation of equality, it is an open question whether the principle of utility would be acknowledged. Offhand it hardly seems likely that persons who view themselves as equals, entitled to press their claims upon one another, would agree to a principle which may require lesser life prospects for some simply for the sake of a greater sum of advantages enjoyed by others. Since each desires to protect his interests, his capacity to advance his conception of the good, no one has a reason to acquiesce in an enduring loss for himself in order to bring about a greater net balance of satisfaction. In the absence of strong and lasting benevolent impulses, a rational man would not accept a basic structure merely because it maximized the algebraic sum of advantages irrespective of its permanent effects on his own basic rights and interests. Thus it seems that the principle of utility is incompatible with the conception of social cooperation among equals for mutual advantage. It appears to be inconsistent with the idea of reciprocity implicit in the notion of a well-ordered society. Or, at any rate, so I shall argue.

I shall maintain instead that the persons in the initial situation would choose two rather different principles: the first requires equality in the assignment of basic rights and duties, while the second holds that social and economic inequalities, for example inequalities of wealth and authority, are just only if they result in compensating benefits for everyone, and in particular for the least advantaged members of society. These principles rule out justifying institutions on the grounds that the hardships of some are offset by a greater good in the aggregate. It may be expedient but it is not just that some should have less in order that others may prosper. But there is no injustice in the greater benefits earned by a few provided that the situation of persons not so fortunate is thereby improved. . .

One should not be misled, then, by the somewhat unusual conditions which characterize the original position. The idea here is simply to make vivid to ourselves the restrictions that it seems reasonable to impose on arguments for principles of justice, and therefore on these principles themselves. Thus it seems reasonable and generally acceptable that no one should be advantaged or disadvantaged by natural fortune or social circumstances in the choice of principles. It also seems widely agreed that it should be impossible to tailor principles to the circumstances of one's own case. We should insure further that particular inclinations and aspirations, and persons' conceptions of their good do not affect the principles adopted. The aim is to rule out those principles that it would be rational to propose for acceptance, however little the chance of success, only if one knew certain things that are irrelevant from the standpoint of justice. For example, if a man knew that he was wealthy, he might find it rational to advance the principle that various taxes for welfare measures be counted unjust; if he knew that he was poor, he would most likely propose the contrary principle. To represent the desired restrictions one imagines a situation in which everyone is deprived of this sort of information. One excludes the knowledge of those contingencies which sets men at odds and allows them to be guided by their prejudices. In this manner the veil of ignorance is arrived at in a natural way. This concept should cause no difficulty if we keep in mind the constraints on arguments that it is meant to express. At any time we can enter the original position, so to speak, simply by following a certain procedure, namely, by arguing for principles of justice in accordance with these restrictions. . .

Two Principles of Justice

I shall now state in a provisional form the two principles of justice that I believe would be chosen in the original position. . .

> First: each person is to have an equal right to the most extensive basic liberty compatible with a similar liberty for others.
> Second: social and economic inequalities are to be arranged so that they are both (a) reasonably expected to be to everyone's advantage, and (b) attached to positions and offices open to all. . .

The basic liberties of citizens are, roughly speaking, political liberty (the right to vote and to be eligible for public office) together with freedom of speech and assembly; liberty of conscience and freedom of thought; freedom of the person along with the right to hold (personal) property; and freedom from arbitrary arrest and seizure as defined by the concept of the rule of law. These liberties are all required to be equal by the first principle, since citizens of a just society are to have the same basic rights.

The second principle applies, in the first approximation, to the distribution of income and wealth and to the design of organizations that make use of differences in authority and responsibility, or chains of command. While the distribution of wealth and income need not be equal, it must be to everyone's advantage, and at the same time, positions of authority and offices of command must be accessible to all. One applies the second principle by holding positions open, and then, subject to this constraint, arranges social and economic inequalities so that everyone benefits.

These principles are to be arranged in a serial order with the first principle prior to the second. This ordering means that a departure from the institutions of equal liberty required by the first principle cannot be justified by, or compensated for, by greater social and economic advantages. The distribution of wealth and income, and the hierarchies of authority, must be consistent with both the liberties of equal citizenship and equality of opportunity. . .

It should be observed that the two principles (and this holds for all formulations) are a special case of a more general conception of justice that can be expressed as follows.

> All social values—liberty and opportunity, income and wealth, and the bases of self-respect—are to be distributed equally unless an unequal distribution of any, or all, of these values is to everyone's advantage.

Injustice, then, is simply inequalities that are not to the benefit of all. Of course, this conception is extremely vague and requires interpretation.

As a first step, suppose that the basic structure of society distributes certain primary goods, that is, things that every rational man is presumed to want. These goods normally have a use whatever a person's rational plan of life. For simplicity, assume that the chief primary goods at the disposition of society are rights and liberties, powers and opportunities, income and wealth. These are the social primary goods. Other primary goods such as health and vigor, intelligence and imagination, are natural goods; although their possession is influenced by the basic structure, they are not so directly under its control. Imagine, then, a hypothetical initial arrangement in which all the social primary goods are equally distributed: everyone has similar rights and duties, and income and wealth are evenly shared. This state of affairs provides a benchmark for judging improvements. If certain inequalities of wealth and organizational powers would make everyone better off than in this hypothetical starting situation, then they accord with the general conception.

Now it is possible, at least theoretically, that by giving up some of their fundamental liberties men are sufficiently compensated by the resulting social and economic gains. The general conception of justice imposes no restrictions on what sort of inequalities are permissible; it only requires that everyone's position be improved. We need not suppose anything so drastic as consenting to a condition of slavery. Imagine instead that men forego certain political rights when the economic returns are significant and their capacity to influence the course of policy by the exercise of these rights would be marginal in any case. It is this kind of exchange which the two principles as stated rule out; being arranged in serial order they do not permit exchanges between basic liberties and economic and social gains. The serial ordering of principles expresses an underlying preference among primary social goods. When this preference is rational so likewise is the choice of these principles in this order. . .

ADDITIONAL READINGS

Freeman, Samuel, ed. *The Cambridge Companion to Rawls.* Cambridge UK: Cambridge University Press, 2002.

Jackson, Timothy P. "To Bedlam and Part Way Back: John Rawls and Christian Justice." *Faith and Philosophy* 8.4 (October 1991): 423–447.

Kukathas, Chandran, and Philip Petit. *Rawls: A Theory of Justice and Its Critics.* Stanford, CA: Stanford University Press, 1990.

Rothenberg, Randall. "John Rawls vs. Robert Nozick." *Esquire* (March 1983): 201–09.

Sandel, Michael J. *Liberalism and the Limits of Justice.* Cambridge UK: Cambridge University Press, 1982.

9. AN ENTITLEMENT ALTERNATIVE: ROBERT NOZICK

Karen Lebacqz

If Rawls is right, and justice requires that the basic structures of society be arranged so as to benefit the least advantaged, then a sufficiently strong state will be required to accomplish this end. Indeed, something akin to a modem democratic "welfare" state is envisioned. It is this vision of a strong state that sets the stage for Robert Nozick's alternative proposal in *Anarchy, State, and Utopia*.[1]

Justice is not Nozick's dominant concern. His intent is to argue for a limited role for the state. He wants to show that the minimal state—and *only* the minimal state—is justifiable.[2] Questions of justice arise because distributive justice such as that envisioned by Rawls is often cited as a rationale for the more-than-minimal state. In attempting to show that distributive justice does not provide a rationale for a more-than-minimal state, Nozick offers an intriguing and quite distinctive approach to justice. He calls it an "entitlement" view.

The Role of the State

To see how this theory develops, we must begin with the legitimacy of the minimal state—and the minimal state *only*. Nozick takes a Kantian view that "individuals are ends and not merely means."[3] Individuals are ends in themselves, possessed of certain "natural" rights. This means that there are *constraints* ("side constraints") on action: no actions are permitted that violate fundamental human rights.[4] Thus, for Nozick, a limited set of near absolute rights constitutes the foundation of morality.[5]

Among these fundamental rights is the right not to be killed or assaulted. No one may be "sacrificed" for others. One of the constraints on action brought about by the inviolability of human rights is therefore a prohibition on aggression against another.[6]

But such a prohibition raises interesting questions about the role of the state. If the state becomes the exacter of justice, then it seems to violate this constraint on aggression.[7] This is the anarchist's challenge: the anarchist argues that *any* state violates individual rights. Against this charge, Nozick argues that a minimal state would come into existence by an "invisible hand" process that does not violate individual rights.[8]

In essence, the argument looks something like this: In a Lockean state of nature, the natural law would not provide for all contingencies where human rights conflict: "private and personal enforcement of one's rights . . . leads to feuds. . . . And there is no firm way to *settle* such a dispute."[9] Self-interested and rational persons would therefore form protective agencies to help adjudicate conflicting claims and to make sure that their claims were protected.[10] One such protective agency will tend to become dominant in a territory.

This dominant agency is not yet a state, because it does not claim monopoly on who may legitimately use force to settle disputes nor does it protect all within its territory.[11] However, once the transition is made to include both these elements, then we arrive at the minimal state.

Nozick rejects the idea that there is a single way of life that would constitute utopia for everyone. Since people are so different, a single utopian vision would be absurd. The minimal state leaves people free to form utopian communities within the overall framework without having their rights violated. "Treating us with respect by respecting our rights, it allows us . . . to choose our life and to realize our ends . . . aided by the voluntary cooperation of other individuals possessing the same dignity."[12] The minimal state therefore provides a "framework" for utopia.[13]

We have arrived, then, at the justification for the minimal state. Such a state does not violate anyone's rights, since it arises by an "invisible hand" process coupled with a fundamental moral principle of compensation for loss of freedom. But it remains to establish that only the minimal state is justifiable. Here is where Nozick develops his understanding of justice.

Distributive Justice

Nozick argues that the minimal state is *not* redistributive. No grounds have been established by which the state may take from some persons in order to *assist* others. The minimal state arises through the operation of "negative" rights of nonintervention and related principles of compensation and knowledge; it does not arise through nor imply any "positive" rights of citizens to support by the state.

But is a more extensive state justified in order to provide such support or to achieve distributive justice? Both Rawls and the utilitarians would legitimate a more-than-minimal state in order to ensure that goods are distributed justly— either to protect the least advantaged or to ensure the greatest overall good. Is such a more-than-minimal state entailed by considerations of justice?

Nozick's answer to this question is a resounding no. The pattern of distribution of goods in society, argues Nozick, is not the result of some central agency which distributes everything. Rather, it is the result of myriads of individual exchanges, gifts, and decisions.[14] Lacking such a central distributive or allocative agency, there can be no question of "distributive justice." Instead, we merely have patterns of individual holdings. Hence the question is posed more accurately as a question of "justice in holdings."

When are a person's holdings just? Nozick's answer takes the form of one basic principle: *whatever arises from a just situation by just steps is just*.[15] Picture any original set of holdings or distribution of goods that seems just, e.g., an equal distribution of goods to each person. Then permit people to make choices about exchanging those goods and about giving to each other from their share.

For example, suppose everyone wants to watch Wilt Chamberlain play basketball, and they are willing to give him $1 each for the pleasure of watching him play.[16] Each exchange of $1 to Chamberlain is itself fair. After some time, however, holdings will no longer be equal: Chamberlain will be far richer than everyone else. Yet this discrepancy in holdings is just, says Nozick, since the holdings arise by fair means from an initially just situation. Any attempt to redistribute goods according to some end-goal or pattern (e.g., Rawls' difference principle) must therefore intrude on these free decisions made by people.[17]

Justice in holdings, then, is comprised of the justice of the original acquisition and the justice of the transfers made.[18] This system might be referred to as the principle "from each as they choose; to each as they are chosen."[19] Nozick calls it a "historical" theory, because justice is determined by how the distribution came about, not by what the distribution is.[20]

Indeed, Nozick rejects all "patterned" principles of justice that distribute goods in accord with some chosen "end-state"—e.g., equality of holdings, bettering the position of the least advantaged—or along dimensions suggested by formulae such as "to each according to need" or "to each according to merit." Such principles look only at *what* the final distribution is and ignore the *manner* by which the distribution came into effect.

In contrast to such patterned principles, says Nozick, "*historical principles* of justice hold that past circumstances or actions of people can create differential entitlements or differential deserts to things."[21] Hence, his is an "entitlement" theory. Justice is determined not by the pattern of the final outcome of distribution, but by whether "entitlements" are honored.

Since transfers made in an entitlement system are often done for reasons—e.g., I exchange with others because they will benefit me—"strands of patterns will run through it."[22] That is, the actual distribution will look in part as though it were done on the basis of some formula such as "give to each according to their contributions." But the overall system is not patterned according to any such formulae, but is simply based on the procedural principles of fair acquisition and fair transfer.

Private ownership is the key assumption here. One of the few "positive" rights that Nozick permits as a fundamental human right is the right to acquire and transfer property.[23] Nozick does not elaborate a full theory for fair acquisition and transfer. In general, he seems to support the underlying assumptions of market exchange.

He does accept, however, a "Lockean proviso" on the justice of original acquisition: I am free to acquire by "mixing my labor" with something, *provided* I do not hurt others in the process. Hence, it is not just for me to acquire something that is so limited that my acquisition of it worsens others' condition.[24]

This reasoning about original *acquisition*, suggests Nozick, applies by extension to *transfer* and *purchase*. It would not be just for me to transfer or purchase something so limited that its concentration in the hands of one and its absence to others hurts their situation.[25] "Each owner's title to his holding includes the historical shadow of the Lockean proviso on appropriation."[26] In short, at the root of this system appears to lie a *prohibition against harm* to others deriving from their (Kantian) rights as human beings. One has the right to own goods, but not when that ownership harms others.

However, Nozick gives several interesting twists to the "Lockean proviso." For example, instead of remaining firm on the notion that one may not acquire severely limited goods, he argues that one may indeed acquire them so long as one compensates others so that their situation is not worsened.[27] He argues that a scientist has the right to horde a new compound that she has invented. While there may be some who need the compound in order to live, creating the compound did not *worsen* their state from what it was before. Thus, the scientist is not under any obligation to give or sell the compound, and may exchange it at any price the market will bear.[28]

The notion of what it means to "harm" or "worsen" someone's situation is therefore very central to this theory. Nozick acknowledges that a full theory of justice in holdings needs both a baseline for determining what it means to "harm" others or to make them worse off, and also a theory of property rights.[29]

This approach to justice puts individual liberty and choice in a primary position over any claims for equality of holdings. Indeed, one of Nozick's strongest criticisms of "patterned principles" such as Rawls' difference principle is that they inevitably involve violations of freedom of choice. Since they force arrangements that redistribute the goods that people have chosen to give or exchange, they violate the fundamental Kantian principle of respect for people's autonomy of choice.[30]

One of the interesting implications of this approach is Nozick's understanding of taxes. Taxes, he declares, are equivalent to forced labor.[31] Paying taxes is like being forced to work n hours for someone else. Hence, patterned principles of distributive justice that require taxation (e.g., in order to benefit the least advantaged) are "appropriating" or "seizing" people's labor.[32] To seize another's labor is to use that other as a means, not respecting them as an end in themselves. Taxes violate Kantian "side constraints" and are not morally permissible.

The net result of this reasoning is that no justification can be offered for a more-than-minimal state on grounds that it is necessary to ensure distributive justice. Justice is not "distributive" but depends on just acquisition and transfer of holdings. Freedom of choice is violated by any state or system that imposes "patterns" of "redistribution" or attempts to achieve any "end-state" of allocation of goods. "If the set of holdings is properly generated, there is no argument for a more extensive state based upon distributive justice."[33]

REVIEW

In short, Nozick begins with a minimal state based on a minimal set of fundamental (Kantian) rights: rights against injury by others, rights to freedom of choice and action, and rights to own private property. The state has legitimacy only to ensure protection of these rights and compensation for their violation.

Where Rawls sees the necessity for societal principles to ensure just distribution, Nozick rejects any role for the state in "distributive justice." Justice is limited to the "commutative" sphere of individual exchanges.

Hence, "justice" for Nozick consists in fair exchange. Justice makes no substantive claims, but consists only in procedural requirements for fairness in exchange. One cannot argue that "justice" requires any particular distribution of goods. Whatever distribution of goods results from free choice and exchange is "just" so long as the beginning point and the exchange itself are fair.

Significantly, justice does not consist in promoting the greatest good of the greatest number, nor in protecting the least advantaged. Neither society as a whole nor any individual or group can make claims against the state for a distribution of goods other than that which arises from free exchanges among individuals. It may be "unfortunate" that some are wealthier than others, but it is not "unfair," provided the rules for free choice in exchange have not been violated.

NOTES

1. Robert Nozick, *Anarchy, State, and Utopia* (New York: Basic Books, 1974), p. 153.
2. Ibid., pp. 52–53.
3. Ibid., p. 31.
4. Ibid., pp. 28–29.
5. H. L. A. Hart, "Between Utility and Rights," in *The Idea of Freedom: Essays in Honour of Isaiah Berlin*, ed. Alan Ryan (Oxford: Oxford University Press, 1979), p. 81.
6. Nozick, *Anarchy, State, and Utopia*, p. 33.
7. Ibid., p. 51.
8. An "invisible hand explanation" shows that something that appears to have been produced by intentional design was in fact brought about by a process that did not have that design in mind (ibid., pp. 19–20).
9. Ibid., p. 11.
10. Ibid., p. 13.
11. Ibid., pp. 22–23.
12. Ibid., p. 334.
13. Ibid., p. 333.
14. Ibid., p. 149.
15. Ibid., p. 150.
16. Ibid., pp. 161–162.
17. Ibid., p. 163.
18. Ibid., pp. 150–152. In addition, there will need to be a principle for rectification of injustice in case either the original holdings or the transfer is not just.
19. Ibid., p. 160. Indeed, Nozick claims that most theories of justice consider only the recipients of goods and not the rights of the givers of goods (p. 168).
20. Nozick, *Anarchy, State, and Utopia*, p. 153.
21. Ibid., p. 155.
22. Ibid., p. 157.
23. Hart, "Between Utility and Rights," p. 81.

24. Nozick, *Anarchy, State, and Utopia*, p. 175.
25. Ibid., pp. 178–179.
26. Ibid., p. 180.
27. Ibid., p. 178.
28. Ibid., p. 181.
29. Ibid., pp. 177–178.
30. Ibid., p. 167. Nozick does allow one possible role for such patterned principles. He suggests that a principle such as Rawls' "difference principle" might serve as a "rough rule of thumb" for approximating the principle of rectification in places where acquisition and transfer have not been fair (p. 231).
31. Ibid., p. 169.
32. Ibid., p. 172.
33. Ibid., p. 230.

10. DISTRIBUTIVE JUSTICE

Robert Nozick

Robert Nozick's (1939–2002) famous work, Anarchy, State and Utopia *(1974), published three years after Rawls's* A Theory of Justice, *represents then and now one of the strongest critiques of the egalitarian conception of justice and a compelling defense of libertarianism. Nozick joined with Rawls in his criticism of utilitarianism. However, Rawls and Nozick differ in their understandings of freedom and which rights, in particular, are so compelling that they trump even the general welfare.*

Nozick characterizes Rawls's approach to justice as a "time-slice" theory, where one goes about evaluating the morality of a particular economic distribution by taking a snapshot of that distribution and assessing it according to some concept of justice (e.g., Rawls's Two Principles of Justice). Nozick argues that this approach is deficient, as economic distributions are always the result of an ongoing historical process that involves individual initiative, risk taking, technological development, market forces, and either good or bad luck. Chief among these historical processes is the individual expression of freedom, which often upsets the "neat" categories of time-slice approaches.

Nozick argues that the moral appraisal of economic distributions requires historical principles of justice, and he identifies three such principles: (1) the Principle of Justice in Acquisition; (2) the Principle of Justice in Transfer; and (3) a Principle of Rectification. Economic distributions that embody these three principles of justice will be just distributions (even though they may be highly unequal distributions). In contrast to Rawls's concern that equality and liberty be brought together in such a way that the needs of the "least advantaged" not be overlooked, Nozick's "entitlement theory" emphasizes that everyone possesses exactly what they were entitled to receive, without reference to needs or inequalities. The use of tax dollars, for example, to fund welfare programs is unjust according to Nozick, unless taxpayers voluntarily wish to assign a percentage of their income to help disadvantaged persons. Hence, Nozick's work has provided a significant philosophical foundation for the neo-conservative critique of the modern welfare state. Finally, as a libertarian, Nozick believes that the government should not regulate "recreational" activities such as smoking marijuana or contracting the services of a prostitute. He even goes so far as to argue that one should have the freedom to sell oneself into slavery, that is, if this is done voluntarily. —PB & VW

THE ENTITLEMENT THEORY

The subject of justice in holdings consists of three major topics. The first is the *original acquisition of holdings,* the appropriation of unheld things. This includes the issues of how unheld things may come to be held, the process, or processes, by which unheld things may come to be held, the things that may come to be held by these processes, the extent of what comes to be held by a particular process, and so on. . .

The second topic concerns the *transfer of holdings* from one person to another. By what processes may a person transfer holdings to another? How may a person acquire a holding from another who holds it? Under this topic come general descriptions of voluntary exchange, and gift and (on the other hand) fraud. . .

If the world were wholly just, the following inductive definition would exhaustively cover the subject of justice in holdings.

1.   A person who acquires a holding in accordance with the principle of justice in acquisition is entitled to that holding.
2.   A person who acquires a holding in accordance with the principle of justice in transfer, from someone else entitled to the holding, is entitled to the holding.
3.   No one is entitled to a holding except by (repeated) applications of 1 and 2.

The complete principle of distributive justice would say simply that a distribution is just if everyone is entitled to the holdings they possess under the distribution. . .

Not all actual situations are generated in accordance with the two principles of justice in holdings: the principle of justice in acquisition and the principle of justice in transfer. Some people steal from others, or defraud them, or enslave them, seizing their product and preventing them from living as they choose, or forcibly exclude others from competing in exchanges. None of these are permissible modes of transition from one situation to another. . .

The existence of past injustice (previous violations of the first two principles of justice in holdings) raises the third major topic under justice in holdings: the rectification of injustice in holdings. If past injustice has shaped present holdings in various ways, some identifiable and some not, what now, if anything, ought to be done to rectify these injustices? What obligations do the performers of injustice have toward those whose position is worse than it would have been had the injustice not been done? Or, than it would have been had compensation been paid promptly? How, if at all, do things change if the beneficiaries and those made worse off are not the direct parties in the act of injustice, but, for example, their descendants? Is an injustice done to someone whose holding was itself based upon an unrectified injustice? How far back must one go in wiping clean the historical state of injustices? . . .

Idealizing greatly, let us suppose theoretical investigation will produce a principle of rectification. . .

PATTERNING

Almost every suggested principle of distributive justice is patterned: to each according to his moral merit, or needs, or marginal product, or how hard he tries, or the weighted sum of the foregoing, and so on. The principle of entitlement is *not* patterned. There is no one natural dimension or weighted sum or combination of a small number of natural dimensions that yields the distributions generated in accordance with the principle of entitlement. The set of holdings that results when some persons receive their marginal products, others win at gambling, others receive a share of their mate's income, others receive gifts from foundations, others receive interest on loans, others receive gifts from admirers, others receive returns on investment, others make for themselves much of what they have, others find things, and so on, will not be patterned. . .

To think that the task of a theory of distributive justice is to fill in the blank in "to each according to his ———" is to be predisposed to search for a pattern; and the separate treatment of "from each according to his ———" treats production and distribution as two separate and independent issues. On an entitlement view these are not two separate questions. Whoever makes something, having bought or contracted for all other held resources used in the process (transferring some of his holdings for these cooperating factors), is entitled to it. The situation is *not* one of something's getting made, and there being an open question of who is to get it. Things come into the world already attached to people having entitlements over them. From the point of view of the historical entitlement conception of justice in holdings, those who start afresh to complete "to each according to his ———" treat objects as if they appeared from nowhere, out of nothing. A complete theory of justice might cover this limit case as well; perhaps here is a use for the usual conceptions of distributive justice.

So entrenched are maxims of the usual form that perhaps we should present the entitlement conception as a competitor. Ignoring acquisition and rectification, we might say:

> From each according to what he chooses to do, to each according to what he makes for himself (perhaps with the contracted aid of others) and what others choose to do for him and choose to give him of what they had been given previously (under this maxim) and haven't yet expended or transferred.

This, the discerning reader will have noticed, has its defects as a slogan. So as a summary and great simplification (and not as a maxim with any independent meaning) we have:

> *From each as they choose, to each as they are chosen.*

HOW LIBERTY UPSETS PATTERNS

It is not clear how those holding alternative conceptions of distributive justice can reject the entitlement conception of justice in holdings. For suppose a distribution favored by one of these non-entitlement conceptions is realized. Let us suppose it is your favorite one and let us call this distribution D_1; perhaps everyone has an equal share, perhaps shares vary in accordance with some dimension you treasure. Now suppose that Wilt Chamberlain is greatly in demand by basketball teams, being a great gate attraction. (Also suppose contracts run only for a year, with players being free agents.) He signs the following sort of contract with a team: In each home game, twenty-five cents from the price of each ticket of admission goes to him. (We ignore the question of whether he is "gouging" the owners, letting them look out for themselves.) The season starts, and people cheerfully attend his team's games; they buy their tickets, each time dropping a separate twenty-five cents of their admission price into a special box with Chamberlain's name on it. They are excited about seeing him play; it is worth the total admission price to them. Let us suppose that in one season one million persons attend his home games, and Wilt Chamberlain winds up with $250,000, a much larger sum than the average income and larger even than anyone else has. Is he entitled to this income? Is this new distribution D_2 unjust? If so, why? There is no question about whether each of the people was entitled to the control over the resources they held in D_1 because that was the distribution (your favorite) that (for the purposes of argument) we assumed was acceptable. Each of these persons *chose* to give twenty-five cents of their money to Chamberlain. They could have spent it on going to the movies, or on candy bars, or on copies of *Dissent* magazine, or of *Monthly Review*. But they all, at least one million of them, converged on giving it to Wilt Chamberlain in exchange for watching him play basketball. If D_1 was a just distribution, and people voluntarily moved from it to D_2, transferring parts of their shares they were given under D_1 (what was it for if not to do something with?), isn't D_2, also just? If the people were entitled to dispose of the resources to which they were entitled (under D_1) didn't this include their being entitled to give it to, or exchange it with, Wilt Chamberlain? Can anyone else complain on grounds of justice? Each other person already has his legitimate share under D_1. Under D_1, there is nothing that anyone has that anyone else has a claim of justice against. After someone transfers something to Wilt Chamberlain, third parties *still* have their legitimate shares; their shares are not changed. By what process could such a transfer among two persons give rise to a legitimate claim of distributive justice on a portion of what was transferred, by a third party who had no claim of justice on any holding of the others before the transfer? To cut off objections irrelevant here, we might imagine the exchanges occurring in a socialist society, after hours. After playing whatever basketball he does in his daily work, or doing whatever other daily work he does, Wilt Chamberlain decides to put in *overtime* to earn additional money. (First his work quota is set; he works time over that.) Or imagine it is a skilled juggler people like to see, who puts on shows after hours.

Why might someone work overtime in a society in which it is assumed their needs are satisfied? Perhaps because they care about things other than needs. I like to write in books that I read, and to have easy access to books for browsing at odd hours. It would be very pleasant and convenient to have the resources of Widener Library in my back yard. No society, I assume, will provide such resources close to each person who would like them as part of his regular allotment (under D_1). Thus, persons either must do without some extra things that they want, or be allowed to do something extra to get some of these things. On what basis could the inequalities that would eventuate be forbidden? Notice also that small factories would spring up in a socialist society, unless forbidden. I melt down some of my personal possessions (under D_1) and build a machine out of the material. I offer you, and others, a philosophy lecture once a week in exchange for your cranking the handle on my machine, whose products I exchange for yet other things, and so on. (The raw materials used by the machine are given to me by others who possess them under D_1, in exchange for hearing lectures.) Each person might participate to gain things over and above their allotment under D_1. Some persons even might want to leave their job in socialist industry and work full time in this private sector. I shall say something more about these issues in the next chapter. Here I wish merely to note how private property even in means of production would occur in a socialist society that did not forbid people to use as they wished some of the resources they are given under the socialist distribution D_1. The socialist society would have to forbid capitalist acts between consenting adults.

The general point illustrated by the Wilt Chamberlain example and the example of the entrepreneur in a socialist society is that no end-state principle or distributional patterned principle of justice can be continuously realized without continuous interference with people's lives. Any favored pattern would be transformed into one unfavored by the principle, by people choosing to act in various ways; for example, by people exchanging goods and services with other people, or giving things to other people, things the transferrers are entitled to under the favored distributional pattern. To maintain a pattern one must either continually interfere to stop people from transferring resources as they wish to, or continually (or periodically) interfere to take from some persons resources that others for some reason chose to transfer to them. (But if some time limit is to be set on how long people may keep resources others voluntarily transfer to them, why let them keep these resources for *any* period of time? Why not have immediate confiscation?) It might be objected that all persons voluntarily will choose to refrain from actions which would upset the pattern. This presupposes unrealistically (1) that all will most want to maintain the pattern (are those who don't to be "reeducated" or forced to undergo "self-criticism"?), (2) that each can gather enough information about his own actions and the ongoing activities of others to discover which of his actions will upset the pattern, and (3) that diverse and far-flung persons can coordinate their actions to dovetail into the pattern. Compare the manner in which the market is neutral among persons' desires, as it reflects and transmits widely scattered information via prices, and coordinates persons' activities. . .

11. A Catholic Response: The National Conference of Catholic Bishops

In November 1985, the National Conference of Catholic Bishops in the United States released the second draft of a pastoral letter on "Catholic Social Teaching and the U.S. Economy."[1] In this letter the bishops attempt to give "serious and sustained attention to economic justice."[2] The letter therefore presents one Catholic approach to social and distributive justice.

The bishops are responding to many of the same contemporary concerns as are addressed by philosophers John Rawls and Robert Nozick. Indeed, they share with Robert Nozick a fundamental affirmation that humans have rights that cannot be violated. But there the similarity ends. Where Nozick takes this affirmation as grounds for a minimal theory of the state and an argument against any "distributive justice" broader than strict commutative exchange, Catholic tradition has increasingly affirmed the necessity for a broad understanding of justice that goes beyond commutative exchange into "distributive" and "social" justice.

Moreover, as we shift from philosophical reasoning toward the appropriation of a faith stance as the grounds for a theory of justice, the reader will note some changes in style and mode as well. Mill, Rawls, and Nozick all approach justice with the philosopher's interest in conceptual and analytic categories. We enter now an arena focused more directly on social problems and concrete issues of justice. The language and categories—as well as the substantive conclusions—will differ.

Since the bishops' letter applies "Catholic social teaching" to the U.S. economy, a quick review of several aspects of Catholic social teaching will set the stage for reviewing the bishops' approach to economic justice.

Catholic Social Teaching

Modern Catholic tradition on "social teachings" begins in 1891 with Pope Leo XIII's encyclical *Rerum Novarum*. It includes subsequent papal encyclicals, conciliar documents, and other efforts to provide a systematic, normative theory relating faith to concrete social conditions.

During this century of "social teachings," Catholic tradition has changed greatly. The changes are both general and specific. On the general level, there has been a shift from a "natural law" approach that assumed human reason could derive absolute answers for social problems toward a recognition of the historical conditioning of all human consciousness, including reason. Concomitantly, there is a movement toward increasing use of Scripture as a base for social teachings. On the specific level, the tradition has gone from arguing that private property must be "preserved inviolate" to arguing that, under certain conditions, lands can be justifiably expropriated.[3] In the midst of such radical changes, it is difficult to present this tradition as a unity.

And yet, a unity it is. Certain philosophical and theological affirmations have remained constant within methodological and substantive flux. While those affirmations do not result in a static and unchanging interpretation of the social situation, they do yield a striking continuity at the level of moral principles, and hence of understanding the demands of justice.

The Catholic tradition on social teachings is rooted in three basic affirmations: (1) the inviolable dignity of the human person, (2) the essentially social nature of human beings, and (3) the belief that the abundance of nature and of social living is given for all people.

It is the dignity of the person "created in God's image" that sets the stage. From Leo XIII in 1891 through John Paul II in 1981, the transcendental worth of persons is the foundation on which social structures must be built. People are prior to institutions and institutions exist for the sake of people. People have rights which neither the state nor any institution may infringe.

Thus, from the earliest days of Catholic social teaching, the popes have consistently rejected any economic system that denies the rights of workers or treats them without dignity. As early as 1891, Leo XIII rejected the "free contract" as the basis for a fair wage. "Natural justice," he argued, requires that the worker receive adequate support, not merely what might be forthcoming in a contract.[4] Leo began a long tradition of rejecting "contract" in favor of a "living" or "family" wage.[5]

In later years, the rejection of contract was extended to a rejection of the market system and hence of capitalist and liberal ideology. "The proper ordering of economic affairs cannot be left to free competition alone," declared Pius XI.[6] Noting that economic supremacy had taken the place of free competition, he flatly declared that "free competition is dead."[7] Paul VI spelled out the reasoning: "if the positions of the contracting parties are too unequal, the consent of the parties does not suffice to guarantee the justice of their contract." And he made explicit the implied judgment on liberalism: "One must recognize that it is the fundamental principle of liberalism, as the rule for commercial exchange, which is questioned here."[8]

By 1971, the Synod of Bishops spoke not merely about the injustice of the contract or market system, but about an entire "network of domination, oppression and abuses." It exposed as a "myth" the assumption that economic development alone will help the poor.[9] The focus was no longer simply on wage justice, but on *participation* in the system. The tradition has long supported the right of workers to form unions.[10] Pius XI had suggested that wage contracts should, "when possible," be modified to include a "contract of partnership" that would permit wage earners to become owners.[11]

Thus began a tradition of linking economic justice with issues of participation and political rights. Noting that the dignity of persons includes the whole person, not just economic well-being, John XXIII argued for social as well as economic development.[12] Following this lead, Vatican II (1962–1965) stressed broad representation of people at every level of decision about economic issues.[13] Paul VI continued the trend by declaring that development must be "integral," promoting the good of the whole person and the good of every person.[14] He noted the legitimacy of both "the aspiration to equality and the aspiration to participation."[15]

In short, economic injustices have come to be linked with political and "participatory" rights. The dignity of persons requires not only treating them justly in the determination of wages, but also according them their full measure of total human rights.[16] An economic system that produces large quantities of goods and distributes them fairly will nonetheless be "unjust" if its organization and structure are such that "the human dignity of workers is compromised, or their sense of responsibility is weakened, or their freedom of action is removed."[17]

In the movement from a stress on wage justice to a stress on "participation," the notion of individual worth and dignity has been increasingly linked to the social nature of human beings. Rights are not simply claims to be attributed to individuals apart from community. Because human beings are social by their very nature, human dignity will be addressed in social relationships. "Justice" is not simply a matter of proper distribution of goods (distributive justice) but also of permitting and indeed requiring each person to participate in the production of those goods (social justice).

Thus, concrete historical manifestations of social institutions become an important arena for the expression of human dignity, and human dignity is tied up with the "common good." Nowhere is this better illustrated than in the tradition's handling of questions of ownership and use of property.

The right to own property has been consistently affirmed since the time of Leo XIII. This is a right "conferred by nature" and necessary for the development of the person, e.g., for fulfilling family duties.[18] At the same time, the *use* of property has always been understood to be directed by considerations of the common good. "The just ownership of money is distinct from the just use of money," declared Leo XIII.[19] He therefore urged the wealthy to share their goods as a matter of "charity."[20] For Pius XI and the succeeding tradition, however, sharing is not a matter of charity but of *justice,* and the state may intervene to set limits on the use of private property.[21]

While the tradition has therefore affirmed a right to private property based on the dignity of the person, it has also defended limits on that right based on the common good. In recent decades, it has begun to justify limited circumstances in which private property may be expropriated by others. *Gaudium et Spes* reports the consensus of Vatican II that "a person . . . in extreme necessity . . . has the right to take from the riches of others" to meet basic needs.[22] Paul VI extends this to the expropriation of landed estates that are not well used or that bring hardship to people.[23] The underlying principle is that all creation is given for humankind; therefore each has the right to basic necessities and "all other rights whatsoever, including those of property and of free commerce, are to be subordinated to this principle."[24]

The common good affects not only the legitimacy of ownership, but also the determination of wages. The right to a "living wage" is always put within the context of the common good: "the wage scale must be regulated with a view to the economic welfare of the whole people."[25] Distributive justice in the area of wages therefore becomes a complicated matter of balancing workers' rights and contribution with the requirements of the community, including the impact of wage scales on employment rates.[26] Nonetheless, the tradition affirms the priority of labor over capital.[27]

Perhaps most striking in the tradition is its consistent concern for the plight of the poor. In Leo XIII and Pius XI are found the roots of a tradition that perceives the mere *fact* of inequality of wealth as a sign of injustice. The poor, declares Leo, do not deserve their plight. Rather, "a very few and exceedingly rich . . . have laid a yoke almost of slavery on the unnumbered masses of non-owning workers."[28] Pius XI asserts that the immense numbers of poor, on the one hand, and the super-abundant riches of the few, on the other, are "an unanswerable argument" that goods are "far from rightly distributed and equitably shared."[29] John XXIII argues that there is "manifest injustice" in placing a whole group of citizens (farmers) "in an inferior economic and social status, with less purchasing power than required for a decent livelihood."[30] Vatican II declares that "excessive economic and social differences . . . militate against social justice. . . ."[31] The "uplifting of the proletariat," as Pius XI called it, was a constant theme during this time, and was applied both within cultures and between wealthy First-World and poor Third-World countries.[32] These concerns culminate in what is today called the "option for the poor": "true relationships of justice and equality," declares Paul VI, require "the preferential respect due to the poor."[33]

The grounds for this option, however, have changed. From Leo XIII through John XXIII, the special position of the poor is justified largely on grounds of reason: the poor are not able to fend for themselves; therefore, distributive justice requires that the state take particular care of them.[34] Phrases such as "justice and equity require" are common, but the terms are rarely defined. The reader is left to be persuaded by the logic of the argument. This is the more traditional "natural law" approach and is summarized in the statement from *Gaudium et Spes* that the church "has worked out these principles [of justice and equity] as right reason demanded."[35]

Since the time of Vatican II, however, with increasing consciousness of the historically conditioned nature of human reason, church leaders have turned increasingly to Scripture as the justifying ground for the "option for the poor." In *Justice in the World*, the Synod of Bishops spelled out God's preference for the poor in both Old and New Testaments.[36] Paul VI reiterated that "we are instructed by the Gospel" in the proper respect for the poor.[37]

It is also important to note that the tradition has worked on a model of social consensus. Labor and capital need each other; thus, classes are not in opposition to each other and harmony is possible. In spite of its concern for the poor and its growing emphasis on the priority of labor and the right to participation and political involvement, the tradition has shied away from any suggestion that revolution will be necessary in order to secure the rights of the poor. The vision of justice is a vision grounded in a sense of solidarity, mutual responsibility, and joint benefit. Individual rights and the common good are never in opposition to each other but are mutually supporting basic principles. Similarly, reason and revelation are mutually supporting sources of insight.

The Bishops' Letter

The heritage of this tradition shows strongly in the bishops' letter on the U.S. economy. The dignity of the person, the social nature of humankind, the special position of the poor, stress on participation, assumptions of social consensus, the rejection of "rigid" capitalism—all are present. And they are combined with an effort to provide a more systematic treatment of justice, drawing on tradition, scripture, and philosophical reasoning.

The bishops declare that the fundamental criterion for assessing the economic system is its impact on human dignity: *"The dignity of the human person, realized in community with others, is the criterion against which all aspects of economic life must be measured."*[38] Thus, moral policies for economic life must be shaped by three questions: what they do *for* people, what they do *to* people, and *how* people *participate* in them.[39]

Since the poor are most affected by economic decisions, and since they have a special claim by virtue of being vulnerable, such decisions must be judged by what they do to and for the poor and by what they enable the poor to do for themselves.[40] The treatment of the poor is the "litmus test" for the justice or injustice of a society.[41] Stress on the position of the poor is supported both by Christian conviction and by "the promise of this nation to secure liberty and justice for all."[42]

Hence, the fundamental moral criterion for all economic policies and decisions is simply: "They must be at the service of *all people, especially the poor.*"[43]

Following the post-Vatican II trend, the bishops devote considerable time to developing a scriptural base for this fundamental criterion. While they stress that "philosophical reflection" and "common human experience" confirm these religious convictions, it is the religious convictions themselves that are developed at length.

Israelite tradition provides a theological framework through themes of creation, covenant, and community.[44] The creation stories affirm the "alien dignity" of every human being.[45] They also give us fundamental themes of common use of goods: "From the Patristic period to the present, the Church has affirmed that misuse of the world's resources or appropriation of them by a minority of the world's population betrays the gift of creation since 'whatever belongs to God belongs to all.'"[46]

From the covenant tradition we understand God to be a God of justice. *Justice* in Scripture has several nuances. Most fundamentally, it means a sense of "what is right"—including both ṣedaqah (righteousness) and *mishpat* (right judgment and concrete acts of justice).[47] However, there is a distinctive aspect of the biblical presentation of justice: "the justice of a community is measured by its treatment of the powerless in society."[48]

The New Testament affirms these themes of creation and covenant: Jesus brings a "new creation" and a "new covenant."[49] The new covenant calls for discipleship or service, summed up in the great commandment to love one's neighbor as oneself.[50] In Luke's gospel in particular, the "poor" are blessed and are the objects of God's special love.[51] Thus, the foundation is laid for a "preferential option for the poor."[52]

This scriptural foundation provides a basic vision. It does not yield direct policy imperatives. On the conviction that this vision is "intelligible to those who do not share Christian religious convictions,"[53] the bishops seek an ethical framework drawn from generally accepted norms.

Among these are norms of "basic justice." These norms state minimal levels of mutual care and respect; they are not as all-encompassing as the biblical vision.[54] But they provide a common grounding for judgments about economic justice. Here the bishops draw specifically on the Catholic tradition of commutative, social, and distributive justice.

Commutative justice requires fairness in agreements and exchanges between private parties. It is commutative justice that requires a fair wage and adequate working conditions.[55] *Social* justice requires people to participate in the creation of the common good. It therefore also requires society to enable them to do so.[56] The requirement for full employment, for example, can be drawn from social justice. *Distributive* justice deals with the allocation of social goods. The bishops propose that distributive justice requires special attention to needs, prohibits discrimination, and provides for a minimal welfare floor.[57]

These fundamental requirements of "basic justice" are summarized in a requirement for *"the establishment of minimum levels of participation in the life of the human community for all persons."*[58] The "ultimate injustice" is for people or groups to be treated as if they were "nonmembers" of the human race.[59] Hence, all people have fundamental human rights as enumerated, for example, in Pope John XXIII's *Pacem in Terris* and in the U.N. *Declaration of Human Rights.*[60]

These convictions also give rise to three priority principles. First, fulfilling the basic needs of the poor is of the highest priority.[61] Second, increasing participation for the marginalized is a high priority.[62] Third, investment policies should be directed to benefiting those who are poor or economically insecure.[63]

These priorities are not economic policies per se, but "norms" against which policies can be judged.[64] The movement from norm to policy is complex, and the bishops do not assert the same moral authority for their policy judgments as for their normative claims.[65] Nonetheless, in view of the importance they attach to labor and to the plight of the poor, a quick review on each of these issues will round out the bishops' understanding of economic justice.

Because of the importance of work for the fulfillment of human life, people have a right to work.[66] Thus, the first specific policy recommendation made by the bishops is a call for "full employment."[67] High levels of unemployment are unacceptable because of their impact on human life.[68] The bishops therefore call for the establishment of a right to work, urging that it is a joint task between private enterprise and government.[69] They propose targeted employment programs, expanding job training, the development of new strategies for job sharing, and other such efforts.[70]

As has become traditional in Catholic social teaching, the bishops walk a line between acceptance and critique of capitalism as the context for work. On the one hand, they support "the freedom of entrepreneurship, business, and finance."[71] At the same time, they follow Catholic tradition in arguing that there is a "social mortgage" on private property.[72] They also contend that the "free market" gives employers greater bargaining power, and therefore that justice requires certain minimal guarantees for workers.[73] Hence, they reject the notion that a free market automatically produces justice.[74]

Employment alone, however, will not solve the problems of poverty given high priority by the bishops. Here, the bishops review statistics and analyses to demonstrate the depth and nature of poverty in the United States.[75] Our economy is "marked by a very uneven distribution of wealth and income."[76] Since Catholic tradition has taken such disparities to represent a form of injustice, the question must be raised whether justice requires equality of wealth and income. To this, the bishops answer no.[77] However, following Catholic tradition, they suggest that there is a "presumption" against extreme inequalities which are detrimental to social solidarity.[78] Such inequalities are therefore to be rectified.

In doing so, the "principle of participation" must be honored.[79] That is, programs that do things "with" the poor are to be preferred to those that do things "for" the poor in a paternalistic manner. The bishops give special attention to problems of stigmatization of poverty.[80] Tax reforms, removing discriminatory barriers, education, and welfare programs are all supported.[81]

REVIEW

Justice, for the bishops, is neither the result of societal consensus nor of rational deduction or calculation alone. It is rooted in a faith tradition that responds to a loving and just God. God's intentions for human life determine what is just and what is unjust.

Hence, the justice or injustice of discrepancies in wealth is not determined by assessing the fairness of the exchanges involved historically. Nor is it determined by principles of autonomous choice or calculations of the greatest overall good. Discrepancies of wealth indicate a situation in which some fail to remember that the goods of the earth are given for use by all; such a situation is unjust because it violates both the social nature of human beings and the purposes for which God gives the riches of the earth.

Because Catholic tradition advocates the common good, at first glance it appears similar to utilitarianism. But the common good means something different from the greatest good of the greatest number. The common good is judged by the plight of the poor; never would the greater good of some justify deprivation of others. Thus, far from justifying abuses of the powerless, the "common good" and the social nature of human beings becomes a corrective against such abuses.

Because Catholic tradition advocates certain "rights" of the individual that are prior to the interests of the state and that cannot be abrogated by the state, at first glance it also appears similar to Nozick. But where Nozick's rights are primarily "negative" rights against interference, Catholic tradition upholds "positive" rights to welfare. One of these is the right to a "living" wage. But acceptance of this right means precisely rejection of the unfettered market exchange system that Nozick lauds. Thus, taking a perspective that advocates individual rights does not yield the same understanding of economic justice.

Because protections for the disadvantaged loom large in the bishops' view, at first glance it also appears that they share much with Rawls. Indeed, substantively they do. The plight of the worst off becomes the measuring stick for the justice of a society. Again, however, this seeming agreement masks numerous underlying differences. The bishops appear to recognize more explicitly than Rawls does that economic differences will result in political inequalities. The grounding for protection of the disadvantaged is very different. For Rawls, protection of the least advantaged is the result of a self-interested calculation under conditions of ignorance; for the bishops, it is the result of acknowledgment of the presence and will of a loving God.

APPENDIX

THE PRINCIPLE OF SUBSIDIARITY

Origin and meaning

185. *Subsidiarity is among the most constant and characteristic directives of the Church's social doctrine* and has been present since the first great social encyclical. It is impossible to promote the dignity of the person without showing concern for the family, groups, associations, local territorial realities; in short, for that aggregate of economic, social, cultural, sports-oriented, recreational, professional and political expressions to which people spontaneously give life and which make it possible for them to achieve effective social growth. This is the realm of *civil society,* understood as the sum of the relationships between individuals and intermediate social groupings, which are the first relationships to arise and which come about thanks to "the creative subjectivity of the citizen."[82] This network of relationships strengthens the social fabric and constitutes the basis of a true community of persons, making possible the recognition of higher forms of social activity.

186. *The necessity of defending and promoting the original expressions of social life is emphasized by the Church in the Encyclical* Quadragesimo Anno, *in which the principle of subsidiarity is indicated as a most important principle of "social philosophy."* "Just as it is gravely wrong to take from individuals what they can accomplish by their own initiative and industry and give it to the community, so also it is an injustice and at the same time a grave evil and disturbance of right order to assign to a greater and higher association what lesser and subordinate organizations can do. For every social activity ought of its very nature to furnish help to the members of the body social, and never destroy and absorb them."[83]

On the basis of this principle, all societies of a superior order must adopt attitudes of help ("subsidium")—therefore of support, promotion, development—with respect to lower-order societies. In this way, intermediate social entities can properly perform the functions that fall to them without being required to hand them over unjustly to other social entities of a higher level, by which they would end up being absorbed and substituted, in the end seeing themselves denied their dignity and essential place.

Subsidiarity, understood *in the positive sense* as economic, institutional or juridical assistance offered to lesser social entities, entails a corresponding series of *negative* implications that require the State to refrain from anything that would de facto restrict the existential space of the smaller essential cells of society. Their initiative, freedom and responsibility must not be supplanted.

Concrete indications

187. *The principle of subsidiarity protects people from abuses by higher-level social authority and calls on these same authorities to help individuals and intermediate groups to fulfil their duties. This principle is imperative because every person, family and intermediate group has something original to offer to the community.* Experience shows that the denial of subsidiarity, or its limitation in the name of an alleged democratization or equality of all members of society, limits and sometimes even destroys the spirit of freedom and initiative.

The principle of subsidiarity is opposed to certain forms of centralization, bureaucratization, and welfare assistance and to the unjustified and excessive presence of the State in public mechanisms. "By intervening directly and depriving society of its responsibility, the Social Assistance State leads to a loss of human energies and an inordinate increase of public agencies, which are dominated more by bureaucratic ways of thinking than by concern for serving their clients, and which are accompanied by an enormous increase in spending."[84] An absent or insufficient recognition of private initiative—in economic matters also—and the failure to recognize its public function, contribute to the undermining of the principle of subsidiarity, as monopolies do as well.

In order for the principle of subsidiarity to be put into practice there is a *corresponding need* for: respect and effective promotion of the human person and the family; ever greater appreciation of associations and intermediate organizations in their fundamental choices and in those that cannot be delegated to or exercised by others; the encouragement of private initiative so that every social entity remains at the service of the common good, each with its own distinctive characteristics; the presence of pluralism in society and due representation of its vital components; safeguarding human rights and the rights of minorities; bringing about bureaucratic and administrative decentralization; striking a balance between the public and private spheres, with the resulting recognition of the *social* function of the private sphere; appropriate methods for making citizens more responsible in actively "being a part" of the political and social reality of their country.

188. *Various circumstances may make it advisable that the State step in to supply certain functions.* One may think, for example, of situations in which it is necessary for the State itself to stimulate the economy because it is impossible for civil society to support initiatives on its own. One may also envision the reality of serious social imbalance or injustice where only the intervention of the public authority can create conditions of greater equality, justice and peace. In light of the principle of subsidiarity, however, this institutional substitution must not continue any longer than is absolutely necessary, since justification for such intervention is found only in the *exceptional nature* of the situation. In any case, the common good correctly understood, the demands of which will never in any way be contrary to the defence and promotion of the primacy of the person and the way this is expressed in society, must remain the criteria for making decisions concerning the application of the principle of subsidiarity.

NOTES

1. National Conference of Catholic Bishops, *Pastoral Letter on Catholic Social Teaching and the U.S. Economy,* second draft (Washington, D.C., October 7, 1985), hereafter cited as "Bishops' Letter"; numbers in the text are given. The third draft of the letter was published while this book was in press.
2. Bishops' Letter, 32.
3. For the former position, see Leo XIII, *Rerum Novarum* (1891), §23; for the latter, see Paul VI, *Populorum Progressio* (1967) §§23, 24.
4. *Rerum Novarum* §63. The sentiment was echoed by John XXIII when he declared that workers must receive a wage "sufficient to lead a life worthy of man . . ." (*Mater et Magistra* 1961, §71).
5. The phrase "living wage" can be attributed to John A. Ryan; the concept, however, was clearly present in *Rerum Novarum*, and has continued to permeate the tradition. More recently, phrases such as "family wage" are used. See Pope John Paul II, *Laborem Exercens* (1981), §19.
6. *Quadragesimo Anno* (1931), part II, section 5.
7. Ibid., part III, section I.
8. *Populorum Progressio*, §§58–59.
9. *Justice in the World* (1971), §§3, 16.

10. John Paul II, in *Laborem Exercens*, §20, declared that unions are a "mouthpiece for the struggle for social justice."
11. *Quadragesimo Anno*, §34.
12. *Mater et Magistra*, §73.
13. *Gaudium et Spes* (1965), §§67 and 65.
14. *Populorum Progressio*, §14.
15. *Octogesima Adveniens* (1971), §22. The 1971 Synod of Bishops summarized this trend by declaring that "economic injustice and lack of social participation keep a [person] from attaining his [or her] basic human and civil rights" (*Justice in the World*, §9).
16. A rather complete listing of rights is provided by Pope John XXIII in *Pacem in Terris* (1963), §§11–27. "The right to take an active part in public affairs and to contribute one's part to the common good" is explicitly mentioned (§26).
17. John XXIII, *Mater et Magistra*, §83.
18. Cf. Leo XIII, *Rerum Novarum*, §§10 and 19; John XXIII, *Mater et Magistra*, §§109 and 71.
19. *Rerum Novarum*, §35.
20. Ibid., §36.
21. *Quadragesimo Anno*, part II, section 1.
22. *Gaudium et Spes*, §69.
23. *Populorum Progressio*, §24.
24. Ibid., §22.
25. Pius XI, *Quadragesimo Anno*, part II, section 4.
26. John XXIII, *Mater et Magistra*, §71.
27. John Paul II, *Laborem Exercens*, §12.
28. *Rerum Novarum*, §§5, 6.
29. *Quadragesimo Anno*, part II, section 3.
30. *Mater et Magistra*, §140.
31. *Gaudium et Spes*, §29.
32. Pius XI, *Quadragesimo Anno*, part II, section 3. In *Mater et Magistra* John XXIII extends the principle to the obligation of the rich nations to help the poor (§161).
33. *Octogesimo Anno*, §23.
34. *Rerum Novarum*, §54. See also *Pacem in Terris*, §56.
35. *Gaudium et Spes*, §63.
36. *Justice in the World*, §§30–31.
37. *Octogesimo Anno*. §23.
38. Bishops' Letter, 49; emphasis in the original.
39. Ibid., 1.
40. Ibid., 28.
41. Ibid., 120.
42. Ibid., 22.
43. Ibid., 28.
44. Ibid., 36.
45. Ibid., 38.
46. Ibid., 40.

47. Ibid., 45, 43.

48. Ibid., 44.

49. Ibid., 47.

50. Ibid., 49–51.

51. Ibid., 58. The bishops stress that early Christianity did not therefore "canonize" poverty; poverty is always cause for sadness.

52. Ibid., 59.

53. Ibid., 67.

54. Ibid., 73.

55. Ibid., 74.

56. Ibid., 75.

57. Ibid., 76–78.

58. Ibid., 81; emphasis in the original.

59. Ibid.

60. Ibid., 83.

61. Ibid., 92.

62. Ibid., 93.

63. Ibid., 94.

64. Ibid., 95.

65. Ibid., 132–133.

66. Ibid., 97–102. The bishops here draw on Pope John Paul II's *Laborem Exercens,* in which he argued that work was both a right and a duty.

67. Ibid., 135: "Full employment is the foundation of a just economy."

68. Ibid., 140–142.

69. Ibid., 152, 153.

70. Ibid., 157–168. The bishops' specific policy recommendations remain rather general and have the air of urging rather than specifying action.

71. Ibid., 108.

72. Ibid., 113.

73. Ibid., 102.

74. Ibid., 113.

75. Ibid., 169–182.

76. Ibid., 181.

77. Ibid., 183: "Some degree of inequality is not only acceptable, but may be considered desirable for economic and social reasons."

78. Ibid.

79. Ibid., 186.

80. Ibid., 192.

81. Ibid., 194–211.

82. John Paul II, Encyclical Letter *Sollicitudo Rei Socialis,* 15: *AAS* 80 (1988), 529.

83. Pius XI, Encyclical Letter *Quadragesimo Anno: AAS* 23 (1931), 203.

84. John Paul II, Encyclical Letter *Centesimus Annus,* 48: *AAS* 83 (1991), 854.

12. A PROTESTANT ALTERNATIVE: REINHOLD NIEBUHR

Karen Lebacqz

During much of the time that Catholic social teachings were developing, American Protestant Christianity was being pushed and prodded by the prodigious works of Reinhold Niebuhr. Like the Catholic tradition during the same period, Niebuhr's own thought underwent considerable change. Nonetheless, a core understanding of justice permeates his long career and provides a significant Protestant alternative to the Catholic view.

Niebuhr respected his Catholic peers, but thought that they, like their liberal counterparts in the philosophical world, were not sufficiently "realistic" about the necessity for struggle in history. Hence, his own "Christian realism" attempts to take seriously the limits of political and social possibilities.

Love and Sin

For Niebuhr, prophetic religion combines an utmost seriousness about history with a transcendent norm. It never permits us to ignore history or to seek escape from it; yet it does not find its ultimate goals or standards within history. Therein lies the special gift of prophetic religion.

In Christianity, Jesus is the "perfect fruit of prophetic religion": he is both in history and points beyond history.[1] Jesus represents seriousness about history (incarnation) and yet a normative realm beyond history (the kingdom). From Jesus, we get the supreme ethical command: love. His ethical ideal is one of complete obedience to God's will.[2] This is perfect love, which Jesus both embodies and commands.

For Niebuhr, therefore, Christian ethics begins with love. Love is, first, a derivation of faith. At the same time, love is a "natural" requirement for humans. Individuals can realize themselves only in community, or "brotherhood." The "kingdom of God" indicates our fulfillment in a world of perfect harmony. Love, therefore, is "the primary law" of human nature and the highest principle of Christian ethics.[3]

What is love? Niebuhr distinguishes "mutual" love from "self-sacrificial" love.[4] Mutual love is not simply a calculating reciprocity; it springs from concern for the other. But it is never free from prudential concern for oneself as well. It is therefore never the purest form of love. Self-sacrificial love requires a selfless identification with the needs of the other.[5] It is characterized by "disinterestedness," meaning a lack of self-interest and a concern only for the life and well-being of the other.[6] Its ideal is perfect harmony; its purest expression, self-sacrifice. Hence, for Christians, the cross is the symbol of this ultimate perfection.[7]

If such selflessness were a simple possibility in history, there would be no need for justice, since all would coexist in a perfect harmony of love.[8] Unfortunately, claims Niebuhr, there is no such possibility: "the love commandment stands in juxtaposition to the fact of sin."[9] It is the attempt to be "realistic" about sin that grounds Niebuhr's approach to social ethics. Where Catholic tradition stresses the creation of humans in God's image, Niebuhr stresses another part of the creation story: the fact that humans are "fallen" sinners.

Sin for Niebuhr has two dimensions. The religious dimension of sin is idolatry: "The sin of man is that he seeks to make himself God."[10] We are creatures, but we are constantly tempted to forget that fact and to attempt to be God. A common form of this sin of idolatry is identifying our interests with the general interests, or thinking that our perception of truth is *the* truth.[11]

But sin also has a moral dimension. "The ego which falsely makes itself the centre of existence in its pride and will-to-power inevitably subordinates other life to its will."[12] If perfect love is the sacrifice of self, sin is the assertion of self against others: "sin is always trying to be strong at the expense of someone else."[13] The moral dimension of sin, therefore, is *injustice*—an unwillingness to value the claims of the other or to see one's own claims as equal but not superior to the other's. The root injustice is exploitation: "exploiting, enslaving, or taking advantage of other life."[14]

In the face of these "historical realities" of self-interest and exploitation, sacrificial love is not an adequate social ethic. Its ethical ideal of disinterestedness "is too rigorous and perfect to lend itself to application in the economic and political problems of our day."[15] Niebuhr's constant theme is that a profound faith must appreciate "the recalcitrance of sin on every level."[16] He rails against those who underestimate the power of sin both in individual life and especially in collective life. Even for the individual, a life of selfless giving is impossible.

But when we move from the individual to the collective level, the impossibility of disinterestedness is compounded. For here, the one who would act out of self-sacrifice is sacrificing not only his or her own interests, but the interests of others. Thus, self-sacrifice becomes "unjust betrayal" of the other.[17] Groups, therefore, must never be expected to behave altruistically: "groups have never been unselfish in the slightest degree."[18] This is particularly true of nations: "no nation in history has ever been known to be purely unselfish in its actions."[19] It is also true of classes.[20]

Love remains for Niebuhr an "impossible possibility"—relevant as the ultimate standard by which actions may be judged, but not possible of immediate implementation in the social world. Economic and political affairs must therefore be governed by what Niebuhr calls the "nicely calculated less and more" of justice.[21]

Justice

Justice is for Niebuhr a multifaceted term having something of the character of paradox. Indeed, it might be said that he uses the term rather loosely to cover a plethora of functions. He speaks of the "spirit of justice,"[22] of "rules" and "structures" of justice,[23] of calculating rights,[24] and, most often, of balancing forces or competing interests.[25] He declares that "justice that is only justice is less than justice."[26] To understand these diverse uses of the term and the seeming contradictions involved, one must understand the dialectic of love and justice in Niebuhr's thought.

Perfect justice would be a state of "brotherhood" in which there is no conflict of interests.[27] But such a state is no more possible in the world of sin than is a state of perfect love. Indeed, perfect justice would be love. But since love cannot be fully realized, neither can perfect justice. To be "realistic," justice must assume the continued power of self-interest.[28] In history we live always within the realm of "imperfect" or "relative" justice.[29] It is the inevitability of these relative distinctions in history that is so often ignored by Christian thinkers, says Niebuhr.[30] Relative justice involves the calculation of competing interests, the specification of duties and rights, and the balancing of life forces.

Such relative justice has a dialectical relationship to love. On the one hand, rules of justice extend our obligations toward dealing with complex, continuing, and socially recognized obligations that go far beyond the immediate boundaries of what we would naturally feel for others.[31] In doing so, such rules serve the "spirit of brotherhood" or love. In this sense, then, rules of justice support love and must not be excluded from the domain of love. Complex relations require justice.

Yet, because justice is always relative, it is always capable of improvement. Any historical manifestation or rule of justice could always approximate more closely the ideal of love. Justice is the best *possible* harmony within the conditions created by sin, but it is not the best *imaginable* harmony. Indeed, the laws and rules of justice themselves will always reflect the partiality of human perspectives; they are not "unconditionally" just.[32]

Hence, all historical enactments of justice stand under the judgment of love. Love requires justice for the complex realities of the sinful social world. Yet, love also transcends, fulfills, negates, and judges justice. It transcends justice because it goes beyond, exceeding the demands of justice.[33] It fulfills justice because it never implies less than justice: where life affirms life, justice is done.[34] It negates and judges justice because every historical justice is imperfect and stands under the judgment of more perfect possibilities of human community.[35]

This explains why "justice that is only justice is less than justice." The minimal justice of equal rights before the law, for example, is indeed justice. But it never fulfills the total spirit of the willing affirmation of life with life that is required for "perfect justice" or love.

Niebuhr's ethical stance is therefore dualistic, affirming the necessity for norms of both justice and love, neither of which is sufficient in itself.

But what, then, are the requirements of justice? Niebuhr elaborates these in terms of rules or laws (the more "theoretical" side of justice) and in terms of structures.

Rules of Justice

Because every historical justice is less than love and is therefore capable of improvement, there are for Niebuhr no universal or absolute standards of justice. Indeed, Niebuhr suggests that any attempt to codify justice—for example, into a listing of rights—always develops into injustice because "the perspective of the strong dictates the conceptions of justice by which the total community operates."[36]

But this does not imply a relativism that acknowledges no standards at all. For Niebuhr, there are generally valid principles that inform and judge historical choices. The two most important of these are freedom and equality.[37]

Freedom is the essence of human nature and therefore always stands as a crucial value. But unfettered freedom in the economic sphere too often means that the poor are priced out of the market.[38] Thus, freedom cannot stand alone as a social principle: it must always be "relegated" to justice, community, and equality.[39]

Equality emerges as Niebuhr's highest standard of justice: "a religion which holds love to be the final law of life stultifies itself if it does not support equal justice as a political and economic approximation of the ideal of love."[40] Equality is the "regulative principle" of justice, a "principle of criticism under which every scheme of justice stands."[41] "Equal justice" is the best approximation of "brotherhood"—or love—under the conditions of sin.[42] Equal justice is therefore "the most rational possible social goal."[43] The rule of equality includes both concerns for process (e.g., impartiality in the calculation of needs) and also for equality as a substantive goal (e.g., equal civil rights).

Even equality, however, can be modified. Indeed, in historical societies, differences of need and social function make inequality a necessity.[44] In addition, "imaginative justice" goes beyond simple equality to note the needs of the neighbor.[45] And equal justice will itself issue in a kind of "option for the poor":

> A social conflict which aims at greater equality has a moral justification which must be denied to efforts which aim at the perpetuation of privilege. . . . The oppressed have a higher moral right to challenge their oppressors than these have to maintain their rule by force.[46]

Structures of Justice

But how is justice to be established? It is obvious from Niebuhr's elaboration of freedom and equality that *reason* has a role to play in bringing about justice. It is "constitutive" in the rules of justice.[47] Its canons of consistency will lead us to condemn special privileges that cannot be justified.[48] It enables us to judge things from a more inclusive perspective.[49] It helps provide a penetrating analysis of factors in the social situation.[50] Moreover, it can destroy illusions.[51]

But reason alone cannot bring about justice. First, reason itself is not free from the influence of human passions and interests. Reason, too, is "fallen."[52] All rational estimates of rights and interests are "contingent" and "finite," "tainted" by passion and self-interest.[53] Thus, "even the most rational" of people will propose corrupted definitions of justice.[54] *Our* truth is never *the* truth.[55]

Indeed, Niebuhr suggests that the development of rationality has actually injured the search for social justice by "imparting universal pretensions" to partial social interests.[56] The privileged classes are particularly guilty of this form of sin; they do not realize how much their presumed rational calculations are affected by their economic interests.[57] Indeed, Niebuhr gives a kind of "epistemological privilege" to the oppressed, suggesting that "those who benefit from social injustice are naturally less capable of understanding its real character than those who suffer from it."[58]

It is partly because of the distortions of reason that there can be no universal "rational" standards of justice. It is also for this reason that "neutrality" in social struggle is impossible, and that efforts to remain "neutral" really have the effect of working to the advantage of entrenched interests.[59]

Second, reason alone is not adequate to establish justice because justice involves the totality of human life which includes both reason and passion. The realist knows, claims Niebuhr, that "history is not a simple rational process but a vital one."[60] Justice in history therefore requires not merely rules and principles but the balancing of competing forces, the taming and ordering of human "vitalities."[61] This is to say that justice requires the use of power or coercion to establish order: "justice is achieved only as some kind of decent equilibrium of power is established."[62] Niebuhr is perhaps best known for his constant stress on the balance of power: "Any justice that the world has ever achieved rests upon some balance between the various interests."[63] This, he declares, is a "clear lesson of history."[64]

This also means that, for Niebuhr, *power* yields injustice. Niebuhr speaks frequently of the injustice of power: "it may be taken as axiomatic that great disproportions of power lead to injustice."[65] Justice in social systems, therefore, is not simply a matter of how goods are distributed, but is also a question of the proper ordering and balancing of power. The struggle for justice is a struggle to increase the power of the victims of injustice.[66]

Political and Economic Implications

Since justice requires a balance of power, the centers of power are crucial to the historical enactment of justice. Two such centers loom large for Niebuhr: the political and the economic.

In response to the threat of fascism, much of Niebuhr's energies went to arguing for and supporting forms of strong democratic government. The "structures of justice" needed for balancing vitalities in society require both a strong organizing power, or government, and a balance of powers. Too little organizing power results in anarchy; too much becomes tyranny.[67] Government must always be understood as both necessary and oppressive.[68]

But government is not the only important center of power. Niebuhr's concern for social justice took root during his pastorate in a church in Detroit; it was the struggles of the workers during hard economic times that set the agenda for his life-long passion. In contemporary society, argues Niebuhr, centers of power are largely economic.[69] In his early years, Niebuhr saw political power as so dependent on economic power that "a just political order is not possible without the reconstruction of the property system."[70] While he later modified this seemingly trenchant Marxism, he never lost his concern about the power of the economic sphere. The diffusion of political power in democracy makes for justice, he declared; yet the political power of the individual does not eliminate "flagrant forms of economic injustice" in capitalist democratic countries.[71]

Thus, economic justice is a prime concern for Niebuhr. Both liberalism and Marxism, Niebuhr charges, fail to understand property as a form of power.[72] Because property is power, "inequalities in possession have always made for an unjust distribution of the common social fund."[73] Niebuhr therefore is a staunch critic of contemporary capitalism, which he finds "a particularly grievous form of social injustice."[74] "Modern capitalism breeds injustice because of the disproportions of economic power that it tolerates and upon which it is based."[75]

Since justice requires a balance of power, Niebuhr asserts early on what Catholic tradition later affirmed: economic justice requires political participation and the use of power.[76] But, for Niebuhr, political participation will be won only by the conflict of force with force. Sinful people will never voluntarily give up their power and self-interest. Justice requires coercion.

Therefore, Niebuhr refused to deny the possibility of revolution or other violent approaches to the establishment of justice. The balance of power that represents justice always involves a tension; tension is covert conflict, and covert conflict can become overt.[77] While Niebuhr often argued on pragmatic grounds against violence, he found no absolute arguments against it in principle: "Once we have made the fateful concession of ethics to politics, and accepted coercion as a necessary instrument of social cohesion, we can make no absolute distinctions between nonviolent and violent types of coercion."[78] Hence, "the fight for justice will always be a fight."[79]

To those who would say, "*If only* we loved each other violence would not be necessary," Niebuhr would retort that they underestimate that *if*.[80] To those who advocate nonviolence as the "Christian" way, he would retort that they fail to observe the ways in which they *are already* involved in violence: "the whole of society is constantly involved in both coercion and violence."[81] For Niebuhr, government especially was a source of injustice and violence: in preserving "peace" it always does so by enforcing certain injustices.[82] Niebuhr rails against modern "robber states" who deny to the poor the very privileges that they have seized for themselves.[83]

In brief, Niebuhr's understanding of justice might be summed up in the phrase "love compromising with sin." Justice is derivative from love, yet distinct from it. The demands of justice are, in the end, the demands of love. Perfect love is a harmony in which human wills are not in conflict. Justice approximates that harmony through norms of equality and liberty. Yet, there can be no absolute rules of justice, since any approximation always stands under the possibility of correction. Justice requires constant attention to the distortions in our perspectives. It also requires the use of coercion to achieve balance of power.

For Niebuhr, the Protestant affirmation of justification by faith alone does not make efforts for justice irrelevant. Rather, it means that "we will not regard the pressures and counterpressures, the tensions, the overt and covert conflicts by which justice is achieved and maintained, as normative in the absolute sense; but neither will we ease our conscience by seeking to escape involvement in them."[84]

REVIEW

Niebuhr's approach to justice differs from all those considered above because of his emphasis on sin. For Niebuhr, sin or conflict among people is a persistent and enduring aspect of human life. Hence, both the utilitarians and the Catholics would be "unrealistic" in assuming a harmony between individual interests and the greater or common good. Rawls' dependence on reason is fallacious, because reason itself is tainted by sin and thus cannot alone yield valid principles of justice. Nozick's trust in the "free" exchanges of market systems ignores the fact that humans will always seek unfair advantage in exchange so that resulting divisions of goods are unjust. In a world permeated by sin, no single principle or approach can yield eternally valid principles of justice.

Instead, justice must be characterized first by a balance of power. The ideal is harmony of self with self; justice approximates this ideal by balancing powers so that the weak are protected against the strong. Such a balance is only a relative harmony, but it is a necessary and just harmony. Even Rawls' first principle of equal liberty would probably not satisfy Niebuhr, since it does not ensure a balance of power between classes. Similarly, Niebuhr would argue contra the bishops that justice does not consist in meeting the needs of the poor but in ensuring that they have enough power to meet their own needs.

But a balance of power is not itself the ideal. Thus, every historical enactment of justice for Niebuhr also involves injustice. Justice is never finished or achieved. Every relative justice is a relative injustice as well. One can never rest satisfied that justice has been done simply because "the greatest good" has been done or the disadvantaged are better off than they were before, or exchanges are fair, or living wages are granted. Each of these forms a part of justice, but each holds within it also a perversion of justice. All structures and arrangements of justice are temporary and partial. They always await the better balance, the closer approximation of the harmony of love that is perfect justice.

NOTES

1. Reinhold Niebuhr, *An Interpretation of Christian Ethics* (New York: Seabury, 1979; first published 1935), p. 22.
2. Reinhold Niebuhr, *The Nature and Destiny of Man*, 2 vols. (New York: Scribner, 1943, 1964), vol. 2, *Human Destiny*, p. 73.
3. D. B. Robertson, ed., *Love and Justice: Selections from the Shorter Writings of Reinhold Niebuhr* (Gloucester, Mass.: Peter Smith, 1976), p. 25; Niebuhr, *Nature and Destiny*, 2:244; Reinhold Niebuhr, *The Children of Light and the Children and Darkness* (London: Nisbet, 1945), p. 11.
4. Niebuhr, *Nature and Destiny*, 2, chap. 3.
5. Niebuhr, *Christian Ethics*, p. 100: "The complete identification of life with life which the law of love demands."
6. Robertson, *Love and Justice*, p. 31.
7. Niebuhr, *Nature and Destiny*, 2:72.
8. Robertson, *Love and Justice*, p. 27.
9. Niebuhr, *Christian Ethics*, p. 39; cf. Robertson, *Love and Justice*, p. 27.
10. Reinhold Niebuhr, *Nature and Destiny*, vol. 1, *Human Nature*, p. 179; see also p. 140.
11. Reinhold Niebuhr, *Moral Man and Immoral Society* (New York: Scribner, 1932, 1960), p. 117.
12. Niebuhr, *Nature and Destiny*, 1:179.
13. Robertson, *Love and Justice*, p. 164; cf. Niebuhr, *Nature and Destiny*, 2:252.
14. Robertson, *Love and Justice*, p. 282; cf. Niebuhr, *Christian Ethics*, p. 90.
15. Robertson, *Love and Justice*, p. 30.
16. Robertson, *Love and Justice*, p. 212.
17. Niebuhr, *Nature and Destiny*, 2:88; cf. Reinhold Niebuhr, *Moral Man*, p. 267.
18. Robertson, *Love and Justice*, p. 243.
19. Niebuhr, *Moral Man*, p. 75; cf. p. 84: "The selfishness of nations is proverbial." Niebuhr notes that loyalty to the nation is a high form of individual altruism, but that it becomes transmuted into patriotism, which is national egoism. Thus, "the unselfishness of individuals makes for the selfishness of nations" (*Moral Man*, p. 91).
20. Cf. Niebuhr, *Moral Man*, p. 213.
21. Niebuhr, *Christian Ethics*, p. 62; *Moral Man*, p. 68; *Nature and Destiny*, 1:295.
22. Robertson, *Love and Justice*, p. 25.
23. Niebuhr, *Nature and Destiny*, 2:247.
24. Ibid., p. 252.
25. E.g., Robertson, *Love and Justice*, p. 207: "Some balance of power is the basis of whatever justice is achieved in human relations."
26. Ibid., p. 32; cf. Niebuhr, *Moral Man*, p. 258.
27. Robertson, *Love and Justice*, p. 49.
28. Ibid., p. 28.
29. Ibid., p. 162: ". . . Maintaining a relative justice in an evil world."
30. Niebuhr, *Nature and Destiny*, 2:280.
31. Ibid., 2:248.

32. Niebuhr, *Nature and Destiny*, 2:252.

33. Niebuhr, *Christian Ethics*, p. 112; *Nature and Destiny*, 1:295.

34. Niebuhr, *Christian Ethics*, pp. 90, 128; *Nature and Destiny*, 1:295.

35. Niebuhr, *Christian Ethics*, p. 85; *Nature and Destiny*, 1:285, 2:246.

36. Robertson, *Love and Justice*, p. 32.

37. Niebuhr, *Nature and Destiny*, 2:254.

38. Robertson, *Love and Justice*, p. 87.

39. Ibid., p. 95.

40. Niebuhr, *Christian Ethics*, p. 80.

41. Ibid., pp. 65–66; cf. p. 121.

42. Niebuhr, *Nature and Destiny*, 2:254.

43. Niebuhr, *Moral Man*, p. 171.

44. Niebuhr, *Children of Light*, p. 55; *Nature and Destiny*, 2:255.

45. Niebuhr, *Christian Ethics*, p. 66.

46. Niebuhr, *Moral Man*, p. 234.

47. Niebuhr, *Nature and Destiny*, 2:248.

48. Niebuhr, *Christian Ethics*, p. 125.

49. Niebuhr, *Moral Man*, pp. 30–31.

50. Ibid., p. 32; cf. Niebuhr, *Christian Ethics*, p. 100.

51. Niebuhr, *Moral Man*, p. 237.

52. Niebuhr, *Christian Ethics*, pp. 79f.; Robertson, *Love and Justice*, p. 47; Niebuhr, *Nature and Destiny*, 1:284.

53. Niebuhr, *Nature and Destiny*, 2:252.

54. Robertson, *Love and Justice*, p. 48.

55. Niebuhr, *Nature and Destiny*, 2:214.

56. Niebuhr, *Christian Ethics*, p. 137.

57. Niebuhr, *Moral Man*, p. xiv.

58. Ibid., p. 80.

59. Robertson, *Love and Justice*, p. 254.

60. Ibid., p. 207.

61. Niebuhr, *Nature and Destiny*, 2:257.

62. Robertson, *Love and Justice*, p. 52. In Niebuhr's view, two things are necessary for the establishment of social justice: (1) a balance of powers, and (2) a central organizing power. Each of these can become distorted and contradict the law of love— the first by dissolving into anarchy, the second by becoming tyranny (*Nature and Destiny*, 2:257–258).

63. Robertson, *Love and Justice*, p. 173.

64. Ibid., p. 36.

65. Ibid., p. 199; Niebuhr, *Nature and Destiny*, 2:262; cf. *Nature and Destiny*, 1:223; Robertson, *Love and Justice*, pp. 173, 199.

66. Bennett, "Reinhold Niebuhr's Social Ethics," p. 60.

67. Niebuhr, *Nature and Destiny*, 2:257–258.

68. Ibid., 2:269; Niebuhr speaks of "both the vice and the necessity of government" (ibid., p. 278).

69. Niebuhr, *Christian Ethics*, p. 113; cf. Niebuhr, *Moral Man*, p. 163.

70. Niebuhr, *Christian Ethics*, p. 113.
71. Niebuhr, *Nature and Destiny*, 2:262–263.
72. Niebuhr, *Children of Light*, p. 76.
73. Niebuhr, *Christian Ethics*, p. 113.
74. Robertson, *Love and Justice*, p. 46.
75. Robertson, *Love and Justice*, p. 257; cf. Niebuhr, *Christian Ethics*, p. 90.
76. Robertson, *Love and Justice*, pp. 92–93.
77. Ibid., p. 276; cf. pp. 261 and 53.
78. Niebuhr, *Moral Man*, p. 179.
79. Robertson, *Love and Justice*, p. 38.
80. "It is because men are sinners that justice can be achieved only by a certain degree of coercion on the one hand, and by a resistance to coercion and tyranny on the other hand" (Reinhold Niebuhr, *Christianity and Power Politics* [New York: Scribner, 1946], p. 14).
81. Niebuhr, *Moral Man*, p. 192.
82. Niebuhr, *Nature and Destiny*, 2:275.
83. Robertson, *Love and Justice*, p. 167.
84. Niebuhr, *Nature and Destiny*, 2:284.

13. LOVE AND JUSTICE: SELECTIONS FROM THE SHORTER WRITINGS OF REINHOLD NIEBUHR

D. B. Robertson (ed.)

Reinhold Niebuhr (1892–1971) began his ministry as the pastor of Bethel Evangelical Church in Detroit, Michigan. As the congregation grew it attracted parishioners from the emerging Detroit professional class. As a pastor he spoke prophetically against the labor practices of Henry Ford, the automobile manufacturer. In 1928 Niebuhr became a professor at Union Theological Seminary in New York where he remained until his retirement in 1960. During his Union years he was active in addressing social issues in both religious and political contexts.

Niebuhr's first influential work, Moral Man and Immoral Society *(1932) analyzed collective human behavior and how it is influenced by power and self-interest. At the time of that writing Niebuhr was committed to socialism and pacifism. In 1935 he published* An Interpretation of Christian Ethics *in which he argued that Christian faith is a viable alternative to the liberal optimism of modern culture. By 1936 Niebuhr severed his ties to socialism, abandoned his pacifist stance, and later advocated United States involvement in the war effort against the Nazis.*

In 1939 he was invited to the University of Edinburgh to deliver the Gifford Lectures. These lectures would later be published under the title The Nature and Destiny of Man *(1941, 1943). In this two-volume work, Niebuhr juxtaposed the Christian understanding of human experience against classic and modern expressions of human experience. His scholarship and political activism made him a leading public intellectual. Niebuhr's theological perspective began with the human experience (anthropology). This point of departure allowed him to develop a Christian approach to social issues that could be practically applied to real-world situations. —NC*

THE SPIRIT OF JUSTICE

In the Christian faith the final law in which all other law is fulfilled is the law of love. But this law does not abrogate the laws of justice, except as love rises above justice to exceed it demands. The ordinary affairs of the community, the structure of politics and economics, must be governed by the spirit of justice and by specific and detailed definitions of rights and duties.

American Christianity tends to be irrelevant to the problems of justice because it persists in presenting the law of love as a simple solution to every communal problem. It is significant that the "social gospel," which sought to overcome the excessive individualism of the Christian faith in America, never escaped this sentimentality and irrelevance because it also preached the same ethic that it pretended to criticize. It insisted that Christians should practice the law of love not only in personal relations but in the collective relations of mankind. In these relations love as an ecstatic impulse of self-giving is practically impossible. Nations, classes, and races do not love one another. They may have a high sense of obligation to one another. They must express this sense of obligation in the desire to give each one his due.

The effort to substitute the law of love for the spirit of justice instead of recognizing love as the fulfillment and highest form of the spirit of justice, is derived from the failure to measure the power and persistence of self-interest. It is because self-interest is not easily overcome in even the life of the "redeemed" that most of the harmonies of life are not the perfect harmonies of fully co-ordinated wills but the tolerable harmonies of balanced interests and mutually recognized claims. Even in the family, in which the spirit of love may prevail more than in any other human institution, the careful calculation of rights is an important element in the harmony of the whole, though it must be observed that rights are so complexly intertwined in intimate relations that the calculations of justice lead to friction if love is not constantly infused into them.

Christian businessmen are more frequently characterized by a spirit of philanthropy than by a spirit of justice in assessing the claims and counterclaims of economic groups. Love in the form of philanthropy is, in fact, on a lower level than a high form of justice. For philanthropy is given to those who make no claims against us, who do not challenge our goodness or disinterestedness. An act of philanthropy may thus be an expression of both power and moral complacency. An act of justice on the other hand requires the humble recognition that the claim that another makes against us may be legitimate.

The pronouncements of church bodies and the preachments of the pulpit still tend to smell of sentimentality in our day because the law of love is presented without reference to the power of the law of self-love. "All coercion," wrote a Christian businessman recently, "is foreign to the Christian life because we Christians know that only uncoerced goodness is real goodness." This does not take into account that we need a great deal of second-rate goodness to get along with one another. We have to have a taxation system that demands more of us than we are inclined to give voluntarily; and we must maintain a social security system that holds us responsible for the security of other families than our own beyond our natural inclination.

JUSTICE AND LOVE

"A Christian," declared an eager young participant in a symposium on Christianity and politics, "always considers the common welfare before his own interest." This simple statement reveals a few of the weaknesses of moralistic Christianity in dealing with problems of justice. The statement contains at least two errors, or perhaps one error and one omission.

The first error consists in defining a Christian in terms which assure that consistent selflessness is possible. No Christian, even the most perfect, is able "always" to consider the common interest before his own. At least he is not able to do it without looking at the common interest with eyes colored by his own ambitions. If complete selflessness were a simple possibility, political justice could be quickly transmuted into perfect love; and all the frictions, tensions, partial co-operations, and overt and covert conflicts could be eliminated.

The other error is one of omission. To set self-interest and the general welfare in simple opposition is to ignore nine tenths of the ethical issues that confront the consciences of men. For these are concerned not so much with the problem of the self against the whole as with problems of the self in its relation to various types of "general welfare." "What do you mean by common interest?" retorted a shrewd businessman in the symposium referred to. Does it mean the family or the nation? If I have to choose between "my family " and "my nation," is the Christian choice inevitably weighted in favor of the nation since it is the larger community? And if the choice is between "my" nation and another nation, must the preference always be for the other nation on the ground that concern for my own nation represents collective self-interest? Was the young pacifist idealist right who insisted that if we had less "selfish concern for our own civilization" we could resolve the tension between ourselves and Russia, presumably by giving moral preference to a communist civilization over our own?

Such questions as these reveal why Christian moralism has made such meager contributions to the issues of justice in modern society. Justice requires discriminate judgments between conflicting claims. A Christian justice will be particularly critical of the claims of the self as against the claims of the other, but it will not dismiss them out of hand. Without this criticism all justice becomes corrupted into a refined form of self-seeking. But if the claims of the self (whether individual or collective) are not entertained, there is no justice at all.

In so far as justice admits the claims of the self, it is something less than love. Yet it cannot exist without love and remain justice. For without the "grace" of love, justice always degenerates into something less than justice.

But if justice requires that the interests of the self be entertained, it also requires that they be resisted. Every realistic system of justice must assume the continued power of self-interest, particularly of collective self-interest. It must furthermore assume that this power will express itself illegitimately as well as legitimately. It must therefore be prepared to resist illegitimate self-interest, even among the best men and the most just nations. A simple Christian moralism counsels men to be unselfish. A profounder Christian faith must encourage men to create systems of justice which will save society and themselves from their own selfishness.

But justice arbitrates not merely between the self and the other, but between the competing claims upon the self by various "others." Justice seeks to determine what I owe my family as compared with my nation; or what I owe this segment as against that segment of a community.

The realm of justice is also a realm of tragic choices, which are seldom envisaged in a type of idealism in which all choices are regarded as simple. Sometimes we must prefer a larger good to a smaller one, without the hope that the smaller one will be preserved in the larger one. Sometimes we must risk a terrible evil (such as an atomic war) in the hope of avoiding an imminent peril (such as subjugation to tyranny). Subsequent events may prove the risk to have been futile and the choice to have been wrong. If there is enough of a world left after such a wrong choice we will be taxed by the idealists for having made the wrong choice; and they will not know that they escaped an intolerable evil by our choice.

THE ETHIC OF JESUS AND THE SOCIAL PROBLEM

Since Walter Rauschenbusch aroused the American church to the urgency of the social problem and its relation to the ethical ideals of the gospel, it has been rather generally assumed that it is possible to abstract an adequate social ethic for the reconstruction of society from the social teachings of Jesus. Dozens of books have been written to prove that Jesus' ideals of brotherhood represented an outline of the ideal society, that his law of service offered an alternative to the competitive impulse in modern society, that guidance for the adjustment of every political and economic problem could be found in his words, and that nothing but a little logic would serve to draw out the "social implications " of his teachings.

Most of this energy has been vainly spent and has served to create as much confusion as light. There is indeed a very rigorous ethical ideal in the gospel of Jesus, but there is no social ethic in the ordinary sense of the word in it, precisely because the ethical ideal is too rigorous and perfect to lend itself to application in the economic and political problems of our day. This does not mean that the ethic of Jesus has no light to give to a modern Christian who faces the perplexing economic and political issues of a technological civilization. It means only that confusion will be avoided if a rigorous distinction is made between a perfectionist and absolute ethic and the necessities of a social situation.

In terms of individual life his ethical ideal was one of complete disinterestedness, religiously motivated. No one was to seek his own. The man who asked him to persuade his brother to divide an inheritance with him was rudely rebuked. Evil was not to be resisted, the borrower was to be given more than he asked for without hope of return.

Jesus did not deny that disinterested action would result in rewards; "all these things" would be added, and the man who forgot himself completely would find himself most truly. Here is the recognition of the basic ethical paradox that the highest result of an action can never be its desired result. It must be a by-product. If it is desired, the purity of the action is destroyed. If I love to be loved or to be socially approved, I will not be loved or approved in the same way as if my fellow men caught in me a glimpse of pure disinterestedness. Obviously the only way to achieve such pure disinterestedness is to have actions motivated purely by religious motives. But this very emphasis upon religious motives lifts the ethic of Jesus above the area of social ethics. We are asked to love our enemies, not because the social consequences of such love will be to make friends of the enemies, but because God loves with that kind of impartiality. We are demanded to forgive those who have wronged us, not because a forgiving spirit will prove redemptive in the lives of the fallen, but because God forgives our sins.

It is not difficult to draw conclusions in regard to the social ideal implied by such disinterestedness. In practical terms it means a combination of anarchism and communism dominated by the spirit of love. Such perfect love as he demands would obviate the necessity of coercion on the one hand because men would refrain from transgressing upon their neighbor's rights, and on the other hand because such transgression would be accepted and forgiven if it did occur. That is anarchism, in other words. It would mean communism because the privileges of each would be potentially the privileges of all. Where love is perfect the distinctions between mine and thine disappear. The social ideal of Jesus is as perfect and as impossible of attainment as is his personal ideal. But again it is an ideal that cannot be renounced completely. Whatever justice men attain in the society in which they live is always an imperfect justice.

Whether we view the ethical teachings of Jesus from the perspective of the individual or of society we discover an unattainable ideal, but a very useful one. It is an ideal never attained in history or in life, but one that gives us an absolute standard by which to judge both personal and social righteousness. It is a standard by comparison with which all human attainments fall short.

Valuable as this kind of perfectionism is, it certainly offers no basis for a social ethic that deals responsibly with a growing society. Those of us who believe in the complete reorganization of modern society are not wrong in using the ideal of Jesus as a vantage point from which to condemn the present social order, but I think we are in error when we try to draw from the teachings of Jesus any warrant for the social policies which we find necessary to attain to any modicum of justice. We may be right in believing that we are striving for a justice which approximates the Christian ideal more closely than the present social order, but we are wrong when we talk about achieving a "Christian social order." The Barthians are quite right, I think, in protesting against the easy identification of the Kingdom of God with every movement of social reform and social radicalism that has prevailed in American Christianity in particular and in liberal Protestantism in general.

The struggle for social justice in the present economic order involves the assertion of rights, the rights of the disinherited, and the use of coercion. Both are incompatible with the pure love ethic found in the Gospels.

The Negro has been forgiving in his subordinate position in society for a long time, but he has not persuaded the white man to grant him larger privileges in society. Whatever place the industrial worker has won in society has been won by the assertion of his rights through his trade-union organizations.

No one who looks realistically at the social scene can fail to discover that economic, racial, and national groups stand on a moral level considerably lower than that of the most sensitive individuals. They are not easily persuaded to a voluntary sacrifice of privileges, and an attitude of pure nonresistance on the part of those who suffer from their exactions does not produce the spirit of repentance among them.

The social struggle involves a violation of a pure ethic of love, not only in the assertion of rights, but in the inevitable use of coercion. Here again one need but state the obvious; but the obvious is usually not recognized by academic moralists. No society can exist without the use of coercion, though every intelligent society will try to reduce coercion to a minimum and rely upon the factor of mutual consent to give stability to its institutions. Yet it can never trust all of its citizens to accept necessary social arrangements voluntarily. It will use police force against recalcitrant and antisocial minorities, and it will use the threat of political force against a complacent and indifferent group of citizens which could never be relied upon to initiate adequate social policies upon its own accord. No government can wait upon voluntary action on the part of the privileged members of a community for an adequate inheritance or income tax. It will use political force created by the votes of the disinherited and less privileged to initiate and enforce taxation policies, designed to equalize privileges. Privileged groups may accept such legislation without violent revolt, but they will probably argue against its justice until the day of their death.

The necessity of this kind of coercion, based upon the assertion of interest on the part of the less privileged, is such a clear lesson of history that one hesitates to belabor the point and would refrain from doing so were it not for the fact that half of the academic treatises on social ethics and Christian ethics were written as if no such necessity existed. In this respect secular moralists are frequently as naïve as religious ones. In the one case it is expected that a change in educational technique will eliminate the drive of self-interest which determines economic life and in the other case there is a naive confidence in the possibility of changing human nature by religious conversion or religious inspiration.

One of the most unfortunate facts about our contemporary moral situation is that the church has ceased to convict men of selfishness at the precise moment in history when human greed is more obvious and more dangerous than at any previous time. Nowhere has the liberal church played more false to its generation than in its optimistic and romantic interpretation of human nature, just when an industrial civilization revealed the drive of self-interest in all its antisocial power. The part of the Christian church that has tried to convict the generation of sin knows too little about the problems of modern life to convict men of their significant sins. Thus religion has on the whole produced moral complacency rather than the spirit of repentance.

If we dealt realistically with the facts of human nature, we might be able to create an attitude of complacency toward increasing social restraint, based upon the realization that few, if any, of us are wise enough to restrain our expansive desires voluntarily in a degree sufficient for the needs of our highly interdependent society.

True religion could mitigate the cruelties of the social struggle by its creation of the spirit of love as well as the spirit of repentance. The love ideal which Jesus incarnates may be too pure to he realized in life, but it offers us nevertheless an ideal toward which the religious spirit may strive.

Real religious imagination is able, furthermore, to create an attitude of trust and faith toward human beings, in which the potentialities rather than the immediate realities are emphasized. Through such imagination the needs of the social foe are appreciated, his inadequacies are understood in the light of his situation, and his possibilities for higher and more moral action are recognized.

The fight for justice in society will always be a fight. But wherever the spirit of justice grows imaginative and is transmuted into love, a love in which the interests of the other are espoused, the struggle is transcended by just that much.

Neutrality in a social struggle between entrenched and advancing social classes really means alliance with the entrenched position. In the social struggle we are either on the side of privilege or need. No ethical perfectionism can save us from that choice.

14. A LIBERATION CHALLENGE: JOSE PORFIRIO MIRANDA

Like Reinhold Niebuhr, liberation theologians stress the reality of conflict in society. Like Niebuhr, they argue for sin—and hence for justice—to be understood as *structural* phenomena. And like Niebuhr, they emphasize the importance and meaning of history. And yet "Christian realism" and "liberation theology" have come to be understood as opposing camps in the theological world. For all of the similarities, a different—and quite distinctive—view of justice emerges from liberation theology.

A sustained attempt to provide a theory of justice from the liberation perspective is Jose Porfirio Miranda's *Marx and the Bible*.[1] However, because this work consists largely of scriptural exegesis, I will both set the stage for it and supplement it by drawing on the liberation approach more generally. In particular, I will draw heavily on the work of Gustavo Gutierrez, who is acknowledged as one of the first theologians to have given shape to the liberation approach.[2] It should be remembered, however, that liberation theology is not solely a Latin American phenomenon. It is also important to remember that it is largely a spoken, not written, theology; it has an elusive character difficult to render with vitality on paper.

A NEW METHOD

"God chose from birth to live the same as the poorest, didn't he? . . . [H]e was born poor and wants us all to be poor. Isn't that so? or rather, he wants us all to be equal."[3]

These words spoken by a poor woman in Latin America make an appropriate place to begin an examination of liberation theology, for liberation theology is first and foremost a new *method* for doing theology. "Latin American theology does not start with existing theologies but with the real and concrete totality of what is taking place."[4] It starts with "praxis"—with passionate and committed involvement in the struggle for liberation.[5] It is a dialectical reflection: reflecting on practice in the light of faith and on faith in the light of practice. Theology is therefore the "second movement," after involvement.

Moreover, this involvement has a clear bias: the perspective of the poor and oppressed. Its beginning place is the perspective of the poor. "The theology of liberation is an attempt to understand the faith from within the concrete historical, liberating, and subversive praxis of the poor of this world—the exploited classes, despised ethnic groups, and marginalized cultures."[6] The "poor" are variously defined. The term is used both literally and in an extended meaning that applies not only to those who are materially deprived but also to those who are "marginated" in society, lacking full access to and participation in socio-economic and political processes. Thus, the "poor" include laborers, peasants, the elderly and young, the unemployed, women, those from oppressed ethnic and racial groups, and others.[7] These people have become, in Gutierrez's words, "nonpersons," "suffering misery and exploitation, deprived of the most elemental human rights, scarcely aware that they are human beings at all."[8]

Thus, two important circumstances set the stage for liberation theology: first, the realities of poverty and oppression, and second, the commitment of Christians to the struggle for liberation. In the Latin American context, the two elements of oppression and struggle for liberation are sharply defined.[9]

Latin America is characterized by oppression, repression, and dependence. The realities of oppression—"untenable circumstances of poverty, alienation and exploitation"[10]—are everywhere evident: "It leaps out at you. It is impossible not to see it."[11] Former colonialization has simply been replaced by new forms of oppression. Internationalization of capitalism and proliferation of multinational corporations has resulted in a situation in which Third World countries have relatively little power or autonomy in the bargaining process; if they refuse to provide the desired cheap labor, corporations simply go elsewhere. Military regimes and "national security states" have arisen to ensure compliance of the masses with this economic agenda. The gap between rich and poor is growing.[12] Scholarship in the social sciences confirms that Latin America has been "from the beginning and constitutively" dependent.[13] Thus Dussel calls colonial domination the "original sin" of the prevailing world system.[14]

Based on their involvement in these realities, many Christians and church leaders have denounced the grave social injustices in Latin America. They have also formed "comunidades eclesiales de base"—small grass-roots organizations that educate and raise consciousness about social justice issues. As a result of these activities, Christians in Latin America have suffered persecution.[15] To economic poverty is added political repression. Such persecution merely reinforces the perception of the deep social ills plaguing Latin America.

Thus, liberation theology refuses "to conceal the conflictive nature of society under the cloak of generic, innocent-looking terminology."[16] Social conflict implies class struggle: history today is characterized by a division "into oppressors and oppressed, into owners of the means of production and those dispossessed of the fruit of their work, into antagonistic social classes."[17] Hence, "only a class analysis will enable us to see what is really involved in the opposition between oppressed countries and dominant peoples."[18] Here, most liberation theologians turn explicitly to Marxist analysis of class conflict.

Such an analysis implies the need for a paradigm adequate to the situation of dependence. "Development" will not do, since it implies no conflict. Gutierrez excoriates those who fail to perceive that lack of equitable distribution of goods is not simply an "unfortunate" circumstance that will be overcome in time, but is "the fault of the system itself."[19] In a situation characterized not by "underdevelopment" but by oppression, "liberation" is the proper paradigm. "The concerns of the so-called Third World countries revolve around the social injustice-justice axis, or, in concrete terms, the oppression-liberation axis."[20]

Recognizing the realities of dependence, oppression, and repression, Christians who have joined the struggle for liberation are calling for new interpretations of Scripture and new bases for Christian ethics. Too often, theology has been a tool justifying oppression.[21] From the "praxis" perspective, Christians argue that "salvation" is not simply a "spiritual" phenomenon, but is a unitary concept that includes social justice as well as spiritual well-being. Liberation implies social revolution, not merely reform.[22] Its goal is the creation of a "new person" in a "new society." Nor is "sin" to be understood as an individual, internal phenomenon: "Latin American theology does not start . . . with a relationship of the solitary self with another individual self but considers the structure in which the sin of the world conditions our own personal sin."[23]

Out of their perspective of involvement in liberation struggles, liberation theologians no longer trust mainline (European-dominated) readings of either the situation or of Scripture. They have developed a "hermeneutic of suspicion."[24]

Thus, for example, they seek not the "balance of power" lauded by Niebuhr, but a transfer of power.[25] And "violence" must be understood differently: the violence of the subjugator is evil, while the violence used by those who seek liberation from oppression is not.[26] No general judgments against violence can be levied, but only judgments from within the "praxis" seeking liberation. Liberation theology is thus contextual in its ethics.

Out of these commitments and reflections emerges a new kind of rationality—"the rationality of a concrete, historical undertaking."[27] This rationality dares to posit the vision of a social revolution that others find "utopian." Gutierrez charges that these "dominators" of the system simply are not familiar with the scientific rigor and rationality of concrete theology. Praxis gives a perception of aspects of the Christian message that escapes other approaches.[28] Dominant among these is an understanding of the central biblical concern for justice.

JUSTICE

Above all, Christians involved in liberating praxis are gleaning from Scripture and praxis a new understanding of justice. In the Bible they find eloquent testimony to God's concern for the poor and oppressed and evidence for a view of salvation that includes the struggle for a just society as part of salvation history.[29] In particular, they find that Scripture is clear that to know and to love God is to do justice for our neighbor.[30]

Miranda's analysis reflects several aspects typical of liberation theology: he begins with injustice; he uses Marxist analysis to develop perspective on the situation; he finds capitalism as a system to be a core locus of injustice; he finds agreeable sources within Christian (in his case, Catholic) tradition; and he turns to Scripture for confirmation of the centrality of justice and the condemnation of injustice.[31]

Liberation theology starts with prophetic denunciation of "the grave injustices rampant in Latin America."[32] To understand what "justice" is and what it demands, one begins with a review of those injustices experienced by the oppressed. Liberation theology presents in the first place, therefore, *a theory of injustice*. "In the underdeveloped countries one starts with a rejection of the existing situation, considered as fundamentally unjust and dehumanizing."[33]

A number of terms emerge as descriptions of injustice in the situation of the oppressed: slavery, humiliation, exploitation, repression—and, above all, poverty itself.[34]

But "injustice" is not simply a condition or circumstance. It is structured and institutionalized. It is *systematized*. The misery and exploitation of the poor do not just "happen." They are due "not to 'neglect' but to the very logic of the system."[35] The existence of the poor is "not politically neutral, and it is not ethically innocent. The poor are a by-product of the system in which we live."[36] Thus, the cry for liberation and justice is an attack on the entire system or social order, not merely on isolated instances of injustice. "More than anything else, it is the system itself that is being called into question by the exploited."[37]

Particularly crucial here is the capitalist system that undergirds the modern "security states" in Latin America. For Miranda, "capitalist oppression carries with it the weight of thousands of years of injustice and hardening of hearts and obstinacy of spirit."[38] The issue, therefore, is not simply to weed out injustices within the system, but to change the system itself: "it is a question not only of attacking the prevailing distribution of ownership, but the very right of differentiating ownership, especially of the means of production."[39] Noting that whether capitalism rises or languishes, "the outlook for the poor is dismal," Gutierrez also argues that capitalism is "of its very nature" detrimental to the poor.[40]

Miranda draws explicitly on Catholic social tradition to ground his judgment on the "injustice" of the situation in Mexico. Leo XIII's great encyclical *Rerum Novarum* argued for the right of workers to contract freely for wages. But it also noted that workers accept harder conditions than they should because they are victims of force and injustice—i.e., because they have no alternative. Justice presumes some freedom of choice; the fact that something is chosen or agreed to does not mean that it is "just."

Miranda suggests that the same logic be applied on the macroeconomic level. Where 75% of a population receives only one-third of the national income, we can presume that the "choices" that led to this situation were not altogether voluntary. "No one would say that the workers freely accept the national system of contracts and transactions in virtue of which they are kept in a state of perpetual disempowerment and the capitalists in a perpetual situation of privilege."[41] The justice of a wage system depends on the supposition of free choice. But the "violence" of the system forces capitulation: "the man has no choice but to accept or to die of hunger."[42] Thus the prevailing distribution is due to injustice.[43]

Since the distribution of ownership is simply the accumulated distribution of income, private ownership of the means of production is the result of this coercive distribution of income—i.e., it is the result of injustice.[44] Moreover, Miranda argues that this kind of "differentiating ownership" that divides people into classes could not come to be without a system of violence and spoliation: "the accumulation of capital in a few hands could not and cannot be achieved without an institutional violence exercised over wages and prices."[45] Private ownership as we know it therefore is "robbery—legalized, institutionalized, civilized, canonized robbery."[46] Dussel makes a similar argument: I have a right to what I work for, he suggests, "and it is always relatively little. If I have a lot, it is because I robbed someone."[47]

It is for this reason, declares Miranda, that both the Bible and the early church fathers understood "almsgiving" to be "justice." In the Bible, this act is not a supererogatory "charity" but "a restitution that someone makes for something that is not his."[48] As one early church father put it, "You are not making a gift of your possessions to the poor person. *You are handing over to him what is his.*"[49] Thus, suggests Miranda, the Bible confirms what can also be seen from economic study: the kind of private ownership that differentiates rich from poor is unacquirable without violence and spoliation.[50]

Ultimately, therefore, for Miranda, we need to free ourselves from the false ways of thinking that we have acquired in Western society. Hence, the bulk of his work is an examination of Scripture, intended to offer "the 'way of thinking' proper to the Bible."[51] Liberation theology seeks a genuinely biblical justice. As Gutierrez puts it, "justice and right cannot be emptied of the content bestowed on them by the Bible."[52] However, this genuinely biblical justice will not be simply a new set of rules for distribution. Rather, it will be new ways of understanding the meaning of justice. Understood from the praxis of those struggling for justice and liberation, new meanings emerge from Scripture.

Miranda isolates three central messages of Scripture. First, one can know God only through effecting justice. Using established techniques of scriptural exegesis, Miranda argues, for example, that the prohibition against making "graven images" of God arises from the conviction that God cannot be separated from the hearing of God's commands. There is no "God" apart from God's injunctions. Thus, there is no way to "image" God or to know or to speak about God apart from God's commands. God is known only in the response to God's commands.

These commands are commands of justice. Hence, there is no knowledge of God apart from involvement in acts of justice. "To do justice" is used synonymously in Scripture with "to know God."[53] Thus, liberation theology presents a fundamental epistemological challenge: How is God known? The liberationist answers: not through propositions or deductions or theories, but only in the act of doing justice. As Dussel puts it, "theology does not demonstrate from axioms but from the poor."[54]

Second, the biblical God is a God of liberation: "In the view of the Bible, Yahweh is the God who breaks into human history to liberate the oppressed."[55]

Miranda points out that in the "P" or priestly strand of the Hebrew Scriptures, God's name is given at the moment of liberation.[56] Indeed, the term *justice* is used interchangeably with the term for God, *Yahweh* (e.g., Jer. 23:6, "Yahweh our justice").[57] In the "J" or Yahwist strand, God is the one who hears the cries of the oppressed.[58] Thus, as Boesak puts it, "the all-surpassing characteristic of Yahweh is his acts in history as the God of justice and liberation for the sake of those who are weak and oppressed."[59]

Two terms are used for justice in the Hebrew Scriptures: *ṣedaqah* and *mishpat*. For Miranda, the term *mishpat* is central. He points out that it is the root both of the laws (*mishpatim*) and also of the word usually translated "judgment." Hence, the meaning of the "last judgment" as well as the discrimination of the true laws of Israel will depend on the meaning of *mishpat*. Linguistic and exegetical study suggests that *mishpat* means eliminating injuries based on injustice.[60] Careful examination of its use in the Hebrew Scriptures suggests that "*mishpat* consists in doing justice to the poor, neither more nor less."[61]

Hence, biblical justice means justice for the poor. Jesus follows this tradition by proclaiming *mishpat* (Matt. 12:18, 20).[62] As Gutierrez affirms, "The work of Christ is present simultaneously as a liberation from sin and from all its consequences: despoliation, injustice, hatred."[63] Salvation cannot be separated from social justice. According to Miranda, Paul continues this emphasis on social sin and salvation.[64]

"Justice" is what God does. But what God does is to liberate and love the poor. From the Exodus event to the Beatitudes, God is liberator of the poor. "For the Bible, the root of behavior that can be called 'just' is in the historical fact that constitutes a resume of its faith: God delivered us from Egypt."[65] Jesus is God become poor: born into poverty, living with the poor, addressing "good news" to the poor, lashing out against the rich, and being "poor" or humble in spirit.[66] Jesus' gospel, e.g., the beatitude "blessed are the poor," tells us that God loves the poor, not because they are good, but simply because they are poor.[67]

The poor, therefore, become the litmus test for justice: "To deal with a poor man or woman as Yahweh dealt with his people—this is what it is to be just."[68] This statement must not be misunderstood. In spite of its affinity with Marxist analytic methods and social goals, the view of justice provided in liberation theology is not simply a new version of "to each according to need." Justice is not a simple formula for distribution. Justice would not be accomplished merely by offering programs that meet basic needs of the poor. Justice requires the kind of liberating activity that characterizes God's behavior toward the poor and oppressed.

This sets up the third central affirmation of the liberation approach to justice: there is no separation of "love" and "justice." God's justice is God's love or compassion on those who suffer.[69] God's love is God's justice or liberation of the oppressed.[70] As Boesak maintains, there is no reconciliation without liberation, no loving harmony not based on justice. At the same time, as Dussel maintains, there can be no justice without love. True justice means giving what is due to the other as a *person,* not merely as part of *system,* and this requires love.[71] Hence, differentiating justice and love is "one of the most disastrous errors in the history of Christianity," argues Miranda.[72]

The gospel attacks the roots of all injustice—all breach of love, or sin, and all the "consequences and expressions" of this cleavage in friendship.[73] Gutierrez therefore claims that liberating activity has a threefold dimension: (1) economic, political, and social justice; (2) the emergence of a "new person" in a "new society"; and (3) liberation from sin or selfishness.[74]

Thus, although the capitalist system is seen as unjust by its very nature, socialism or a new economic order is not the sole sum and substance of the "justice" sought by liberation theology. The goals of justice and liberation are "not only to obtain a better standard of living, but also to be able to participate in the socio-economic resources and the decision-making process of the country."[75] Nor is liberation theology concerned merely to support revolution.[76] Understanding of the "totality and complexity" of liberation permits Gutierrez to declare that "the only possible justice is definitive justice."[77]

The justice that is sought by liberation theology is therefore not a formula for distribution. Justice is not a norm or law, but the establishment and maintenance of right relationships or "righteousness."[78] If misery, exploitation, deprivation of basic rights, and lack of respect represent those "grave injustices" that are "rampant" in Latin American society, then "justice" is the opposite. "Justice" would be a condition characterized by adequate structures at all these levels—economic support, political access, and fundamental respect as human beings. As Miranda puts it, "the injustice, the mercilessness, the oppression, and the exploitation to which all cultures have learned to resign themselves are precisely what Yahweh wants to abolish in the world."[79]

REVIEW

Like the bishops and Niebuhr, the liberation approach to justice is grounded in faith. But there are striking differences in the working out of that faith and its implications for justice. For Niebuhr, a biblical view puts stress on the sinfulness of people. For the bishops, a biblical view yields an affirmation of the worth of people and of their interdependence. Miranda would no doubt share these affirmations. But reading Scripture with the eyes of the poor, he finds in it a primary concern for justice focused on God's special love for the poor and oppressed. Justice begins in rejection of injustice. God is a God of justice above all; God is known only in the doing of justice; the doing of justice means doing justice for the poor.

Doing justice for the poor is not, for Miranda, the same as "meeting the needs" of the poor. It is not, as with Rawls, ensuring that the poor benefit from social arrangements that permit others to have more than they do. Nor is it, as with Nozick, ensuring that economic exchanges are fair. Nor is it, as with Niebuhr, ensuring a balance of power. For Miranda, justice for the poor is summed up in

God's liberating activity in the Exodus. It is nothing short of liberation of the poor from all forms of oppression. There can be no divisions of economic and political spheres, for justice is all-encompassing.

NOTES

1. Jose Porfirio Miranda, *Marx and the Bible: A Critique of the Philosophy of Oppression* (Maryknoll, N.Y.: Orbis, 1974).
2. Note, however, that Allan Aubrey Boesak, *Farewell to Innocence* (Maryknoll, N.Y.: Orbis, 1977), p. 16, gives credit to James Cone as the first black theologian to focus on liberation as the central message of the gospel.
3. Ernesto Cardinal, "The Gospel in Solentiname," *Concilium* 5 (May 1974): 107, here quotes a woman identified as "Rebecca."
4. Enrique Dussel, *Ethics and the Theology of Liberation,* (Maryknoll, N.Y.: Orbis, 1983), p. 37.
5. Boesak, *Farewell*, p. 12: "Theology is passionately involved."
6. Gustavo Gutierrez, *The Power of the Poor in History* (Maryknoll, N.Y.: Orbis, 1977), p. 50.
7. Ibid., pp. 137, 193. In *A Theology of Liberation* (Maryknoll, N.Y.: Orbis, 1973), p. 291, Gutierrez reviews the various biblical applications of the term *poor* to the beggar, the weak one, the one bent over or laboring under a weight.
8. Gutierrez, *Power of the Poor,* p. 50.
9. Black South African theologian Allan Aubrey Boesak, *Farewell,* p. 29, gives a parallel description of his situation: "This is the situation in which black people find themselves. Slavery, domination, injustice; being forced to live a life of contradiction and estrangement in their own country and 'in exile,' where fear and the urge to survive made deception a way of life; being denied a sense of belonging; discrimination—all these were realities which have almost completely broken down the sense of worth of black personhood."
10. Gutierrez, *Theology,* p. 89.
11. Gutierrez, *Power,* p. 93.
12. Ibid., pp. 84, 192.
13. Gutierrez, *Theology,* p. 84.
14. Dussel, *Ethics,* p. 26.
15. Gutierrez, *Theology,* p. 133.
16. Gutierrez, *Power,* p. 92.
17. Gutierrez, *Theology,* p. 273.
18. Ibid., p. 87.
19. Gutierrez, *Power,* p. 117.
20. Gutierrez, *Theology,* p. 174.
21. Boesak, *Farewell,* p. 34.
22. Gutierrez, *Theology,* p. 88.
23. Dussel, *Ethics,* p. 2.
24. An extensive discussion of the hermeneutic of suspicion is provided by Juan Luis Segundo, *Liberation of Theology* (Maryknoll, N.Y.: Orbis, 1976), Chap. 1.

25. Jose Miguez Bonino, *Toward a Christian Political Ethic* (Philadelphia: Fortress, 1983), p. 32.
26. Dussel, *Ethics,* p. 43.
27. Gutierrez, *Power,* p. 45.
28. Ibid., p. 197.
29. Gutierrez, *Theology,* p. 168.
30. Ibid., p. 195.
31. What distinguishes Miranda's work is, first, his explicit intention to defend Marxist theory, in contrast to many liberation theologians who criticize that theory; and, second, his explicit focus on modes of thinking.
32. Gutierrez, *Theology,* p. 114.
33. Ibid., p. 174.
34. Gutierrez, *Power,* pp. 18, 54.
35. Ibid., p. 117.
36. Ibid., p. 44; cf. p. 155.
37. Ibid., p. 192.
38. Miranda, *Marx,* p. xx.
39. Ibid., p. 2.
40. Gutierrez, *Power,* p. 85.
41. Miranda, *Marx,* p. 7.
42. Ibid., p. 8.
43. Ibid., pp. 5–6.
44. Ibid., pp. 10–11.
45. Ibid., p. 14.
46. Ibid., p. 11.
47. Dussel, *Ethics,* p. 25. He argues (ibid., p. 49) that a piece of land measuring a thousand square miles cannot be "natural" private property.
48. Miranda, *Marx,* p. 15.
49. Miranda, quoting Ambrose (ibid., p. 16; emphasis in Miranda).
50. Ibid., p. 19. Miranda suggests that when the popes defend private property it is because they assume it can be acquired legitimately—and even so they set limits on its use and accumulation. The presumption about legitimate acquisition is, of course, rebuttable.
51. Ibid., p. 35.
52. Gutierrez, *Power,* p. 211.
53. Miranda, *Marx,* p. 45.
54. Dussel, *Ethics,* p. 176.
55. Miranda, *Marx,* p. 77.
56. Ibid., p. 78.
57. Ibid., p. 86.
58. Ibid., pp. 88f. Miranda emphasizes that the same God who rescues the oppressed is outraged against the oppressors. Thus, for him liberation and judgment go together (see pp. 47, 100–103).
59. Boesak, *Ethics,* p. 19.
60. Miranda, *Marx,* p. 112.

61. Ibid., p. 127. Miranda is here quoting biblical scholar Hertzberg.
62. Ibid., p. 128.
63. Gutierrez, *Theology,* p. 158.
64. Miranda, *Marx,* pp. 176–182.
65. Gutierrez, *Power,* p. 8.
66. Ibid., p. 13.
67. Ibid., pp. 95, 116, and 141.
68. Ibid., p. 8. At this point we see how deeply the National Conference of Catholic Bishops was influenced by liberation theology, since it follows suit by making the poor the litmus test of justice.
69. Miranda, *Marx,* p. 99.
70. Boesak, *Farewell,* p. 19.
71. Dussel, *Ethics,* p. 46.
72. Miranda, *Marx,* p. 61.
73. Gutierrez, *Theology,* p. 106; cf. *Power,* p. 14.
74. Gutierrez, *Theology,* p. 235.
75. Ibid., p. 110.
76. Gutierrez, *Power,* p. 61.
77. Ibid., pp. 7, 14; emphasis added.
78. Bonino, *Toward a Christian Political Ethic,* p. 85.
79. Miranda, *Marx,* p. 168.

15. LIBERATION THEOLOGY: SELECTED READINGS OF JAMES CONE

Dwight N. Hopkins (ed.)

INTRODUCTION

In 1969, James H. Cone published his ground-breaking book, *Black Theology and Black Power*,[1] inaugurating black faith as public talk. Cone situated the African American faith tradition as a challenge to at least three publics: the church, the broader society, and the academy.

It was as if Cone had entered a dark bell tower, stumbled, accidentally pulled a bell rope, and awakened the entire village population. The reverberation of the bell, inadvertently pulled, not only changed the course of theology and our perception and belief in God, it also impacted the global process of doing theology. Therefore, on two accounts, Cone's first published effort created echoes both in its depth and its breadth. First, *Black Theology and Black Power* was the first book in the history of the United States to perceive and position liberation as the heart and theological center of the Christian gospel. Second, *Black Theology and Black Power* was the first book in the world written on liberation theology. In fact, Cone's first two books (e.g., *Black Theology and Black Power*[2] and *A Black Theology of Liberation*, 1970) as companion volumes preceded any other books on liberation theology from Africa, Asia, or Latin America.

When he sat down to write his book in 1968, Cone was acutely concerned with speaking truth to power in the public realm. That is why he addressed the black and white churches, the media, and those concerned with public policy making. However, he chose not to write a sociology of the black church or to offer an economic or cultural analysis. He, instead, sought a theological approach. Theology deals with what one believes and whether or not what one believes is the same as what God has called one to believe and do. To this end, he engaged the following questions: What does the gospel of Jesus Christ have to do with the struggle against white supremacy and for the liberation of black poor folk? What was the relation of Christianity to black power or the lack of it? What did it mean to be black and Christian? And, what was the linkage between the particular faith of black people and universal humanity?

During the period in which Cone was writing, America had the rare experience of confronting directly the current and future status of African Americans. Civil rights, human rights, and black power agendas were national topics of debate and decision making. Drawing on the role of the Hebrew scripture prophets and the Christian scripture role of Jesus as standing for those at the bottom of society, Cone aimed his theological undressing at both liberal and conservative Christians. The liberal white Christians, in Cone's eyes, wanted to talk about integration, nonviolence, and universal love for all of humankind. But, for Cone, this group failed to take seriously the gospel call of liberation of the oppressed; thus, what white liberals truly wanted was to maintain the structures in which they lived, which Cone characterized as monopolized white power over black life and death. Conservative white Christians openly linked the gospel with keeping black folk "in their place."

As for the black church, Cone chided it for its conservative interpretation (and, hence, misreading) of the Bible and the faith. The black church failed to take on the principalities and powers of this earth; it failed to risk all for the gospel by standing "in the gap" for the black poor and the least in society. Moreover, the black church too often imitated the white church. Consequently, the African American faith community did not draw enough on the rich sources from black history, including Africa. White theology (for example, the interpretation of Christianity as the theological support for capitalism) deeply permeated the black church.

In addition, the pioneering position of *Black Theology and Black Power* was how Cone linked black power and religion. For many at that time, it was not possible to be black and Christian. Black power advocates in the larger American society derided Christianity as "the white man's religion;" therefore, to be black was to be a non-Christian, and to be Christian was, for black power activists, to be an "Uncle Tom." For white conservatives, Christianity was a white man's religion. For white liberals, "Negroes" (using the language of that time) could be Christian as long as they modeled themselves after whites and did not challenge the structural relations between the races where whites had a monopoly on power and wealth. The Nation of Islam, given the prominent legacy of Malcolm X, offered a clear alternative to Christianity and showed what faith and blackness could mean, only if one did not become a Christian. And the mainstream black church leadership dismissed the possibility of being "black" and Christian. Because they were integrationists and considered themselves "Negroes," they felt it was impossible to be black and Christian because of their definition of "black." For them, "black" meant violence, revolution, radical changes in the status quo, criminal and uncivilized elements within the Negro community, anti-U.S. government, and secular, nonreligious people. A "Negro" was one who believed in Jesus Christ as a turn-the-other-cheek figure, who suffered innocently as other people beat and killed him. A "Negro" was one who upheld the U.S. Constitution and the Declaration of Independence.

Thus Cone concluded a whole new way of viewing the black freedom struggle and interpreting the good news of Jesus Christ. He embraced several sources from which he gathered his argument and drew his conclusions. He looked at the progressive parts of the black church tradition, where he found the

Bible calling on enslaved African Americans to use any means necessary to fight for freedom. Similarly, he applied the thought of various black church leaders such as Henry McNeal Turner who said God was a black, and Marcus Garvey who set up his own black denomination and also perceived God as black. Cone adopted the black folk tradition of survival and resistance heard in Br'er Rabbit tales and in the blues. On the global stage, he observed the movements for national liberation in Africa and Asia. Closer to home, Cone looked at contemporary events taking place throughout the nation. From the Civil Rights and Black Power movements, he redefined the church as one that struggles in the streets against unjust laws and systems aimed at the weak in society. From these same movements, he understood black power as black poor people having the right of self-identity in their culture and self-determination in politics and redistribution of wealth. Even whites presented an obvious contradiction for Cone; he saw how white scholars and churches had always utilized religion and politics but now argued against black churches involving themselves in the politics of black power.

But most importantly and most decisively, Cone felt called by God, through his encounter with the Bible and his own personal faith experience, to see the liberation of the oppressed and the poor as the heartbeat of the biblical message and the sole definition of what it meant to be a Christian. In addition to other biblical stories, Cone saw this message in the Exodus, in the Hebrew prophets, in Mary's Magnificat, in Luke chapter four, and in Matthew chapter twenty-five. Thus the message of liberation in the Bible was the same message of liberation advanced by poor blacks in their struggle to practice total freedom. And if the white community as well as middle-class-minded churches wanted to find Jesus, then they would all have to base their ministry and their humanity on the complete spiritual, cultural, material, and political freedom of poor blacks in America. Anything short of that, for Cone, was the work of the Anti-Christ and its agents.

Cone felt called by God to redefine revelation and the presence of the Spirit among and within humanity. For him, spiritual revelation was an event within creation. It was not a hocus-pocus invisible mystery. God offered liberation and love and came to earth in the material and visible reality of humanity and creation; and, there, God took sides with the oppressed and the poor, who are the majority population. Therefore, this revelation sided with the least in society in their efforts for liberation into a new reality of communal life and control of all of God's wealth and other resources. More specifically, Jesus was God becoming human for the poor, the marginalized, and the broken-hearted. The Incarnation was concrete and not mystifying. For Cone, the poor and the marginalized were the black poor and marginalized. Because the gospel of Jesus was liberation for the poor and the disadvantaged and because poor blacks were oppressed and marginalized and desired liberation, there was therefore a need for a black theology of liberation.

At the same time, Cone opened up the connection between the particular situation of the black poor (and other poor people) on the one hand, and the vocation of black middle-class-minded Christians and whites on the other. If they all sided with Jesus in Jesus' presence in the freedom movement of the poor, then that liberation called for by the Spirit would eventually change structures and individuals. Once individuals and structures changed, then there would not be white power over black life and other poor people. Without the oppressive white power structures, and with all sharing equally in the ownership and use of God's wealth on earth (including cultural, political, and emotional power), then oppressors would no longer have the systems to oppress others. And the least in society, along with everyone else in society, could express their full potential as human beings.

LIBERATION AS THE CONTENT OF THEOLOGY

Christian theology is a theology of liberation. It is *a rational study of the being of God in the world in light of the existential situation of an oppressed community, relating the forces of liberation to the essence of the gospel, which is Jesus Christ.* This means that its sole reason for existence is to put into ordered speech the meaning of God's activity in the world, so that the community of the oppressed will recognize that its inner thrust for liberation is not only *consistent with* the gospel but *is* the gospel of Jesus Christ. *There can be no Christian theology that is not identified unreservedly with those who are humiliated and abused. In fact, theology ceases to be a theology of the gospel when it fails to arise out of the community of the oppressed.* For it is impossible to speak of the God of Israelite history, who is the God revealed in Jesus Christ, without recognizing that God is the God *of* and *for* those who labor and are over laden. . .

The definition of theology as the discipline that seeks to analyze the nature of the Christian faith in the light of the oppressed arises chiefly from biblical tradition itself.

(1) Though it may not be entirely clear why God elected Israel to be God's people, one point is evident. The election is inseparable from the event of the exodus:

> You have seen what I did to the Egyptians, and how I bore you on eagles' wings and brought you to myself. Now therefore, if you will obey my voice and keep my covenant, you shall be my own possession among all peoples . . . [Exodus 19:4-5a].

Certainly this means, among other things, that God's call of this people is related to its oppressed condition and to God's own liberating activity already seen in the exodus. *You have seen what I did!* By delivering this people from Egyptian bondage and inaugurating the covenant on the basis of that historical event, God is revealed as the God of the oppressed, involved in their history, liberating them from human bondage.

(2) Later stages of Israelite history also show that God is particularly concerned about the oppressed within the community of Israel. The rise of Old Tes-

tament prophecy is due primarily to the lack of justice within that community. The prophets of Israel are prophets of social justice, reminding the people that Yahweh is the author of justice. It is important to note in this connection that the righteousness of God is not an abstract quality in the being of God, as with Greek philosophy. It is rather God's active involvement in history, making right what human beings have made wrong. The consistent theme in Israelite prophecy is Yahweh's concern for the lack of social, economic, and political justice for those who are poor and unwanted in society. Yahweh, according to Hebrew prophecy, will not tolerate injustice against the poor; God will vindicate the poor. Again, God is revealed as the God of liberation for the oppressed.

(3) In the New Testament, the theme of liberation is reaffirmed by Jesus himself. The conflict with Satan and the powers of this world, the condemnation of the rich, the insistence that the kingdom of God is for the poor, and the locating of his ministry among the poor-these and other features of the career of Jesus show that his work was directed to the oppressed for the purpose of their liberation. To suggest that he was speaking of a "spiritual" liberation fails to take seriously Jesus' thoroughly Hebrew view of human nature. Entering into the kingdom of God means that Jesus himself becomes the ultimate loyalty of humankind, for *he is the kingdom.* This view of existence in the world has far-reaching implications for economic, political, and social institutions. They can no longer have ultimate claim on human life; human beings are liberated and thus free to rebel against all powers that threaten human life. That is what Jesus had in mind when he said:

> The Spirit of the Lord is upon me, because he has anointed me to preach good news to the poor. He has sent me to proclaim release to the captives and recovering of sight to the blind, to set at liberty those who are oppressed, to proclaim the acceptable year of the Lord [Luke 4:18-19].

In view of the biblical emphasis on liberation, it seems not only appropriate but necessary to define the Christian community as the community of the oppressed which joins Jesus Christ in his fight for the liberation of humankind. The task of theology, then, is to explicate the meaning of God's liberating activity so that those who labor under enslaving powers will see that the forces of liberation are the very activity of God. *Christian theology is never just a rational study of the being of God. Rather it is a study of God's liberating activity in the world. God's activity in behalf of the oppressed.*

If the history of Israel and the New Testament description of the historical Jesus reveal that God is a God who is identified with Israel because it is an oppressed community, the resurrection of Jesus means that all oppressed peoples become his people. Herein lies the universal note implied in the gospel message of Jesus. *The resurrection-event means that God's liberating work is not only for the house of Israel but for all who are enslaved by principalities and powers.* The resurrection conveys hope in God. Nor is this the "hope" that promises a reward in heaven in order to ease the pain of injustice on earth. Rather it is *hope* which focuses on the future in order to make us refuse to tolerate present inequities. To see the future of God, as revealed in the resurrection of Jesus, is to see also the contradiction of any earthly injustice with existence in Jesus Christ. That is why Camilo Torres was right when he described revolutionary action as "a Christian, a priestly struggle."

The task of Christian theology, then, is to analyze the meaning of hope in God in such a way that the oppressed community of a given society will risk all for earthly freedom, a freedom made possible in the resurrection of Jesus. The language of theology challenges societal structures because it is inseparable from the suffering community.

Theology can never be neutral or fail to take sides on issues related to the plight of the oppressed. For this reason it can never engage in conversation about the nature of God without confronting those elements of human existence which threaten anyone's existence as a person. Whatever theology says about God and the world must arise out of its sole reason for existence as a discipline: to assist the oppressed in their liberation. Its language is always language about human liberation, proclaiming the end of bondage and interpreting the religious dimensions of revolutionary struggle. . .

WHAT IS THE GOSPEL OF JESUS?

Christianity begins and ends with the man Jesus—his life, death, and resurrection. He is the Revelation, the special disclosure of God to man, revealing who God is and what his purpose for man is. In short, Christ is the essence of Christianity. Schleiermacher was not far wrong when he said that "Christianity is essentially distinguished from other faiths by the fact that everything in it is related to the redemption accomplished by Jesus of Nazareth." In contrast to many religions, Christianity revolves around a Person, without whom its existence ceases to be. . .

One has only to read the gospel to be convinced of the central importance of Jesus Christ in the Christian faith. According to the New Testament, Jesus is the man for others who views his existence as inextricably tied to other men to the degree that his own Person is inexplicable apart from others. The others, of course, refer to all men, especially the oppressed, the unwanted of society, the "sinners." He is God himself coming into the very depths of human existence for the sole purpose of striking off the chains of slavery, thereby freeing man from ungodly principalities and powers that hinder his relationship with God. Jesus himself defines the nature of his ministry in these terms:

The Spirit of the Lord is upon me,
because he has anointed me to preach the good news to the poor.
He has sent me to proclaim release to the captives
and recovering of sight to the blind,
To set at liberty those who are oppressed,
To proclaim the acceptable year of the Lord.
Luke 4:18-19, RSV

Jesus' work is essentially one of liberation. Becoming a slave himself, he opens realities of human existence formerly closed to man. Through an encounter with Jesus, man now knows the full meaning of God's action in history and man's place within it.

The Gospel of Mark describes the nature of Jesus' ministry in this manner: "The time is fulfilled, the Kingdom of God is at hand; repent and believe the Gospel" (1:14-15). On the face of it, this message appears not to be too radical to our twentieth-century ears, but this impression stems from our failure existentially to bridge the gap between modern man and biblical man. Indeed, the message of the Kingdom strikes at the very center of man's desire to define his own existence in the light of his own interest at the price of his brother's enslavement. It means the irruption of a new age, an age which has to do with God's action in history on behalf of man's salvation. It is an age of liberation, in which "the blind receive their sight, the lame walk, the lepers are cleansed, the deaf hear, the dead are raised up, the poor have the good news preached to them" (Luke 7:22). This is not pious talk, and one does not need a seminary degree to interpret the message. It is a message about the ghetto, and all other injustices done in the name of democracy and religion to further the social, political, and economic interests of the oppressor. In Christ, God enters human affairs and takes sides with the oppressed. Their suffering becomes his; their despair, divine despair. Through Christ the poor man is offered freedom now to rebel against that which makes him other than human.

It is ironical that America with its history of injustice to the poor (especially the black man and the Indian) prides itself as being a Christian nation. (Is there really such an animal?) It is even more ironic that officials within the body of the Church have passively and actively participated in these injustices. With Jesus, however, the poor were at the heart of his mission: "The last shall be first and the first last" (Matt. 20:16). That is why he was always kind to traitors, adulterers, and sinners and why the Samaritan in the parable came out on top. Speaking of Pharisees (the religious elite of his day), Jesus said: "Truly I say to you, the tax collectors [traitors] and harlots go into the kingdom—but not you" (Matt. 21:31). Jesus had little toleration for the middle- or upper-class religious snob whose attitude attempted to usurp the sovereignty of God and destroy the dignity of the poor. The Kingdom is for the poor and not the rich because the former has nothing to expect from the world while the latter's entire existence is grounded in his commitment to worldly things. The poor man may expect everything from God, while the rich man may expect nothing because he refuses to free himself from his own pride. It is not that poverty is a precondition for entrance into the Kingdom. But those who recognize their utter dependence on God and wait on him despite the miserable absurdity of life are typically the poor, according to Jesus. And the Kingdom which the poor may enter is not merely an eschatological longing for escape to a transcendent reality, nor is it an inward serenity which eases unbearable suffering. Rather, it is God encountering man in the very depths of his being-in-the-world and releasing him from all human evils, like racism, which hold him captive. The repentant man knows that though God's ultimate

Kingdom be in the future, yet even now it breaks through like a ray of light upon the darkness of the oppressed. . .

If the gospel of Christ, as Moltmann suggests, frees a man to be for those who labor and are heavily laden, the humiliated and abused, then it would seem that for twentieth-century America the message of Black Power is the message of Christ himself.

To be sure, that statement is both politically and religiously dangerous; politically, because Black Power threatens the very structure of the American way of life; theologically, because it may appear to overlook Barth's early emphasis on "the infinite qualitative distinction between God and man." In this regard, we must say that Christ never promised political security but the opposite; and Karl Barth was mainly concerned with the easy identification of the work of God with the work of the state. But if Luther's statement, "We are Christ to the neighbor," is to be taken seriously, and, if we can believe the New Testament witness which proclaims Jesus as resurrected and thus active even now, then he must be alive in those very men who are struggling in the midst of misery and humiliation. If the gospel is a gospel of liberation for the oppressed, then Jesus is where the oppressed are and continues his work of liberation there. Jesus is not safely confined in the first century. He is our contemporary, proclaiming release to the captives and rebelling against all who silently accept the structures of injustice. If he is not in the ghetto, if he is not where men are living at the brink of existence, but is, rather, in the easy life of the suburbs, then the gospel is a lie. The opposite, however, is the case. Christianity is not alien to Black Power; it is Black Power.

There are secular interpretations which attempt to account for the present black rebellion, as there have been secular interpretations of the exodus or of the life and death of Jesus. But for the Christian, there is only one interpretation: Black rebellion is a manifestation of God himself actively involved in the present-day affairs of men for the purpose of liberating a people. Through his work, black people now know that there is something more important than life itself. They can afford to be indifferent toward death, because life devoid of freedom is not worth living. . .

THE CHURCH AND BLACK POWER[3]

The Church has not only failed to render service to the poor, but also failed miserably at being a visible manifestation of God's intention for humanity and at proclaiming the message of the gospel to the world. It seems that the Church is not God's redemptive agent but rather an agent of the old society. It not only fails to create an atmosphere for radical obedience to Christ, but also precludes the possibility of becoming a loyal, devoted servant of God. How else can we explain that some church fellowships are more concerned with nonsmoking principles or temperances than with children who die of rat bites or men who are shot while looting a TV set. Men are dying of hunger, children are maimed from rat bites, women are dying of despair, and churches pass resolutions. While we may have difficulty in locating the source of evil, we know what must be done against evil in order to relieve the suffering of the poor. We know why men riot. Perhaps we cannot prevent riots, but we can fight against conditions that cause them. The Church is placed in question because of its contribution to a structure that produces riots.

Some churchmen may reply: "We do condemn the deplorable conditions which produce urban riots. We do condemn racism and all the evils arising from it." But to the extent that this is true, the Church, with the exception of a few isolated individuals, voices its condemnation in the style of resolutions that are usually equivocal and almost totally unproductive. If the condemnation was voiced, it was not understood! The Church should speak in a style that avoids abstractions. Its language should be backed up with relevant involvement in the affairs of people who suffer. It must be a grouping whose community life and personal involvement are coherent with its language about the gospel.

The Church does not appear to be a community willing to pay up personally. It is not a community that views every command of Jesus as a call to the cross—death. Rather, it is an institution whose existence depends on the evils that produce the riots in the cities. With this in mind, we must say that when a minister blesses by silence the conditions that produce riots and condemns the rioters, he gives up his credentials as a Christian minister and becomes inhuman. He is an animal, just like those who, backed by an ideology of racism, order the structure of this society on the basis of white supremacy. We need men who refuse to be animals and are resolved to pay the price, so that all men can be something more than animals.

Whether Black Power advocates are that grouping, we will have to wait and see. But the Church has shown many times that it loves life and is not prepared to die for others. It has not really gone where the action is with a willingness to die for the neighbor, but remains aloof from the sufferings of men. It is a ministry to middle-class America! How else can one explain its snail-like pace toward an inclusive membership? Even though Paul says that Christ "has broken down the dividing walls of hostility" (Eph. 2:14), the Church's community life reflects racism through and through. It is still possible to be a racist, a black-hater, and at the same time a member of the Church. It is my contention that the Church cannot be the Church of Christ and sponsor or even tolerate racism. The fact that the Church does indeed tolerate or sponsor racism is evidenced by its *whiteness*.

This leads me to conclude that Christ is operating outside the denominational Church. The real Church of Christ is that grouping that identifies with the suffering of the poor by becoming one with them. While we should be careful in drawing the line, the line must nevertheless be drawn. The Church includes not only the Black Power community but all men who view their humanity as inextricably related to every man. It is that grouping with a demonstrated willingness to die for the prevention of the torture of others, saying with Bonhoeffer, "when Christ calls a man, he bids him come and die."

WHITE THEOLOGY REVISITED (1998)

Even when white theologians reflect on God and suffering, the problem of theodicy, they almost never make racism a central issue in their analysis of the challenge that evil poses for the Christian faith. If they should happen to mention racism, it is usually just a footnote or only a marginal comment. They almost never make racism the subject of a sustained analysis. It is amazing that racism could be so prevalent and violent in American life and yet so absent in white theological discourse.

President Clinton's call for a national dialogue on race has created a context for public debate in the churches, the academy, and the broader society. Where are the white theologians? What guidance are they providing for this debate? Are they creating a theological understanding of racism that enables whites to have a meaningful conversation with blacks and other people of color? Unfortunately, instead of searching for an understanding of the great racial divide, white religion scholars are doing their searching in the form of a third quest for the historical Jesus. I am not opposed to this academic quest. But if we could get a significant number of white theologians to study racism as seriously as they investigate the historical Jesus and other academic topics, they might discover how deep the cancer of racism is embedded not only in the society but also in the narrow way in which the discipline of theology is understood.

Although black liberation theology emerged out of the Civil Rights and Black Power movements of the 1960s, white theologians ignored it as if it were not worthy to be regarded as an academic discipline. It was not until Orbis Books published the translated works of Latin American liberation theologians that white North American male theologians cautiously began to talk and write about liberation theology and God's solidarity with the poor. But they still ignored the black poor in the United States, Africa, and Latin America. Our struggle to make sense out of the fight for racial justice was dismissed as too narrow and divisive. White U.S. theologians used the Latin American focus on class to minimize and even dismiss the black focus on race. African-Americans wondered how U.S. whites could take sides with the poor out there in Latin America without first siding with the poor here in North America. It was as if they had forgotten about their own complicity in the suffering of the black poor, who often were only a stone's throw from the seminaries and universities where they taught theology . . .

Most whites do not like to talk about white supremacy because it makes them feel guilty, a truly uncomfortable feeling. They would rather forget about the past and think only about the present and future. I understand that. I only ask whites to consider how uncomfortable the victims of white supremacy must feel, as they try to cope with the attitudes of whites who act as if white supremacy ceased with the passage of the 1964 Civil Rights Bill. At least when people express their racism overtly, there is some public recognition of its existence and a possibility of racial healing. Silence is racism's best friend.

"A time comes when silence is betrayal," Martin King said. That time has come for white theologians. White supremacy is one of the great contradictions of the gospel in modern times. White theologians who do not oppose racism publicly and rigorously engage it in their writings are a part of the problem and must be exposed as the enemy of justice. No one, therefore, can be neutral or silent in the face of this great evil. We are either for it or against it.

Black theologians must end their silence too. We have opposed racism much too gently. We have permitted white theological silence in exchange for the rewards of being accepted by the white theological establishment. This is a terrible price to pay for the few crumbs that drop from the white master's table. We must replace theological deference with courage, and thereby confront openly and lovingly silent white racists or be condemned as participants in the betrayal of our own people.

In 1903 W.E.B. Du Bois prophesied, "The problem of the twentieth century is the problem of the color-line,—the relation of the darker to the lighter races of [people] in Asia and Africa, in America and the islands of the sea." As we stand at the threshold of the next century, that remarkable prophesy is as relevant today as it was when Du Bois uttered it. The challenge for black theology in the twenty-first century is to develop an enduring race critique that is so comprehensively woven into Christian understanding that no one will be able to forget the horrible crimes of white supremacy in the modern world.

NOTES

1. James H. Cone, *Black Theology and Black Power* (New York: Harper & Row, 1969; Maryknoll, N.Y.: Orbis Books, 1997).
2. James H. Cone, *A Black Theology of Liberation* (Philadelphia: J.B. Lippincott Co., 1970; Maryknoll, N.Y.: Orbis Books, 1990).
3. "Christianity and Black Power" from *Is Anybody Listening to Black America?* Edited by C. Eric Lincoln (Seabury Press, Inc., 1968).

16. CONCLUSION FROM
SIX THEORIES OF JUSTICE

Karen Lebacqz

So where have we come with our explorations of the elephant? What are the gifts and legacies of each approach? What are the possibilities for a theory of justice? Let us begin with a quick review.

SIX FRAGMENTS ON JUSTICE

From Mill and the utilitarians, we get a vision of a good that transcends and yet incorporates individual rights. Claims are accepted as the core of justice, but claims are always derived from and dependent on the maximizing of utility. To be sure, justice for Mill includes a fundamental sense of equality, since each person's good is to count as much as each other's. Yet there is no standard of equality as the goal or pattern of distribution. Instead, the possibilities of the greater good overall present the challenge that all subsequent theories of justice must encounter.

It is this challenge to which Rawls responds. Rawls, too, acknowledges the possibility of inequality in distribution for the sake of a greater gain. However, not just any gain will do: it matters who receives the benefits and who bears the burdens. Whereas utilitarians would have us picture society as an individual "writ large," making choices about gains and losses, for Rawls the gains to some do not compensate for losses to others. The vision of a common good is not alone sufficient, and must be tempered by a distributive principle that benefits the least advantaged. In Rawls' own view, the theory ultimately works toward an equality of distribution, though it does not require equality as its distributive principle.

Nozick wants to begin from the same Kantian principles as Rawls, respecting the rights and reason of individuals. But he rejects utterly any substantive equalitarianism as the requirement of justice. Rather, justice becomes the product of free choice and exchange. To set any requirements for equality of distribution is to violate human freedom. It is therefore freedom, not equality, that constitutes the core of justice. This is the insurmountable challenge that Nozick raises: is freedom to be sacrificed in the interests of equality?

Neither do the bishops call for substantive equality. Yet, they reject any simple notion that free choice alone—especially in the market system—yields justice. Drawing on a long Catholic tradition, they propose three principles of justice: commutative fairness in exchange, distributive attention to need, and, perhaps most important, social requirements for participation. Theirs is a vision of justice based on the notion that human dignity is achieved only in community and that the resources of the earth "belong" ultimately only to God.

Niebuhr adds to this synthetic picture the discordant note of sin. Individual rights and group interests are not so easily compatible with the "greater good" or with the "common good" as Mill, on the one hand, and Catholic tradition, on the other, might have it. Justice is not the result of philosophical theory, for reasoning and theory themselves become suspect. Justice in the "real" world is a constant process of compromise with the realities of sin and injustice. Niebuhr leaves us distressingly without clear rules for justice, though equality emerges as both a procedural and a substantive principle. What he does leave us with is a sense of the necessity for historical compromise and hence of the inadequacies of every concrete achievement of justice.

Miranda and other liberation theologians accept and advance Niebuhr's focus on sin. Justice begins, not with theory, but with the concrete realities of injustice experienced by the oppressed and illumined by the God of the Bible. Niebuhr's distrust of reason is carried to its full implications of the "epistemological privilege" of the poor: only those who suffer injustice and are involved in the struggle for justice can know what justice is. Justice has become not merely structural, but systemic.

OF ELEPHANTS AND JUSTICE

Here, in brief, are six fragments of justice—six descriptions of the elephant. What, then, is the nature of the beast? These theories can be assessed from the perspective of substance and of method. Let us begin with substance.

Tradition has it that the formal principle of distributive justice is "to each what is due."[1] In one way or another, most of the authors considered here would accept that formula, at least to a point. But when it comes to deciding what is "due," they would give the formal statement of justice radically different content. If justice is "to each according to . . . ," then our six theories might look like this:

- *Mill:* to each according to those tendencies of actions that maximize overall utility;
- *Rawls:* to each according to a basic structure that benefits the least advantaged (within limits set by equal political rights, equal opportunity, and just savings for future generations);
- *Nozick:* to each according to the choices that have given them entitlements;
- *Bishops:* to each according to their dignity as creatures made in the image of God (with duties and rights consonant with that image, and spelled out in a threefold notion of justice);
- *Niebuhr:* to each according to principles of freedom, and especially of equality, tempered by love or equity;

- *Miranda:* to each according to God's interventions in history to liberate the poor and oppressed.

The differences are striking. Does justice require maximizing utility, benefiting the least advantaged, accepting the consequences of choice, honoring human dignity, treating equally, or liberating the poor and oppressed? Striking, too, is the absence of some traditional notions such as the Aristotelian claim that justice means distribution in accord with merit.

The differences are just as striking if we turn from substance to method. How are we to arrive at a theory of justice? Here, our authors might complete the sentence, "the requirements of justice are derived by . . ." as follows:

- *Mill:* the requirements of justice are derived by looking for the common core in accepted notions of what is just and unjust;
- *Rawls:* the requirements of justice are derived by rational choice in a "fair" setting;
- *Nozick:* the requirements of justice are those minimal rights derived by deduction from the Kantian maxim to treat each person as an end and not merely as a means;
- *Bishops:* the requirements of justice are derived by embodying a faith-based vision of justice in traditional philosophical and theological principles of duties and rights;
- *Niebuhr:* the requirements of justice are derived by the faith-based principle of love compromising with the realities of sin;
- *Miranda:* the requirements of justice are derived by biblical confirmation of Marxist analysis of injustices experienced by the oppressed.

Again, the differences are striking. Are the requirements of justice derived by observations of the elite, by reason abstracted from history, by deduction, by reason complementing revelation, by faith compromising with history, or by biblical and Marxist analysis? Not only have those examining the elephant come to different conclusions about the nature of the beast named "justice," but they use such different tools for their examination that it is only to be expected that sometimes they appear to be describing different beasts altogether.

These characterizations of our six blindfolded explorers are gross oversimplifications, bordering on, if not slipping into, caricature. Yet if there is any truth in these characterizations, they suggest a serious problem for all those interested in this elephant. As stated, they imply that there is no common ground for a theory of justice. Neither in method nor in substance is there sufficient agreement to think that even within our limited historical context we can have a theory of justice. As Macintyre suggests, we do appear to be left with moral fragments that no longer have and are incapable of having a common ground or supporting base.

Perhaps this is due in part to the different concerns of our theorists. Rawls' attention is directed to the basic structure of society, while Niebuhr's was directed toward a fundamental view of human nature. Nozick's attention is directed to the necessities and limits of the state, while Miranda's is focused on biblical ways of thinking. Mill's attention was focused on criteria for right action in general, while the bishops focus more directly on poverty in the United States. Different starting places yield different fragments on justice.

OF BLINDFOLDED EXPLORATION

The differences do not divide neatly along philosophical and theological lines. In some ways, there is as much difference between Rawls and Nozick as between Rawls and the National Conference of Catholic Bishops. Both the bishops and Niebuhr could be and have been accused of adopting many of the "liberal" presuppositions that permeate the philosophical theories considered here. Thus, in spite of striking differences, there are also striking similarities.

Yet, at one point, which is worth considering, there does seem to be a division along the line of philosophy versus theology. It is the point of assessment of fundamental assumptions of the capitalist market and private property system.

All three philosophical systems considered here represent support for and affirmation of a market-based, capitalist economic system. With its reliance on the "greatest net good," utilitarianism became the base for much economic theory that supports capitalism. Problems experienced by workers in such a system are not easily recognized by a theory in which gains to some can outweigh losses to others. As long as the overall economic system is thought to work for the "greater good" in the long run, losses to the poor in the short run are deemed a "necessary trade-off" that does not make a system unjust. This is seen very clearly in some of the responses from the business community to the bishops' letter.

Rawls, too, appears to defend democratic capitalism. Although he argues that his principles of justice are compatible with both capitalist and socialist economic systems, basic acceptance of capitalism is assured. So long as the least advantaged are thought to "benefit" from the market system, no injustice has been done. On what is dubbed the "trickle down" theory, benefits to those at the top in a capitalist economy are always thought to "trickle down" to some benefits for those at the bottom. By Rawls' theory, this makes capitalism basically a just economy.

Nozick gives the most explicit support for a capitalist market exchange system based on the right of private property. Indeed, he indicates that he believes contemporary capitalist societies do not violate the principles of justice in exchange that he offers. Whatever distribution of goods occurs within an economy is just, so long as it is the consequence of proper market exchanges. There is no sense of any limits necessary to protect the poor.

Thus, although the utilitarians, Rawls, and Nozick hold very different basic theories of justice, in practice they all support forms of capitalist "free market" exchange and private property.

The picture changes quickly when we turn to the theological theories. None of them gives such unqualified support to capitalism or to private property.

Though the Catholic tradition continues to support the right of private ownership, that right has always been subject to the constraints of the common good on the use of property. Writing within the North American context, the bishops do not address strongly the growing tendency in Catholic social teaching to support expropriation of lands. Nor do they offer a fundamental criticism of capitalism. Yet their support is clearly qualified, and they raise grave concerns about the impact of capitalism on the poor.

Niebuhr in his early years adopted explicitly Marxist critiques of capitalism. To be sure, he was also critical of socialist alternatives. Nonetheless, it is clear that a "free exchange" system based on private property would not for him represent economic justice. It gives too much power to those in control of capital, and, for Niebuhr, justice always required a balancing of such power.

Miranda is one of the liberation theologians most outspokenly opposed to capitalism. For him, the capitalist system that permits "differentiating" ownership and the development of classes is intrinsically evil. Justice is antithetical to any system that permits the poor to suffer so.

Once again, although all three Christian perspectives offer quite different approaches to, and theories of, justice, in practice they appear to agree at least on the question of capitalism.

Thus, it seems that a clear line can be drawn at least on this one issue, if not on others. Even here, however, I venture to suggest that those who describe the elephant so differently nonetheless may profit from dialog with each other.

Surely the most radically different approaches are those of Nozick and Miranda. They seem to be at opposite ends of the economic—and possibly the political—spectrum. As different and irreconcilable as their views appear, however, there are some interesting common grounds.

Liberation theology arises out of historical injustices. But what is the nature of these injustices? Miranda suggests that the micro-level injustices of wage contracts can be used to develop a macro-level analogy: the poor would not have agreed to the system that puts them in their current poverty. These claims make sense if one assumes a base akin to Nozick's theory of commutative justice. If the original acquisition is fair, and if the exchange is fair, then the resulting division is fair. Surely the liberation charge is either that the original acquisition was not fair (e.g., lands and goods were stolen rather than purchased) or that the exchange was not fair (coercion was involved, grounds for setting a fair price were not mutually agreed).

Miranda acknowledges this when he says that "commutative justice itself carries within it the whole problem of distribution."[2] Thus, in order for the charges of "injustice" leveled by liberation theology to be established, there must be some theory about right exchange and fairness in choice. Nozick's theory might provide some base for liberation accusations. In this sense, the liberation perspective needs Nozick.

But Nozick also needs the liberation perspective. Nozick claims to establish a historical approach to justice. But he provides no mechanisms by which that approach can be tested. His conclusion that capitalism meets the demands of justice rests on speculation, not evidence. Liberation theology provides the historical experiences necessary to test the truth of Nozick's claim. If liberation theology needs Nozick to demonstrate why the situation in Latin America is genuinely "unfair" and not just "unfortunate," Nozick needs liberation theology to put flesh on the bones of his historical approach to justice.

But then if it turns out that liberation theology is correct, and that the world situation is characterized largely by injustice, something else will be needed. Nozick nods toward the necessity for a theory of rectification of injustice, but fails to develop that theory. Yet, it is precisely this that may be the most important clue toward establishing distributive justice in our age.

If injustice is the beginning point, then we may need different theories of justice. In rejecting the classical distinction of distributive, retributive, and commutative justice, Feinberg suggests that "an equally useful" way of classifying the data of justice and one which promises "more rewarding theoretical insights" is a classification according to types of injustice.[3] Perhaps another perspective for exploring the elephant is needed. A theory of justice is needed that is truly historical and that takes seriously the problem of rectification of injustice. If *mishpat* is to be the measure, then *ṣedaqah* must be the plumb line. It is toward that plumb line that my next volume will move.

NOTES

1. This formal notion is widely accepted in both theological and philosophical circles. See, for example, Emil Brunner, *Justice and the Social Order* (London: Lutterworth, 1945), p. 23: "From time immemorial the principle of justice has been defined as the *suum cuique*—the rendering to each man of his due."
2. Jose Porfirio Miranda, *Marx and the Bible: A Critique of the Philosophy of Oppression* (Maryknoll, N.Y.: Orbis, 1974), p. 26.
3. Joel Feinberg, "Noncomparative Justice," in *Justice: Selected Readings*, ed. J. Feinberg and H. Gross (Belmont, Calif.: Wadsworth, 1977), p. 55. A. D. Woozley, "Injustice," in *Studies in Ethics:* American Philosophical Quarterly Monograph Series 7 (1973), also suggests that injustice is "more interesting" than justice, and has been little analyzed.

17. INTRODUCTION: JUSTICE AND GENDER

Susan Moller Okin

We as a society pride ourselves on our democratic values. We don't believe people should be constrained by innate differences from being able to achieve desired positions of influence or to improve their well-being; equality of opportunity is our professed aim. The Preamble to our Constitution stresses the importance of justice, as well as the general welfare and the blessings of liberty. The Pledge of Allegiance asserts that our republic preserves "liberty and justice for all."

Yet substantial inequalities between the sexes still exist in our society. In economic terms, full-time working women (after some very recent improvement) earn on average 71 percent of the earnings of full-time working men. One-half of poor and three-fifths of chronically poor households with dependent children are maintained by a single female parent. The poverty rate for elderly women is nearly twice that for elderly men.[1] . . . Until there is justice within the family, women will not be able to gain equality in politics, at work, or in any other sphere. . .

The typical current practices of family life, structured to a large extent by gender, are not just. Both the expectation and the experience of the division of labor by sex make women vulnerable. As I shall show, a cycle of power relations and decisions pervades both family and workplace, each reinforcing the inequalities between the sexes that already exist within the other. Not only women, but children of both sexes, too, are often made vulnerable by gender-structured marriage. One-quarter of children in the United States now live in families with only one parent—in almost 90 percent of cases, the mother. Contrary to common perceptions—in which the situation of never-married mothers looms largest—65 percent of single-parent families are a result of marital separation or divorce.[2] Recent research in a number of states has shown that, in the average case, the standard of living of divorced women and the children who live with them plummets after divorce, whereas the economic situation of divorced men tends to be better than when they were married.

A central source of injustice for women these days is that the law, most noticeably in the event of divorce, treats more or less as equals those whom custom, workplace discrimination, and the still conventional division of labor within the family have made very unequal. Central to this socially created inequality are two commonly made but inconsistent presumptions: that women are primarily responsible for the rearing of children; and that serious and committed members of the workforce (regardless of class) do not have primary responsibility, or even shared responsibility, for the rearing of children. The old assumption of the workplace, still implicit, is that workers have wives at home. It is built not only into the structure and expectations of the workplace but into other crucial social institutions, such as schools, which make no attempt to take account, in their scheduled hours or vacations, of the fact that parents are likely to hold jobs.

Now, of course, many wage workers do not have wives at home. Often, they *are* wives and mothers, or single, separated, or divorced mothers of small children. But neither the family nor the workplace has taken much account of this fact. Employed wives still do by far the greatest proportion of unpaid family work, such as child care and housework. Women are far more likely to take time out of the workplace or to work part-time because of family responsibilities than are their husbands or male partners. And they are much more likely to move because of their husbands' employment needs or opportunities than their own. All these tendencies, which are due to a number of factors, including the sex segregation and discrimination of the workplace itself, tend to be cyclical in their effects: wives advance more slowly than their husbands at work and thus gain less seniority, and the discrepancy between their wages increases over time. Then, because both the power structure of the family and what is regarded as consensual "rational" family decision making reflect the fact that the husband usually earns more, it will become even less likely as time goes on that the unpaid work of the family will be shared between the spouses. Thus the cycle of inequality is perpetuated. Often hidden from view within a marriage, it is in the increasingly likely event of marital breakdown that the socially constructed inequality of married women is at its most visible.

This is what I mean when I say that gender-structured marriage *makes* women vulnerable. These are not matters of natural necessity, as some people would believe. Surely nothing in our natures dictates that men should not be equal participants in the rearing of their children. Nothing in the nature of work makes it impossible to adjust it to the fact that people are parents as well as workers. That these things have not happened is part of the historically, socially constructed differentiation between the sexes that feminists have come to call *gender*. We live in a society that has over the years regarded the innate characteristic of sex as one of the clearest legitimizers of different rights and restrictions, both formal and informal. While the legal sanctions that uphold male dominance have begun to be eroded in the past century, and more rapidly in the last twenty years, the heavy weight of tradition, combined with the effects of socialization, still works powerfully to reinforce sex roles that are commonly regarded as of unequal prestige and worth. The sexual division of labor has not only been a fundamental part of the marriage contract, but so deeply influences us in our formative years that feminists of both sexes who try to reject it can find themselves struggling against it with varying degrees of ambivalence. Based on this linchpin, "gender"—by which I mean the *deeply, entrenched institutionalization of sexual difference*—still permeates our society. . .

During these same two decades, there has been a great resurgence of theories of social justice. Political theory, which had been sparse for a period before the late 1960s except as an important branch of intellectual history, has become a flourishing field, with social justice as its central concern. Yet, remarkably, major contemporary theorists of justice have almost without exception ignored the situation I have just described. They have displayed little interest in or knowledge of the findings of feminism. They have largely bypassed the fact that the society to which their theories are supposed to pertain is heavily and deeply affected by gender, and faces difficult issues of justice stemming from its gendered past and present assumptions. Since theories of justice are centrally concerned with whether, how, and why persons should be treated differently from one another, this neglect seems inexplicable. These theories are about which initial or acquired characteristics or positions in society legitimize differential treatment of persons by social institutions, laws, and customs. They are about how and whether and to what extent beginnings should affect outcomes. The division of humanity into two sexes seems to provide an obvious subject for such inquiries. But, as we shall see, this does not strike most contemporary theorists of justice, and their theories suffer in both coherence and relevance because of it. . .

The combined effect of the omission of the family and the falsely gender-neutral language in recent political thought is that most theorists are continuing to ignore the highly political issue of gender. The language they use makes little difference to what they actually do, which is to write about men and about only those women who manage, in spite of the gendered structures and practices of the society in which they live, to adopt patterns of life that have been developed to suit the needs of men. The fact that human beings are born as helpless infants—not as the purportedly autonomous actors who populate political theories—is obscured by the implicit assumption of gendered families, operating outside the range of the theories. To a large extent, contemporary theories of justice, like those of the past, are about men with wives at home.

GENDER AS AN ISSUE OF JUSTICE

For three major reasons, this state of affairs is unacceptable. The first is the obvious point that women must be fully included in any satisfactory theory of justice. The second is that equality of opportunity, not only for women but for children of both sexes, is seriously undermined by the current gender injustices of our society. And the third reason is that, as has already been suggested, the family—currently the linchpin of the gender structure—must be just if we are to have a just society, since it is within the family that we first come to have that sense of ourselves and our relations with others that is at the root of moral development. . .

GENDER AND EQUALITY OF OPPORTUNITY

The family is a crucial determinant of our opportunities in life, of what we "become." It has frequently been acknowledged by those concerned with real equality of opportunity that the family presents a problem.[3] But though they have discerned a serious problem, these theorists have underestimated it because they have seen only half of it. They have seen that the disparity among families in terms of the physical and emotional environment, motivation, and material advantages they can give their children has a tremendous effect upon children's opportunities in life. We are not born as isolated, equal individuals in our society, but into family situations: some in the social middle, some poor and homeless, and some superaffluent; some to a single or soon-to-be-separated parent, some to parents whose marriage is fraught with conflict, some to parents who will stay together in love and happiness. Any claims that equal opportunity exists are therefore completely unfounded. Decades of neglect of the poor, especially of poor black and Hispanic households, accentuated by the policies of the Reagan years, have brought us farther from the principles of equal opportunity. To come close to them would require, for example, a high and uniform standard of public education and the provision of equal social services—including health care, employment training, job opportunities, drug rehabilitation, and decent housing—for all who need them. In addition to redistributive taxation, only massive reallocations of resources from the military to social services could make these things possible.

But even if all these disparities were somehow eliminated, we would still not attain equal opportunity for all. This is because what has not been recognized as an equal opportunity problem, except in feminist literature and circles, is the disparity *within* the family, the fact that its gender structure is itself a major obstacle to equality of opportunity. This is very important in itself, since one of the factors with most influence on our opportunities in life is the social significance attributed to our sex. The opportunities of girls and women are centrally affected by the structure and practices of family life, particularly by the fact that women are almost invariably primary parents. What nonfeminists who see in the family an obstacle to equal opportunity have *not* seen is that the extent to which a family is gender-structured can make the sex we belong to a relatively insignificant aspect of our identity and our life prospects or an all-pervading one. This is because so much of the social construction of gender takes place in the family, and particularly in the institution of female parenting.

Moreover, especially in recent years, with the increased rates of single motherhood, separation, and divorce, the inequalities between the sexes have *compounded* the first part of the problem. The disparity among families has grown largely because of the impoverishment of many women and children after separation or divorce. The division of labor in the typical family leaves most women far less capable than men of supporting themselves, and this disparity is accentuated by the fact that children of separated or divorced parents usually live with their mothers. The inadequacy—and frequent nonpayment—of child support has become recognized as a major social problem. Thus the inequalities of gender are now directly harming many children of both sexes as well as women themselves. Enhancing equal opportunity for women, important as it is in itself, is also a crucial way of improving the opportunities of many of the most disadvantaged children.

As there is a connection among the parts of this problem, so is there a connection among some of the solutions: much of what needs to be done to end the inequalities of gender, and to work in the direction of ending gender itself, will also help to equalize opportunity from one family to another. Subsidized, high-quality day care is obviously one such thing; another is the adaptation of the workplace to the needs of parents. . .

THE FAMILY AS A SCHOOL OF JUSTICE

One of the things that theorists who have argued that families need not or cannot be just, or who have simply neglected them, have failed to explain is how, within a formative social environment that is *not* founded upon principles of justice, children can learn to develop that sense of justice they will require as citizens of a just society. Rather than being one among many co-equal institutions of a just society, a just family is its essential foundation.

It may seem uncontroversial, even obvious, that families must be just because of the vast influence they have on the moral development of children. But this is clearly not the case. I shall argue that unless the first and most formative example of adult interaction usually experienced by children is one of justice and reciprocity, rather than one of domination and manipulation or of unequal altruism and one-sided self-sacrifice, and unless they themselves are treated with concern and respect, they are likely to be considerably hindered in becoming people who are guided by principles of justice. Moreover, I claim, the sharing of roles by men and women, rather than the division of roles between them, would have a further positive impact because the experience of *being* a physical and psychological nurturer—whether of a child or of another adult—would increase that capacity to identify with and fully comprehend the viewpoints of others that is important to a sense of justice. In a society that minimized gender this would be more likely to be the experience of all of us.

Almost every person in our society starts life in a family of some sort or other. Fewer of these families now fit the usual, though by no means universal, standard of previous generations, that is, wage-working father, homemaking mother, and children. More families these days are headed by a single parent; lesbian and gay parenting is no longer so rare; many children have two wage-working parents, and receive at least some of their early care outside the home. While its forms are varied, the family in which a child is raised, especially in the earliest years, is clearly a crucial place for early moral development and for the formation of our basic attitudes to others. It is, potentially, a place where we can *learn* to be just. It is especially important for the development of a sense of justice that grows from sharing the experiences of others and becoming aware of the points of view of others who are different in some respects from ourselves, but with whom we clearly have some interests in common. . .

In a just society, the structure and practices of families must give women the same opportunities as men to develop their capacities, to participate in political power and influence social choices, and to be economically secure. But in addition to this, families must be just because of the vast influence that they have on the moral development of children. The family is the primary institution of formative moral development. And the structure and practices of the family must parallel those of the larger society if the sense of justice is to be fostered and maintained. While many theorists of justice, both past and present, appear to have denied the importance of at least one of these factors, my own view is that both are absolutely crucial. A society that is committed to equal respect for all of its members, and to justice in social distributions of benefits and responsibilities, can neither neglect the family nor accept family structures and practices that violate these norms, as do current gender-based structures and practices. It is essential that children who are to develop into adults with a strong sense of justice and commitment to just institutions spend their earliest and most formative years in an environment in which they are loved *and* nurtured, and in which principles of justice are abided by and respected. What is a child of either sex to learn about fairness in the average household with two full-time working parents, where the mother does, at the very least, twice as much family work as the father? What is a child to learn about the value of nurturing and domestic work in a home with a traditional division of labor in which the father either subtly or not so subtly uses the fact that he is the wage earner to "pull rank" on or to abuse his wife? What is a child to learn about responsibility for others in a family in which, after many years of arranging her life around the needs of her husband and children, a woman is faced with having to provide for herself and her children but is totally ill-equipped for the task by the life she agreed to lead, has led, and expected to go on leading? . . .

NOTES

1. U.S. Department of Labor, *Employment and Earnings: July 1987* (Washington, D.C.: Government Printing Office, 1987); Ruth Sidel, *Women and Children Last: The Plight of Women in Affluent America* (New York: Viking, 1986), pp. xvi, 158.

2. Twenty-three percent of single parents have never been married, an 12 percent are widowed. (U.S. Bureau of the Census, Current Population Reports, *Household and Family Characteristics: March 1987* [Washington, D.C.: Government Printing Office, 1987], p. 79). In 1987, 6.8 percent of children under eighteen were living with a never-married parent. ("Study Shows Growing Gap Between Rich and Poor," *New York Times*, March 23, 1989, p. A24).

3. See esp. James Fishkin, *Justice, Equal Opportunity and the Family* (New Haven: Yale University Press, 1983); Phillips, *Just Social Order*, esp. pp. 346–49, Rawls, *Theory*, pp. 74, 300–301, 511–512.

18. THE MOMMY TAX

Ann Crittenden

In the U.S. we have no way to address women's economic disadvantages except through the concept of gender. We see the problem as discrimination on the basis of gender. But what's really going on is a disadvantaging of *mothers* in the workforce.

—Susan Pedersen, historian

On April 7, 1999, the Independent Women's Forum, a conservative antifeminist organization, held a news conference at the National Press Club in Washington, D.C. Displayed in the corner of the room was a large green "check," made out to feminists, for ninety-eight cents. The point being made was that American women now make ninety-eight cents to a man's dollar and have therefore achieved complete equality in the workplace.

The sheer nerve of this little exercise in misinformation was astonishing. Upon closer examination, it turned out that the women who earn almost as much as men are a rather narrow group: those who are between the ages of twenty-seven and thirty-three and who have never had children. The Independent Women's Forum was comparing young childless women to men and declaring victory for all women, glossing over the real news: that mothers are the most disadvantaged people in the workplace. One could even say that motherhood is now the single greatest obstacle left in the path to economic equality for women.

For most companies, the ideal worker is "unencumbered," that is, free of all ties other than those to his job. Anyone who can't devote all his or her energies to paid work is barred from the best jobs and has a permanently lower lifetime income. Not coincidentally, almost all the people in that category happen to be mothers.

The reduced earnings of mothers are, in effect, a heavy personal tax levied on people who care for children, or for any other dependent family members. This levy, a "mommy tax," is easily greater than $1 million in the case of a college-educated woman. For working-class women, there is increasing evidence both in the United States and worldwide that mothers' differential responsibility for children, rather than classic sex discrimination, is the most important factor disposing women to poverty.

"This is the issue that women's and children's advocates should be raising," argues Jane Waldfogel, a professor at Columbia University School of Social Work.

"Women's equality is not about equal access to education or equal job opportunities anymore—those things are done. The part that's left is the part that has to do with family responsibilities."

The much-publicized earnings gap between men and women narrowed dramatically in the 1980s and early 1990s. All a girl had to do was stay young and unencumbered. The sexual egalitarianism evident in so many television sitcoms, from *Friends* to *Seinfeld* to *Ally McBeal* is rooted in economic reality. Young women don't need a man to pay their bills or take them out, any more than men need a woman to iron their shirts or cook their dinner. Many childless women under the age of thirty-five firmly believe that all of the feminist battles have been won, and as far as they're concerned, they're largely right.

But once a woman has a baby, the egalitarian office party is over. I ought to know.

MILLION-DOLLAR BABIES

After my son was born in 1982, I decided to leave the *New York Times* in order to have more time to be a mother. I recently calculated what that decision cost me financially.

I had worked full-time for approximately twenty years, eight of those at the *Times*. When I left, I had a yearly salary of roughly $50,000, augmented by speaking fees, freelance income, and journalism awards. Had I not had a child, I probably would have worked at least another fifteen years, maybe taking early retirement to pursue other interests. Under this scenario, I would have earned a pension, which I lost by leaving the paper before I had worked the requisite ten years to become vested. (The law has since changed to allow vesting after five years with one employer.)

My annual income after leaving the paper has averaged roughly $15,000, from part-time freelance writing. Very conservatively, I lost between $600,000 and $700,000, not counting the loss of a pension. Without quite realizing what I was doing, I took what I thought would be a relatively short break, assuming it would be easy to get back into journalism after a few years, or to earn a decent income from books and other projects. I was wrong. As it turned out, I sacrificed more than half of my expected lifetime earnings. And in the boom years of the stock market, that money invested in equities would have multiplied like kudzu. As a conservative estimate, it could have generated $50,000 or $60,000 a year in income for my old age.

At the time, I never sat down and made these economic calculations. I never even thought about money in connection with motherhood, or if I did, I assumed my husband would provide all we needed. And had I been asked to weigh my son's childhood against ten or fifteen more years at the *Times*, I doubt whether the monetary loss would have tipped the scales. But still, this seems a high price to pay for doing the right thing.

The mommy tax I paid is fairly typical for an educated middle-class American woman. Economist Shirley Burggraf has calculated that a husband and wife who earn a combined income of $81,500 per year and who are equally capable will lose $1.35 million if they have a child. Most of that lost income is the wages forgone by the primary parent. In a middle-income family, with one parent earning $30,000 per year as a sales representative and the other averaging $15,000 as a part-time computer consultant, the mommy tax will still be more than $600,000. Again, this seems an unreasonable penalty on the decision to raise a child, a decision that contributes to the general good by adding another productive person to the nation.

In lower-income families, the mommy tax can push a couple over the brink. Martha F. Richie, a former director of the U.S. Census Bureau, told me, "There is anecdotal evidence—no real research—that for a lower-earning married couple the decision to have a child, or a second child, throws them into poverty."

WHERE IS THE MOMMY TAX THE LOWEST?

An appreciation of a mother's needs can be added to the list of things, like food and fashion, that the French simply do best. Certainly everyone who has ever studied family policy comes away from France with the same blissful expression that one would wear after a great meal.

The country spends more than twice the percentage of its GDP on social welfare as the United States: 29 percent versus 14 percent. And much of that money goes to mothers and children. *Every* French mother, rich or poor, married or single, receives not only free health care but a cash allowance for each child. The allowance can be spent in any way she wants, including hiring help at home. If she hires a licensed nanny, the government will even cover the costs of her contributions to the nanny's pension program.

Single mothers are also entitled to a package of benefits, including housing subsidies, worth about $6,000 a year. These special benefits are sharply reduced when a child reaches the age of three. But time limits do not have the same harsh effects that they would have in the United States, because of the universal medical care, and because public nursery school is available for every three-year-old. By that age virtually every French child is enrolled in one of the world's best preschool systems, free of charge. These programs, combined with a year-long paid maternity leave, make it easy for French mothers to take care of their infants *and* to be employed.

The mommy tax on French women is consequently one of the lowest in the world. The earnings differential between working mothers and childless working women in France is about 8 to 10 percent, compared with at least 20 percent in the United States and 50 percent in Great Britain and Germany. Put another way, babies are much cheaper in France. They are also better off. The combination of relatively high maternal income and a strong safety net keeps the child poverty rate in France down to 6 percent, compared with 17 percent in the United States—despite similar rates of out-of-wedlock births.

Those who care for elderly relatives also discover that their altruism will be heavily penalized. A small survey of individuals who provided informal, unpaid care for family members found that it cost them an average of $659,139 in lost wages, Social Security, and pension benefits over their lifetimes. The subjects reported having to pass up promotions and training opportunities, use up their sick days and vacations, reduce their workload to part-time, and in many cases even quit their paid jobs altogether. This exorbitant "caring tax" is being paid by an increasing number of people, three-quarters of them women. A 1997 study discovered that one in four families had at least one adult who had provided care for an elderly relative or friend.

The mommy tax is obviously highest for well-educated, high-income individuals and lowest for poorly educated people who have less potential income to lose. All else being equal, the younger the mother, and the more children she has, the higher her tax will be, which explains why women are having fewer children, later in life, almost everywhere.

The tax is highest in the Anglo-Saxon countries, where mothers personally bear almost all the costs of caring, and lowest in France and Scandinavia, where paid maternity leaves and public preschools make it easier for mothers to provide care without sacrificing their income.

Most women never think about the mommy tax until they have an encounter with rude reality. Virginia Daley was an interior designer for Aetna Life & Casualty in Hartford, Connecticut. After almost ten years with the company, and consistently good performance reviews, raises, and promotions, Daley was fired in 1993 from her $46,640-a-year job. The dismissal occurred after she had had a baby and then tried to arrange a more flexible work week, in accordance with the company's stated policies.

Not only were her requests for flexibility denied, her workload was actually increased in the wake of a massive corporate downsizing. Already frustrated, Daley was furious to learn in late 1992 that Aetna's chairman Ronald Compton had been awarded a "Good Guy" award from the National Women's Political Caucus for his support of model family-leave programs. (Aetna also consistently made *Working Mother* magazine's annual list of best companies for employed mothers, and in 1992 was touted as one of the *four* "most family-friendly companies" in America by the Families and Work Institute.)

Daley dashed off a memo to Compton, charging that "when it comes to offering flexible family arrangements, Aetna's performance is far from award-winning." The memo concluded that "realistic options for Aetna employees to meet their family obligations without sacrificing their careers are not generally available today. To continue to represent to Aetna employees and the national media that these options are available is unconscionable."

Three months later Daley was terminated, on the grounds of poor performance.

She sued, and the case went to trial in 1997. Aetna maintained that Daley had lost her position because she wasn't able to handle the additional responsibilities that she was assigned after the downsizing (and the baby). The jury essentially agreed with Aetna. It also agreed with the company that Daley was not speaking out on a matter of public concern when she complained that numerous employees were being denied family-friendly schedules. Her memo to Compton was therefore not "protected speech," i.e., an important statement that entitles an employee to protection from retaliation. Daley lost the case, as well as a subsequent appeal.

(Information obtained from a court-ordered survey of all salaried employees below the level of corporate officer confirmed that *slightly less than half* of the Aetna employees who asked to work at home part of the week had had their request granted, in the period between January 1, 1991, and March 1, 1993. Most requests for job sharing and for compressed work weeks were also denied. On the other hand, the great majority of people who wanted to work part-time, usually a thirty-hour week, were granted such a schedule.)

According to Daley's lawyer, Philip L. Steele, the jury foreman told him after the trial that although the panel was very sympathetic to Daley, its members felt she had probably "overextended" herself. "They believed it was just too hard for a woman to raise little kids and do a good job," Steele told me. "The thinking was, how can a woman do all that, not how could a company do that?"

The decision cost Daley dearly. She calculates that over the next five years following her departure from Aetna, her income as a part-time consultant was from $90,000 to $154,000 lower than if she had stayed at the company. And that doesn't include the loss of Aetna's annual contribution to her 401K retirement plan. "I figure that if I'd stayed at Aetna another ten years," Daley told me, "their contribution to my 401K alone would have been more than $25,000. That could easily become more than six figures by the time I am retirement age . . . People need to know that once you have a child you'll definitely be poorer."

SIXTY CENTS TO A MAN'S DOLLAR

In the Bible, in Leviticus, God instructs Moses to tell the Israelites that women, for purposes of tithing, are worth thirty shekels while men are worth fifty—a ratio of 60 percent. For fifty years, from about 1930 to 1980, the value of employed women eerily reflected that biblical ratio: The earnings of full-time working women were only 60 percent of men's earnings. In the 1980s, that ratio began to change. By 1993, women working full-time were earning an average of seventy-seven cents for every dollar men earned. (In 1997, the gap widened again, as the median weekly earnings of full-time working women fell to 75 percent of men's earnings.)

But lo and behold, when we look closer, we find the same old sixty cents to a man's dollar. The usual way to measure the gender wage gap is by comparing the hourly earnings of men and women who work full-time year-round. But this compares only the women who work like men with men—a method that neatly excludes most women. As we have seen, only about half of the mothers of children under eighteen have full-time, year-round paying jobs.

To find the real difference between men's and women's earnings, one would have to compare the earnings of all male and female workers, both full- and part-time. And guess what one discovers? The average earnings of *all* female workers in 1999 were 59 percent of men's earnings. Women who work for pay are still stuck at the age-old biblical value put on their labor.

My research turned up other intriguing reflections of the 60 percent ratio: A survey of 1982 graduates of the Stanford Business School found that ten years after graduation, the median income of the full- and part-time employed female M.B.A.s amounted to $81,300, against the men's median income of $139,100. Again, the women's share is 58 percent. Another study, of 1974 graduates of the University of Michigan Law School, revealed that in the late 1980s the women's average earnings were 61 percent of the men's—despite the fact that 96 percent of the women were working, and that the men and women were virtually identical in terms of training. The authors of this study concluded that the women's family responsibilities were "certainly the most important single cause of sex differences in earnings."

Conservatives frequently tout women's economic gains in order to charge that women's advocates who haven't folded their tents and gone home must be making up things to complain about. In a polemic titled *Who Stole Feminism?* Christina Hoff Sommers lambasts feminist activists for wearing a button stating that women earn fifty-nine cents to a man's dollar, which, she claims, is "highly misleading and now egregiously out of date." Sommers is right if we skim over what she calls such "prosaic matters" as the fact that people who have primary responsibility for a child have different work patterns from people without caring responsibilities. But if we are interested in the real differences in the earnings of employed men and women, those buttons still tell the real story.

THE COST OF BEING A MOTHER

A small group of mostly female academic economists has added another twist to the story. Their research reveals that working mothers not only earn less than men, but also less per hour than childless women, even after such differences as education and experience are factored out. The pay gap between mothers and nonmothers under age thirty-five is now larger than the wage gap between young men and women.

The first comprehensive estimates of the cost of motherhood in terms of lost income were made in England by Heather Joshi of the City University in London and Hugh Davies of Birkbeck College of the University of London. The two economists estimated that a typical middle-class British mother of two forfeits almost *half* of her potential lifetime earnings.

In the United States, similar work has been done by Jane Waldfogel at Columbia University. Waldfogel set out to assess the opportunity cost of motherhood by asking exactly how much of the dramatic wage gains made by women in the 1980s went to women without family responsibilities. How many of the female winners in the 1980s were people like Donna Shalala, Janet Reno, Elizabeth Dole, and Carole Bellamy, the director of UNICEF: childless women whose work patterns were indistinguishable from those of traditional males.

Back in the late 1970s, Waldfogel found, the difference between men's and women's pay was about the same for all women. Nonmothers earned only slightly higher wages. But over the next decade things changed. By 1991, thirty-year-old American women without children were making 90 percent of men's wages, while comparable women with children were making only 70 percent. Even when Waldfogel factored out all the women's differences, the disparity in their incomes remained—something she dubbed the "family wage gap."

Why do working mothers earn so much less than childless women? Academic researchers have worried over this question like a dog over a bone but haven't turned up a single, definitive answer.

Waldfogel argues that the failure of employers to provide paid maternity leaves is one factor that leads to the family wage gap in the United States. This country is one of only six nations in the world that does not require a paid leave. (The others are Australia, New Zealand, Lesotho, Swaziland, and Papua New Guinea.) With no right to a paid leave, many American mothers who want to stay at home with a new baby simply quit their jobs, and this interruption in employment costs them dearly in terms of lost income. Research in Europe reveals that when paid maternity leaves were mandated, the percentage of women remaining employed rose, and women's wages were higher, unless the leaves lasted more than a few months.

In the United States as well, women who are able to take formal paid maternity leave do not suffer the same setback in their wages as comparably placed women who do not have a right to such leaves. This is a significant benefit to mothers in the five states, including California, New York, and New Jersey, that mandate temporary disability insurance coverage for pregnancy and childbirth.

Paid leaves are so valuable because they don't seem to incur the same penalties that employers impose on even the briefest of unpaid career interruptions. A good example is the experience of the 1974 female graduates of the University of Michigan Law School. During their first fifteen years after law school, these women spent an average of only 3.3 months out of the workplace, compared with virtually no time out for their male classmates. More than one-quarter of the women had worked part-time, for an average of 10.1 months over the fifteen years, compared with virtually no part-time work among the men. While working full-time, the women put in only 10 percent fewer hours than full-time men, again not a dramatic difference.

But the penalties for these slight distinctions between the men's and women's work patterns were strikingly harsh. Fifteen years after graduation, the women's average earnings were not 10 percent lower, or even 20 percent lower, than the men's, but almost 40 percent lower. Fewer than one-fifth of the women in law firms who had worked part-time for more than six months had made partner in their firms, while more than four-fifths of the mothers with little or no part-time work had made partner.

Another survey of almost 200 female M.B.A.s found that those who had taken an average of only 8.8 months out of the job market were less likely to reach upper-middle management and earned 17 percent less than comparable women who had never had a gap in their employment.

Working-class women are also heavily penalized for job interruptions, although these are the very women who allegedly" choose" less demanding occupations that enable them to move in and out of the job market without undue wage penalties. The authors of one study concluded that the negative repercussions of taking a little time out of the labor force were still discernible after twenty years. In blue-collar work, seniority decides who is eligible for better jobs, and who is "bumped" in the event of layoffs. Under current policies, many women lose their seniority forever if they interrupt their employment, as most mothers do. Training programs, required for advancement, often take place after work, excluding the many mothers who can't find child care.

Mandatory overtime is another handicap placed on blue-collar mothers. Some 45 percent of American workers reported in a recent survey that they had to work overtime with little or no notice. In 1994 factory workers put in the highest levels of overtime ever reported by the Bureau of Labor Statistics in its thirty-eight years of tracking the data. Where does that leave a woman who has to be home in time for dinner with the kids? Out of a promotion and maybe out of a job. Increasingly in today's driven workplace, whether she is blue- or white-collar, a woman who goes home when she is supposed to go home is going to endanger her economic well-being.

The fact that many mothers work part-time also explains some of the difference between mothers' and comparable womens' hourly pay. (About 65 percent of part-time workers are women, most of whom are mothers.) Employers are not required to offer part-time employees equal pay and benefits for equal work. As a result, nonstandard workers earn on average about 40 percent less an hour than full-time workers, and about half of that wage gap persists even for similar workers in similar jobs.

Many bosses privately believe that mothers who work part-time have a "recreational" attitude toward work; as one Maryland businessman assured me, presumably, this belief makes it easier to justify their exploitation. But the working conditions they face don't sound very much like recreation. A recent survey by Catalyst, a research organization focused on women in business, found that more than half of the people who had switched to part-time jobs and lower pay reported that their workload stayed the same. Ten percent reported an increase in workload after their income had been reduced. Most of these people were mothers.

Another factor in the family wage gap is the disproportionate number of mothers who operate their own small businesses, a route often taken by women who need flexibility during the child-rearing years. Female-owned small businesses have increased twofold over small businesses owned by men in recent years. In 1999, women owned 38 percent of all U.S. businesses, compared with only 5 percent in 1972, a remarkable increase that is frequently cited as evidence of women's economic success. One new mother noted that conversations at play groups "center as much on software and modems as they do on teething and ear infections."

Less frequently mentioned is the fact that many of these women-owned businesses are little more than Mom-minus-Pop operations: one woman trying to earn some money on the side, or keep her career alive, during the years when her children have priority. Forty-five percent of women-owned businesses are home-based. And the more than one-third of businesses owned by women in 1996 generated only 16 percent of the sales of all U.S. businesses in that year.

In 1997, although women were starting new businesses at twice the rate of men, they received only 2 percent of institutional venture capital, a principal source of financing for businesses with serious prospects for growth. Almost one-quarter of female business owners financed their operations the same way that they did their shopping: with their credit cards.

Some researchers have suggested that mothers earn less than childless women because they are less productive. This may be true for some mothers who work at home and are subject to frequent interruptions, or for those who are exhausted from having to do most of the domestic chores, or distracted by creaky child-care arrangements. But the claim that mothers have lower productivity than other workers is controversial and unproven. It is easier to demonstrate that working mothers face the same old problem that has bedeviled women in the workplace for decades.

IT'S DISCRIMINATION, STUPID

It is revealing that those occupations requiring nurturing skills, such as child care, social work, and nursing, are the most systematically underpaid, relative to their educational and skill demands. These are also, of course, the occupations with the highest percentage of females. But men who are primary caregivers also pay a heavy price: a "daddy tax," if you will. This suggests that at least part of the huge tax on mothers' earnings is due to work rules and practices and habits of mind that discriminate against anyone, of either sex, who cannot perform like an "unencumbered" worker. In other words, discrimination against all good parents, male or female.

Surveys have found that wives may adore husbands who share the parenting experience, but employers distinctly do not. A majority of managers believe that part-time schedules and even brief parental leaves are inappropriate for men. When Houston Oiler David Williams missed one Sunday game to be with his wife after the birth of their first child, he was docked $111,111.

A survey of 348 male managers at twenty Fortune 500 companies found that fathers from dual-career families put in an average of *two* fewer hours per week—or about 4 percent less—than men whose wives were at home. That was the only difference between the two groups of men. But the fathers with working wives, who presumably had a few more domestic responsibilities, earned almost 20 percent less. There it is again: a 20 percent family wage gap.

"Face time still matters as much or more than productivity in many companies," Charles Rodgers, a management consultant in Boston, said. Rodgers told me about a man in a high-tech company who regularly came to work two hours early so that he could occasionally leave early for Little League games with his son. He was given a poor performance rating.

Such discrimination is hard to quantify, but it is potentially a powerful political issue. When the Clinton administration announced that it was banning employment discrimination against *parents* working in the federal government, there were so many calls to a White House staffer assigned to the case that her machine stopped taking messages.

Only eight states currently have laws prohibiting discrimination against parents in the workplace. Examples include taking a primary parent off a career track out of an assumption that the individual couldn't do the work; hiring someone without children over a more qualified person with children; forcing a primary parent to work overtime, or else; and refusing to hire a single parent, though the employer hires single, childless people. In the course of my reporting, I encountered numerous mothers who felt that their employer's refusal to arrange a shorter workweek, particularly after the birth of a second baby, amounted to career-destroying discrimination.

THE SECOND BABY

Cindy DiBiasi, a former reporter for WUSA-TV, a Gannett-owned station in Washington, D.C., is one of the countless mothers who found that the birth of a second baby, and the impossibility of arranging a short workweek to accommodate it, destroyed her career.

DiBiasi is a slim, attractive, dark-haired woman with a brisk air of self-assurance instantly recognizable as the glossy competence displayed every night on the evening news. In 1989, she became the medical reporter for WUSA, a job that she had long coveted. Two days before she was scheduled to begin her new position, DiBiasi discovered that she was pregnant. She hadn't yet signed a contract, and she didn't tell her bosses for seven weeks. But she was able to put her pregnancy to use, producing a series on having a baby, even arranging for a camera crew to be at the hospital when her daughter was born in August of 1990. She remembers being on camera even after her water broke. "They didn't have to worry about me being committed," she commented wryly.

After a ten-week maternity leave, DiBiasi was back on the job from 10:00 A.M. until 6:00 A.M., producing a five-minute live segment for the 4:00 P.M. news show and a taped piece for the 6:00 P.M. news. All went well until just before her child's first birthday, when DiBiasi had to take three days off to visit her sick father in Illinois. A week later, her child's nanny was unable to come to work for two days in a row. DiBiasi was about one hour late on the first day and two hours late on the next. (Her husband took off work on both days to be at home.)

She was subsequently called into her boss's office and told that she would lose vacation time for the days she took to go to Illinois. "I was amazed," she told me. "I asked if it had anything to do with my being late, those two days and explained what had happened. I asked if there was a problem with my work. He said no, but he was getting red in the face . . . A long time ago a female reporter told me that whenever my child got sick, I should always say it was me who was sick. I remember thinking, that's bullshit. How could they want me to be dishonest? But now I wasn't so sure.

"I didn't like the feeling I was getting, so I asked for a meeting with the two top executives. They told me that there was a perception that I was not working 'full days.' I reminded them that I was on the air twice a day, every day, and that nights at home I was reading medical journals to keep up in my field. 'How does the desk know that?' they asked.

"Then they mentioned, almost casually, that they might want to take the medical unit in a different direction, but 'that has nothing to do with you or your work,' they assured me.

"At one point one of them said something like 'the problem is that you think you're the only one who has a family.' . . . Now the guy who said this had a son in college, and the other two men with children had stay-at-home wives. I pointed out that I had a *one-year-old*. And that if had problems dealing with it I'd tell them. They just looked at me, with this blank, flat look."

During the next six months, DiBiasi was asked to do a live segment on the 5:00 P.M. news, along with her pieces for 4:00 P.M. and 6:00 P.M. She agreed, thinking, "As long as I'm not away from my kid any more time, I'll kill myself for them—that'll solve this . . . Then I found out that I was pregnant again. I realized that I couldn't keep up the pace, so I asked if I could switch to a three-day week, with a prorated salary cut. The news director said he would think about it.

"I worked all the way up to my delivery, which was in June of 1992. I had eight weeks of maternity leave. Two days before I was to go back, I had a call from the assistant news director. 'We really need help on general assignment,' he said. So after I get back, for the next two months I'm doing fires, accidents, you name it, and I'm not getting home at six-thirty anymore. One day they asked me to do a live shot in Annapolis at the end of the day, and I said I couldn't—it meant I wouldn't get home until nine P.M. My boss said, 'Can't your nanny just stay?'

"I said, 'Number one, no, she can't stay, and number two, if she *could* stay, I don't want to get home that late. If I do that, I won't see my kids at all.'

"He just looked at me. Then he said, 'So, you'll see them tomorrow.'"

DiBiasi's new position was a demotion, but she continued a while longer, getting home late regularly. Finally, she told the desk that there was no way to be a general assignment reporter if one had to be at home at 6:30 P.M. She was told she had to continue on general assignment.

The managers at WUSA had put DiBiasi in a job they knew she couldn't do. She hired a lawyer and began the process of suing the station. The important thing, her lawyer told her, was to stay on the job, no matter how bad it got. Otherwise, management could argue that she had left voluntarily. However, the demands of staying on the job, and preparing a case, proved overwhelming.

"I was supposed to be secretly tape-recording all our meetings," DiBiasi said, "and then come home and transcribe the tapes at night. I had the job, I had to deal with the attorney, my husband was traveling a lot, and I had two little babies . . . I finally had to quit when it all became just too much of an emotional drain. I would have had to sell short everything in my life I cared about; there would have been no more essence to me."

DiBiasi also decided not to sue: "I knew that if I pursued this, they would say I wasn't a good reporter. And there is a contradiction in these kinds of suits, because in order to get punitive damages, you have to show *damage;* you have to show that you're a wilting flower who has been hurt by all this. If you're strong, and are determined not to be a victim, they can argue, so what's the problem?"

So, after fifteen years in television reporting, DiBiasi lost a job she loved, a six-figure income, her health insurance, and her economic independence. Slowly, she was also losing public recognition, a newsperson's working capital. All because she had had the temerity to try to work for fewer days a week while her two children were young. For all of her talent, energy, and drive, DiBiasi, like millions of other mothers, was suddenly only a husband away from financial disaster.

As Cindy DiBiasi's story illustrates, the most popular form of family planning in the United States and other wealthy countries—two children, spaced not too far apart—is incompatible with most women's careers. Even if a new mother and her employer can cope with one child, the second baby is often the final straw. The most sympathetic employers can prove surprisingly resistant to the second baby. A well-known feminist economist told me that she had gone to great lengths to bend the rules at her university to accommodate one of her graduate students who had become pregnant. The woman was given a year's extension on her schedule and time out to be with her new infant. Then, just before she was due to come back, she became pregnant again.

My friend, who believed she had been as progressive as was humanly possible, felt betrayed. She thinks the woman was foolish not to realize that the system can only accommodate so much deviation. "You have to play by the rules to some extent, especially when other people have stuck their neck out for you," she said. This professor, by the way, has no children herself, but she does have tenure.

HOW TO LOWER THE MOMMY TAX

Until now, narrowing the gender wage gap in the United States has depended almost entirely on what might be called the "be a man" strategy.

Women are told to finish school, find a job, acquire skills, develop seniority, get tenure, make partner, and put children off until the very last minute. The longer a woman postpones family responsibilities, and the longer her "preparental" phase lasts, the higher her lifetime earnings will be.

Ambitious women of the baby-boom generation and younger have by and large tried to be a man in this way. A good example is Susan Pedersen, a historian who achieved tenure at Harvard in the mid-1990s. By that time, she was married and in her late thirties, but she had postponed having children until her academic career was secure. Motherhood was something she wanted very much, she commented during an interview, but it posed a serious threat to her professional dreams and had to be delayed.

As Pedersen's success demonstrates, this strategy does work—for the very small number who are able to pull it off. And women who have their children later in life do have higher lifetime earnings and a wider range of opportunities than younger mothers. The advice dished out by writers like Danielle Crittenden—no relation—an antifeminist ideologue who has urged women to marry and have their babies young, ignores this, along with some other hard truths. Crittenden never tells her readers that young parents tend to separate and divorce much more frequently than older couples, leaving young mothers and children vulnerable to poverty. Large numbers of the women who end up on welfare are there because they have done exactly what she recommends: married and had children young and then been left to support them alone.

But trying to be a man has its own risks. Many baby-boomer women postponed families only to discover that when they wanted to become pregnant, it was too late. (I saw some of the risks associated with this strategy after I had my own child under the wire in 1982. I touted the advantages of late motherhood on a couple of television shows, until I realized that many of my friends over forty were unable to conceive.) And millions of women don't feel that being a man is the way they want to live their lives. Increasingly, young women are saying that they don't want to put off children until they almost qualify for membership in AARP.

An alternative strategy is followed in countries like France and Sweden, where the government, private employers, and/or husbands share much more of the costs of raising children. This makes it far easier for women to be mothers and to work. In France, for example, families with two preschool-age children receive about $10,000 worth of annual subsidies, including free health care and housing subsidies and excellent free preschools. As a result, child poverty is unusual, and the pay gap between mothers and others is much smaller in France than in the United States or the United Kingdom.

Whenever Europe is singled out as a model, the usual response is that Americans would never support such generous social policies. But in fact, the United States already does have an extremely generous social welfare state. But unlike the welfare states of western Europe, the American government doesn't protect mothers; it protects soldiers.

Men who postpone or interrupt civilian employment for military service pay a tax on their lifetime earnings that is quite comparable to the mommy tax. White men who were drafted during the Vietnam War, for example, were still earning approximately 15 percent less in the early 1980s than comparable nonveterans. This "warrior wage gap" is strikingly similar to the family wage gap, again indicating that mothers' lower earnings are not entirely attributable to gender discrimination.

But there is unquestionable discrimination in the way the government has responded to the financial sacrifices that soldiers and parents, particularly mothers, make. All Americans are asked to "make it up" to veterans of the military: The damage to a caregiver's pocketbook is unmitigated, while the damage to a veteran's wallet has legitimized a massive relief effort.

To illustrate this double standard, let's look at two men with identical characteristics. One works as a computer technician, is married to a woman in the same occupation, and has two children. He is a conscientious father, making sure to be home for dinner every night, even helping to cook it. He takes his kids to sporting events, attends teacher conferences, and tries to limit his travel and outside commitments.

This man is legitimately worried about what his dedication to family will do to his career. Let's say he does get fewer promotions and over the years earns 15 to 20 percent less than he would have had he not shared the family obligations. We can realistically say that he pays a significant daddy tax.

Now take a man with the same education and imagine that he spends three or four years in military service. He is worried that these years out of his active professional life will affect his economic future, and they might, although his boss believes that his service was good leadership training. But whatever career losses he suffers will be cushioned by the generous thanks that the nation pays to its ex-servicemen. He discovers that his warrior tax is lowered by these benefits, which are available to him even if he never got near a battlefield:

- He can stay in the military for twenty years as a *part-time reservist* and draw half pay for the rest of his life.
- He will get special preference for government jobs. Extra points will be added to whatever civil service exams he may take, and some rules are written so that he will be chosen over closely ranked nonveterans. In government layoffs, he will have extra protection. Unlike mothers or fathers who find that after a few years out of the job market their credentials are downgraded, his are given a major boost by veterans' preferences.
- If he decides to go back to school for more education, he can qualify for thirty-six months of cash payments worth more than $17,000.
- He also qualifies for a government-guaranteed housing loan, financed at interest rates usually half a percentage point below the going market rate.
- He can make use of a hospital system costing the federal government $17 billion a year.

- He will have access to special low auto insurance rates, available only to individuals with some connection to the military. These come in especially handy when his teenage son begins to drive.
- As long as he remains in the military or works on a military base as a civilian, he can enjoy subsidized child care provided by the best daycare system in the country. For only $37 to $98 a week (in 1997), depending on his income, he can enroll his children in infant and toddler care and preschools staffed by expertly trained and licensed teachers. In the private sector, the fees would be two to four times higher, for often inferior care.

None of these benefits is contingent on service in combat. In 1990, 6.3 million of the 27 million veterans eligible for benefits served only during peacetime. Millions of ex-servicemen, who do not even have a hangnail to show for their harrowing experience in uniform, enjoy the same government largesse that flows to the veterans who were once put in the way of danger.

The benefits paid to military veterans are so lavish that they are now second only to Social Security in terms of government payments to individuals. And they do an excellent job of reducing the warrior tax. The educational benefits in particular help veterans overcome many of the economic disadvantages they suffer by leaving the workplace for a few years.

A congressional study in the early 1990s concluded that the veterans of World War II who took advantage of the G.I. Bill to earn a college degree enjoyed incomes of up to 10 percent more than they might otherwise have earned. Society was also the beneficiary, for the additional taxes paid by the college-educated veterans during their working lives more than paid for the program.

It hardly needs to be said that there is no G.I. Bill, no health care, no subsidized housing, and no job preferences for mothers. As things now stand, millions of women sacrifice their economic independence and risk economic disaster for the sake of raising a child. This says a lot about family values, the nation's priorities, and free riding.

A third way to reduce the mommy tax would be to expand the anti-discrimination laws to cover parents. Joan Williams, a law professor at American University's Washington College of Law, argues that the design of work around masculine norms can be reconceptualized as discrimination. As an example, Williams suggests that if a woman works full-time, with good job evaluations for a significant period, then switches to part-time because of family responsibilities and is paid less per hour than full-time employees doing similar work, she could claim discrimination under the Equal Pay Act. Williams believes that disparate-action suits could also be filed against employers whose policies (including routine and mandatory overtime, promotion tracks, resistance to part-time work) have a disparate impact on women, producing disproportionate numbers of men in top-level positions.

The essential point is that existing laws, and new laws preventing discrimination against people with caregiving responsibilities, could go a very long way toward improving mothers' lifetime earnings.

THE ULTIMATE MOMMY TAX: CHILDLESSNESS

The cost of children has become so high that many American women are not having children at all. One of the most striking findings of Claudia Goldin's survey of white female college graduates is their high degree of childlessness (28 percent). Now that the baby-boomer generation is middle-aged, it is clear that more than one-quarter of the educated women in that age group will never have children. Indeed, the percentage of all American women who remain childless is also steadily rising, from 8 to 9 percent in the 1950s to 10 percent in 1976 to 17.5 percent in the late 1990s.

Is this rising childlessness by choice? Goldin thinks not. She found that in 1978, while in their twenties, almost half of the college-educated boomers who would remain childless had said that they did want children. Goldin calculated that almost one-fifth of this entire generation (19 percent) of white college graduates was disappointed in not having a child. This is the ultimate price of the "be a man" strategy that has been forced on working women. For women in business, the price is staggering. A recent Catalyst survey of 1,600 M.B.A.s found that only about one-fifth of the women had children, compared with 70 percent of the men.

Educated black women have had, if anything, an even harder time combining children with their careers. Many of the most accomplished black women now in their forties and fifties, including Oprah Winfrey, Anita Hill, Eleanor Holmes Norton (the congressional representative for the District of Columbia), and Alexis Herman, secretary of labor in the Clinton administration, have forgone motherhood. These women apparently discovered that the price of success included the lack of parental obligations. And educated black women face an additional problem—an acute shortage of eligible black men.

Americans have a hard time realizing that such deeply personal choices as when or whether to have a child can be powerfully circumscribed by broader social or economic factors. American women, in particular, are stunningly unaware that their "choices" between a career and a family are much more limited than those of women in many European countries, where policies are much more favorable to mothers and children.

Swedish women, for example, enjoy benefits that American women can only imagine in their wildest dreams: a year's paid leave after childbirth, the right to work a six-hour day with full benefits until their child is in primary school, and a stipend from the government to help pay child-care expenses.

And guess what? These pro-family policies dramatically reduce the mommy tax on Swedish mothers; enable a higher percentage of Swedish women, vis-ávis Americans, to have children; and permit more Swedish mothers to stay at home while their children are young.

Germany is an altogether different story. Before the fall of the Berlin Wall, women in East Germany enjoyed many of the same policies that benefit Swedish women, including yearlong paid maternity leaves and free public child care. It was so easy to combine paid work with children that almost every woman had a baby and almost all mothers worked. In 1989 about 91 percent of East German women were biological mothers.

West Germany, on the other hand, offered much less support to working mothers. As a result, only about 80 percent of West German women became biological mothers, and significantly fewer mothers worked.

After German reunification, subsidized child care—and subsidized jobs—were eliminated in East Germany. As a result, birth rates plummeted. Berlin now has one of the lowest birthrates in the world.

In sum, an individual woman's decision whether to have a child or not, and whether to stay home or not, is heavily influenced by her country's willingness to help her bear the costs. In Germany, as in the United States, the official message is *caveat mater,* or "mothers beware": you're on your own.

19. RESTORATIVE JUSTICE, REAL JUSTICE

Erika Bai Siebels

In a courtroom a young man accused of robbery changes his plea to guilty. Another young man asks for undisclosed offenses to be taken into account and as a result gets a stiffer sentence. A drug-trafficker doing time in prison repents and seeks to rebuild his life.

A woman forgives the drunken driver who left her childless and bedridden, and now teaches caregivers how to relate with compassion and patience to people who are disabled. A man partners with the grandfather of his son's killer to launch a foundation that teaches nonviolence and peaceful problem-solving in schools.

At the root of these surprising actions is a practice called restorative justice, a process in which victims and offenders meet to talk about the effects of crime, the harms it causes, and how to make things right. It is a process which allows offenders to put a face on their victims, take responsibility for their crimes, make restitution if possible, and become productive citizens if and when they are released (or emotionally healthy role models should their crime require them to remain incarcerated). It is a process which allows victims to participate in their healing by being heard by and coming to understand the person who caused their trauma, and to experience a new lease on life that comes with the ability to forgive.

When a crime is committed, people are hurt—not only physically and emotionally, but spiritually, too, if they harbor unforgiveness and begin doubting humanity and the system that is supposed to bring justice.

And crime affects more than just the victim and offender. Witnesses to the crime, arresting officers, prison guards, the families and friends both of the convicted person and the victim—all these will experience distress, even upheaval in their lives because of it.

So, when a person is convicted and locked up, has justice taken place? Do contemporary courts and prisons promote true justice? What is real justice? These are the difficult questions that practitioners of restorative justice are daring to articulate and explore.

Restorative justice is an alternative way of considering and responding to crime. Essential to this is the offender's act of taking responsibility and the victim's act of learning to forgive.

In South Africa's prisons, where Joanna Flanders Thomas works with incarcerated men through the Centre for Hope and Transformation, this means encouraging perpetrators to tell the truth in court and restoring to them a sense of dignity by helping them take responsibility for their lives. It also means teaching them how to reconcile with God, their families, their victims, and their communities—whenever possible—and to learn to contribute to society. Most of all, it means the transformation of those in prison, empowering them to break the cycle of crime and violence and to become successfully reintegrated into society upon their release.

While the current system of justice in the United States and other countries is based on retribution—punishing offenders for their crimes—restorative justice focuses on restoration.

"The continuing punitive approach to crime has not worked," says Thomas. She lists the many ways in which the system has failed to bring about true justice. Incarceration, she asserts, neither deters nor prevents crime, which continues to escalate. High recidivism rates are proof that prisoners are not being successfully rehabilitated. Homes, communities, and nations are no longer safe, as crime and corruption—even among police and correctional officers—grow.

Restorative justice, on the other hand, works because it brings healing. Emmett Solomon, executive director of the Restorative Justice Ministry Network of North America, explains the two different approaches: While the traditional criminal justice system in America asks, "Who did this crime?" and "How much pain did they cause?"—essentially spanking its prisoners—restorative justice asks, "What will it take to bring a sense of autonomy to the victim?" and "What will it take to bring the offender back into the community?" These questions lead to healing.

According to Solomon, the present criminal justice system is ineffective because "systems can't love, and only love brings true healing." Government systems cannot love; therefore, they cannot heal. However, community members who reach out with caring hands and hearts can love, and ultimately that brings healing.

"It's healing for the offenders because it helps them understand the damage they caused, and it's healing for the victims to listen and get answers to their questions, like 'Why did you choose to kill my child?'" explains Solomon.

Solomon, a former prison chaplain, at one time wondered why his inmates never prayed for their victims. He eventually came to understand why: Prisoners feel like victims themselves—victims of the criminal justice system.

"They go to jail, are locked up and visited by district attorneys to get into negotiations with the State about their future. By the time they get to prison, they feel hammered down by the system and they forget about the victims," he said.

In 1994, having spent most of his life trying to change the system, Solomon founded the Restorative Justice Ministry of North America. "I was trying to bring healing to a system that went against healing, so I was trying to paddle upstream in that environment," recalls Solomon.

Punishment does not work to right wrongs, proponents of restorative justice say. It can often hurt, destroy, and further break down individuals, communities, and institutions. The process of restorative justice, on the other hand, leads to growth, healing, and a sense of acceptance and community. It does so by seeking to increase the understanding, impact, and consequences of the crime. It asks questions such as, "What circumstances led to the crime? Why? How did you feel?" Forgiveness and reconciliation can result from such soul-searching.

Because crime occurs in a context and affects any number of people, restorative justice encourages all those touched by the crime to participate: victim, offender, family members, and the community itself. Victims, who sometimes initiate the process, typically want answers to their questions and to be involved in the justice process. North Carolina has a well-developed victim-offender program that occurs in the courts, prior to sentencing. Texas, on the other hand, implements restorative justice after the conviction: Once the offender is imprisoned, the Division of Victim Services (a division within the criminal justice system) sometimes sponsors victim-offender mediation programs.

Howard Zehr popularized restorative justice in his 1990 book, *Changing Lenses: A New Focus for Crime and Justice* (Herald Press). In it he proposed that restoration, not retribution, should be the key factor when dealing with crimes. Zehr directed the Mennonite Central Committee U.S. Office on Crime and Justice before moving to Virginia, where he is now professor of sociology and restorative justice in Eastern Mennonite University's graduate conflict-transformation program.

Restorative justice is played out in various arenas—discussion circles, conferences, workshops, and victim-offender mediation—which provide opportunities for people affected by misconduct and crime to talk about what happened.

Practitioners of restorative justice are trained, usually as volunteers, to facilitate the meetings. They learn, among other things, that taking responsibility and accounting for one's actions are key; that the offender needs to take action to repair the harm done through the crime; that forgiveness is a choice; that reconciliation is a process; and that perpetrators are people. They also learn how to listen.

Lorraine Stutzman Amstutz, who heads the Office on Crime and Justice at the Mennonite Central Committee, provides resources and training on many issues of crime and justice, restorative justice being one of them. When she trains people to become facilitators of victim-offender mediation, she tells them that while there is no perfect mediator, good mediators should be able to tolerate varying levels of frustration because it can be difficult—both logistically and emotionally—to bring people together. Furthermore, facilitators don't "make" things happen; they serve only to guide—not control—the process.

In their 1998 curriculum, *Victim Offender Conferencing in Pennsylvania's Juvenile Justice System*, Lorraine Stutzman Amstutz and Howard Zehr write about the risks and benefits of victim-offender conferencing. The knowledge and skills of the mediator will play a critical role in the success of the actual conference. Mediators need to ask themselves questions like: What do you bring to this process? What are your needs? Are there any obstacles to facilitation? How comfortable are you with different levels of anger? These questions are imperative because they help facilitators separate their own issues from those that are pertinent to each case they may mediate.

Other risks include victims having unrealistic expectations of how the offender will respond to their story. Victims might be disappointed if the offender doesn't understand their pain or the offender is unwilling or unable to provide adequate restitution. Additionally, the process of victim-offender mediation may seem unbearable for victims who would rather move on without replaying the crime and reexperiencing the trauma.

Offenders might be afraid of facing their victims; they may imagine the victims want revenge.

Potential benefits far outweigh the risks, however. For offenders, mediation offers a chance to make things right. For victims, it offers an opportunity to participate in the process, which creates a sense of empowerment. It can also mean changed attitudes, increased understanding, and a reduced sense of alienation from the process.

Stutzman Amstutz and Zehr note that mediation can also lead to reduced recidivism rates. When offenders come to see their victims as persons—not just faceless statistics—the high human cost of crime acts as a deterrent to committing a crime again.

How is restorative justice practiced? Joanna Flanders Thomas starts by building relationships with prison management, staff, and prisoners. With the hope of empowering people, she facilitates workshops on such topics as conflict resolution, human dynamics, action learning, productive conversations, strategic planning, trauma debriefing, building support, and restorative justice.

But restorative justice isn't restricted to prisons and courts. It is practiced in schools, companies, and other communities, too. John Bailie, trainer and consultant for Real Justice and the International Institute for Restorative Practices, works with teachers, administrators, and counselors to bring about a restorative culture in the school setting. The program, called SaferSanerSchools, teaches people how to implement restorative practices, showing them how to regulate their abilities to be supportive and nurturing.

"We have to help people change," says Bailie. "That's the end goal—to change their behavior and create a healthy community where people feel safe, are held accountable, and make changes with the support of others without feeling stigmatized, which is what happens if you operate in a punitive system."

SaferSanerSchools started with three pilot schools in southeastern Pennsylvania. After years of implementation, community-building, individual-building, and restorative practices, Bailie says that a decrease occurred in fighting, interruption, and behavior referrals.

Though restorative justice is practiced around the world in secular settings, Christians have promoted it, too. "Jesus' main thing was forgiveness," Emmett Solomon reminds us. "Therefore, we know he was well into restoration."

The message of Christianity is, ultimately, a message of restoration between God and God's people through Jesus Christ. Jesus fulfilled the prophet Isaiah's words: "The Spirit of the Lord is upon me, because He has anointed me to preach good news to the poor. He has sent me to proclaim freedom for the prisoners and recovery of sight for the blind, to release the oppressed, to proclaim the year of the Lord's favor . . ." (Isa. 61:1–2).

The Bible is rich in images of prisoners being set free—free from sin, free from despair, free from prisons of the body, mind, and spirit. The psalmist, King David, wrote, "The Lord sets prisoners free, the Lord gives sight to the blind, the Lord lifts up those who are bowed down" (Ps. 146:7–8).

The following concepts also demonstrate God's commitment to leniency and restoration. Moses describes the year of Jubilee, a year of redemption and freedom in which debts were canceled, slaves freed, and all property returned to original owners (Leviticus 25). Moses set aside cities of refuge, to which anyone who had unintentionally killed someone could flee (Deuteronomy 4).

Lynette Parker, justice initiatives specialist for the International Centre of Justice and Reconciliation (a ministry of Prison Fellowship International), cites Luke 19 to exemplify God's teaching about restorative justice. In that passage, a wealthy tax collector named Zacchaeus climbs a sycamore tree to see Jesus. When he climbs the tree—and takes responsibility—his life is changed.

From that story comes Prison Fellowship International's Project Sycamore Tree, in which victims enter prisons to meet with unrelated offenders over a series of eight to 12 weeks to discuss the effects of crime, the harm it caused, and how to make things right. It helps offenders to understand the impact of crime and victims to express their feelings and gain a sense of power.

Project Sycamore Tree has been used in Rwanda, where it is called the Umuvumu Tree Project. After the 1994 genocide 110,000 people were held in prison without trial—until 2003. Many were to be released, but Prison Fellowship Rwanda began implementing restorative practices through the Umuvumu Tree Project. Genocide survivors met to talk about what happened to them, while relatives of genocide offenders talked about how their lives have been impacted. According to Parker, over 43,000 ex-prisoners have gone through that project. Before the Umuvumu program was implemented, only 5,000 had confessed to their crime. After going through the sessions, less than six months later, the number of confessing prisoners increased to 32,000. Upon release, some have started making amends by building homes for genocide survivors.

Ike Griffin, executive director of Kairos Horizons, volunteered with an ecumenical team of Christians doing prison ministry. The team was made up of all denominations, from Baptists to Catholics and everyone in between. Instead of focusing on their differences, say Griffin, they had one shared mission: to present Christ's love to inmates.

"It was about following Christ's command that we love one another, doing something about it rather than just saying it." Griffin explains that training for the program, called Kairos Prison Ministry, involves 40 hours over an eight-week period. During that time, in order to foster a sense of community, trainees share their lives with other team members in a vulnerable and intimate way. From there the group goes into prisons to meet with inmates and build more community. The groups talk about their goals, forgiveness, and the meaning and origin of agape love.

"People say, 'My view of life has changed. I have never known what love is—never accepted it, given it, or understood it. But now I understand who and what God is all about,'" says Griffin.

"Theological discussions are fine, but they don't change your life," Griffin testifies. "So when you come in and accept people where they are, tell others that God loves you and the proof of that is I love you, people recognize they are a child of God."

And that love brings healing and a true sense of justice.

Erika Bai Siebels is a freelance writer from Troy, N.Y. She can be reached at e.siebels.1 @alumni.nyu.edu.

A PORTRAIT OF RESTORATION

David L. Gustafson

On New Year's Eve, 1997, Bob McIntosh—popular lawyer, triathlon champion, loyal friend, father, husband—was entertaining friends with his wife, Katy, at their home in Squamish, British Columbia. As the evening wore on, Bob became concerned about a raucous party being held down the street in the home of a neighbor whom they knew to be away on vacation. When Bob and his two male guests decided to look in on things, they found over 100 youth partying at the house. Bob climbed the stairs to the master bedroom and protested about kids being in it. One punch knocked Bob out. Four kicks to the head, delivered by a second youth, severed an artery and ended Bob's life.

One youth took responsibility early on for having delivered the punch, but the charge of manslaughter was stayed since he had not delivered the fatal kicks. It was almost five years before sufficient evidence was collected to charge Ryan Aldridge with manslaughter.

Katy had made a video, describing what life had been like for her and her twins during the previous five years. When police played it for Ryan Aldridge, he broke down and confessed. That night he wrote a letter to Katy and the twins, taking responsibility for his part in Bob's death: "The secret has been destroying my life as well as yours."

The next morning, the police brought Katy to meet Ryan. Katy told the *National Post*, "I wanted to pick him up and put him in my arms. He was having a hard time finding words. He started to cry. I said it was going to be okay. He'd have a tough road in the immediate future, but if he dealt with it right now he'd have a chance. I asked him what happened. He didn't remember. He said, 'I was drunk, I kicked him.' It was a recount of a blur, the uselessness of the situation."

Ryan wouldn't look at Katy. The interview was over. "The hardest part," says Katy, "was on the way out I could see him on the TV screen. He was by himself, sobbing. I wanted to make it okay for him . . . He seemed genuinely remorseful."

Katy insists that this encounter helped to heal some of the wounds left by her husband's murder. "I accept what happened. I accept [Ryan] made a fatal error. But what does forgiveness mean? I expect him to make a difference in someone else's life."

Soon after that meeting, Katy began speaking to high school students about the dangers of unsupervised parties, taking her powerful presentation to schools. In an hour-long multi-media presentation, Katy introduces them to Bob: his childhood, passion for sports, their courtship and wedding, the birth of their children, and the sudden death that took him from them. She speaks of risky contexts—drugs, alcohol, unsupervised parties—and how "misguided choices" ended Bob's life. She invites the youth to relationships of respect for self and others, to a life characterized by responsibility, courage, autonomy, dignity, wise choices, and joy. High school students are gripped by her message (to learn more go to www.katyhutchisonpresents.com).

"The only missing link, of course, is having Ryan Aldridge doing it with me," Katy says. "I think it would be a really important thing for him, for me, for the kids."

In the spring of 2003, staff members from Community Justice Initiatives (CJI) met with Katy at her request and listened as she shared aspects of her story that we could never otherwise have known—about the struggles and the growth; about her twins, Sam and Emma, now 10, donating proceeds from a garage sale to an anti-bullying program, winning a poster contest with the theme "Stop the Silence; Stop the Violence," young peacemakers who, after seeing Ryan in court at his sentencing, began to ask about him regularly. "They don't fear him," says Katy. "Ryan has become a character in our home. What happened was a horrible, awful thing, and they hope Ryan can get help."

A few weeks later we arranged to meet with Ryan. He was delighted that a program like the CJI's Victim Offender Mediation Program existed. Katy had sent a letter for Ryan with us, saying she had hoped to meet with him again, believing it would lead to greater healing for them both. She affirmed the direction he had begun to take, saying, "If the letter you wrote to [me] is a reflection of some insight and maturity that you have gained since your incarceration, then I believe you are on the right path."

We began to tailor an approach that would meet the needs expressed by Katy, Sam, and Emma, as well as those Ryan had expressed. A short time later, Katy and Ryan met face-to-face in a board room at the prison. Ryan watched as Katy played her presentation, "The Story of Bob," for us on her notebook computer. There were tears and important dialogue about the need to take responsibility, to confess, as well as to acknowledge each other, the past and present pain, and the hope of healing and life yet to be lived.

Soon after that meeting, Ryan decided to do what he could to assist with Katy's presentation. Shy, reticent, and imprisoned though he was, he wrote a letter for Katy to read as part of the presentations she continues to make. In his letter, Ryan shares the foggy recollections of the events of that New Year's Eve, the awareness of his involvement in Bob's death, the fear and spiral into despair that ensued. He writes movingly, too, about the impact on his family and friends, his rediscovery of the importance of his relationships with his parents, and about the life sentence earned by his choices that night. His letter implores other youth to consider the consequences of their choices, to recognize how easily a wrong choice can lead to tragedy.

Katy says, "We often cannot choose what happens to us in life, but we can always choose how we react to what happens to us. In every situation we can step back, take a deep breath, and think about our reaction and how it is going to shape what is to come. Anger is a dead end. Anger fills us up and consumes us. When we are angry we are paralyzed and cannot move forward. Forgiveness sets you free."

David L. Gustafson is co-director of Community Justice Initiatives in Langley, British Columbia (www.cjibc.org).

"WHAT HAPPENS IN THOSE CIRCLES IS A MIRACLE"

Paula Kurland

I was driving back to Houston from Baton Rouge, listening to a Christian station, and they were talking about forgiveness. I couldn't understand how God would expect me to forgive. It had been nearly eating me alive. But they were talking about how you have to be able to forgive to be able to go on. I knew what they were talking about because I was a walking dead person. I'm driving down the interstate and I'm just crying and I said, "Dear God, how can I forgive Jonathan for what he did?" And this voice was audible in the back of the car: "You don't have to forgive what he *did*; you have to forgive *him*." It was just like something had exploded my heart. I had to pull off the road, I was crying so hard. I don't know how long I sat there, but he just released everything right in that car with just that small statement.

My daughter Mitzi was murdered on her birthday, 1986, along with her roommate. September 13th was Mitzi's birthday, and last year I had my meeting with Jonathan, the man who murdered her, on September 22nd. Two weeks after that, he was executed.

I had felt that every time my life was getting back in order, Jonathan would appear on TV trying something. I'd get a notice that his appeals were coming up, or he was trying to get a new trial because he was an abused child. The list goes on and on. My focal point was keeping him on death row. I couldn't bear the thought that someday he might be released.

But I had also been trying to see him since the minute the trial was over because I wanted to talk to him. I really don't know why: I didn't know what I was going to say to him. But I couldn't get in. Then when someone from victim services asked me if I would like to participate in a new victim-offender mediation program, it was like God answered a prayer. That program literally gave me back my life. The mediation was the hardest thing that I've ever had to do—second only to burying my child. It lasted over five hours and was a life-changing event. I was able to say everything that I felt I needed to say. Now there's a hole in my heart that will always be there, but it doesn't consume my heart anymore.

I had wanted to witness the execution but when I made that decision, it was because I wanted to be the last person he saw. I wanted him to see what kind of pain he was leaving. After the mediation, it was a very difficult thing to watch the execution, because the man I spoke with was not the same man I sat in the courtroom with for 13 months. What Jonathan did was wrong, and he got the sentence he deserved, but it was very difficult to witness his death after Jonathan and I had come to terms with each other. He had become a Catholic and he left me a medal—it's called a miraculous medal. I carry it with me everywhere with my rosary beads.

I walked out of the mediation on death row a different person. Before, I couldn't get involved in any kind of victims' movements—how could I tell somebody else how to heal when I couldn't heal? After the mediation, I said I wanted to become active in victims' things. I didn't care about offenders and I didn't want to talk to somebody else's offender. But people at victim services said, "Just give the [Bridges to Life] victim-offender project a try. Come and meet with victims who have participated in this project in prison." So I went to orientation and heard victims talk about all the things that were happening between them and the offenders in the program. I was absolutely appalled at their wanting relationships with offenders. They're talking about loving those people. I thought they were sick. They started talking about hugging these guys goodbye. I said, "I'll give it a try, but I'm telling you right now, I don't want those people touching me. Don't let them come near me." Well, I went out there and needless to say, I bonded with two of them instantly—one black, one white. They're both out now and I'm following up with them.

I did three of these projects in prison last year, and each lasted for 12 to 14 weeks. And I stay in contact with most of those offenders. Isn't that amazing? I'm telling you, what happens in those circles is a miracle. It is making a change in those offenders. It's healing for me. Every time I come out of there, I've grown by leaps and bounds.

I was at the very pit of the abyss when I got the news that my daughter had been murdered. That is the lowest that anybody could ever go. Now I'm as high as the heavens, and it's only because God has put me there. Now the sky is the limit. I'm still growing. My heart just expands every day.

(Adapted from Transcending *by Howard Zehr [Good Books, 2001]. Reproduced by kind permission of the publisher.)*

"THERE HAD TO BE ROOM FOR UNCONDITIONAL LOVE"

Thomas Ann Hines

In 1985, three months to the day from his college graduation, my son Paul went out to play video games. A young man walked up to him and said, "My mother is dying on the other side of town. Would you give me a ride?" Paul gave him a ride and he shot Paul and left him to bleed to death in the car by himself.

I was angry—I was angry about Paul's murder, I was angry at the lack of justice. I said, "Give him the death penalty." Of course, I ended up shaking hands with Charles, but that was 13 years later.

The way I got here from the hate was that I started asking questions. "Tell me about this guy that killed Paul." I began to get curious about his life. I knew there had to be some factors that influenced who he had become.

The thing that hit like a bolt of lightning was when I was invited by victim services to speak in a prison on a victim impact panel. I was listening to the speakers, watching those guys. I was the last speaker and when I got up to speak, right there was a young, red-headed guy—my Paul frozen in time. He looked at me with what I call hungry eyes: helpless, lonely, filled with pain. I looked at him and thought, "What if that was Paul?" Rather than give my prepared speech about what scum they were and about how I hoped Charles would rot in hell, I looked at that young man and felt like a mother again. I began to talk to them like they were my boys. When I finished speaking, it was almost like a revival meeting. In the front row, one man, 6 foot tall, stood up, tears streaming down his face, and said, "You look just like my mother." What he meant was my compassion and caring. It was a complete turnaround for me. I said, "When can I come back?" That was in 1994, and I'm still going to prisons. The more I go in, the more I want to go in.

I didn't immediately forgive Charles. In fact, I was against starting the victim-offender dialogue program. But the more I went in prisons, the more letters I got from prisoners talking about their childhood, the more curious I got about Charles. As I read those letters, I said, "Yeah, the same thing happened to me." I had an uncle who molested me and a father who told me my uncle wouldn't do that because he was a Christian. All my life, I've had a whole lot of pain, and hurting people often hurt other people or themselves.

At one of the prisons I was leaving and a guy thanked me for coming. I said, "You are such a nice guy. Why are you here?" He started crying and said, "You know. Every time you talked about Paul, you looked at me. When I was 17, I killed a guy to steal his car. I was so desperate to get out of town, just like the guy who murdered your son." I said, "I need to talk to Charles."

[The religious beliefs that I had grown up with] were holding me into this little box of an eye for an eye. I had to get away from all that rigidity. There had to be room for unconditional love. Charles can never give me back my son. Nothing he can do can fix it. At the end of my meeting with Charles, I had the option of putting my hand across that table, knowing he couldn't ever give me anything back.

Shaking hands with Charles, putting my hand out, would be to accept the hand that held the gun that murdered my son. When I took his hand, I was just going to shake it. But I was overwhelmed. I just collapsed on the table with this cry of anguish that took me 13 years to release.

And he let me see inside his soul. Every time I get a letter from him, every time I write to him, I cry. I'm so connected to him. I'm going to go see him again later this month.

It does not make one bit of sense that Paul Hines was murdered by a guy he tried to help. But when I go into that prison, if just one person listens to the message I have to give, then that will be just a little more healing that occurs. It is energizing for me to know I'm in the place that I'm supposed to be. It's not tiresome, and that tells you you're doing the right thing.

(Adapted from Transcending *by Howard Zehr [Good Books, 2001]. Reproduced by kind permission of the publisher.)*

"FATHER, FORGIVE THEM, FOR THEY KNOW NOT WHAT THEY DO"

Kathleen A. O'Shea

Not long ago I spent an afternoon with a friend of mine who was so terribly troubled and grieved that I found myself questioning everything I'd ever learned about forgiveness. This woman, a Christian who really believes the Word of God is meant to be lived, said she felt she was losing her faith because she could not forgive. She was talking about a very specific situation where her eldest daughter, Amy, was raped and almost murdered on her high school graduation night by a total stranger. It happened in a classroom, in the supposedly safe confines of the school building where she was donning her graduation gown and reviewing her valedictorian acceptance speech. The assailant was a man with no personal motivation, no vendetta, a man on drugs who during his trial and confession admitted he did not know why he attacked her. Amy survived the trauma and was able to identify her assailant, who admitted his guilt and was eventually put in prison. While incarcerated, this same man became a Christian, at which point he stopped just doing time and began repenting. In his repentance, and while still incarcerated, he joined a community of Catholic monks which accepts inmates into their order. He now lives in a monastery in Minnesota.

Five years after the attack, Amy, who never recovered emotionally, took her own life. "He killed her that night," her mother said bitterly. "And now he's a monk, free, holy, leading a blessed life? I cannot reconcile this, I cannot forgive this. What more does God want?"

I heard her anger, felt her pain, and offered the words of Christ on the cross: "Father, forgive them, for they know not what they do." She looked at me as if I had just dropped a bomb. "Yes," she said. "God will have to forgive him, because I can't." At home later that night, my mind kept going back to my friend, her pain, and our conversation. What could I have said? What *should* I have said? Finally, without an answer, I went to bed and slept. About 4:00 a.m. I woke up suddenly, saying, "I understand."

What I understood then and what I believe now is that when Christ asked his Father to forgive his assailants, he was speaking out of his humanity, to show us that there are times and situations in which we may not be capable of forgiving and that he understands that.

If Christ had been speaking from his divinity, he would have looked out from the cross and said, "*I* forgive you, for you know not what you do." But Christ's pain was human. He was suffering in his physical body as much as any of us would have suffered with nails in our hands and feet, our flesh tortured beyond recognition. And he was suffering from unimaginable mental anguish as well. Without having ever committed a crime, and certainly without a fair trial, Christ was undergoing a slow and excruciating execution.

At that moment, he needed his Father to do the forgiving for him. This picture of Christ asking God to step in for him led me to consider how we, too, might step in and do the forgiving for people who, for one reason or another, cannot find it in themselves to forgive at the present time, people who have suffered abuse at the hands of those whose job it is to protect them, people who have been maimed by hatred, war, or crime. Most of us feel at a loss as to how to accompany people whose lives have been shattered in these unspeakable ways. Quite often, if they are Christians, their pain is intensified when they cannot find it in their hearts to forgive; they feel they should, but they find they cannot. In instances like these, could we not then be their spiritual companions, stepping in as "delegated forgivers" to lift the burden from their shoulders?

As human beings we may face traumas that alter our lives in ways we could never imagine beforehand. These situations may bring long periods of grief, anger, bitterness, and even a desire for vengeance. If we are to survive these dark and lonesome journeys until we come again into the circle of light, then we might need someone else to do the forgiving for us, at least temporarily, until we are ready to do it ourselves. This is yet another poignant but necessary role we can fill for one another. This is love. This is Christian community.

Kathleen O'Shea is a social worker, writer, and activist. Her most recent book is Women on the Row: Revelations from Both Sides of the Bars *(Firebrand Books, 2000). She is currently working on an anthology of stories of nuns who have befriended death row inmates.*

ORGANIZATIONS

Restorative Justice Ministry Network
www.rjmn.net

International Institute for Restorative Practices
www.iirp.org.www.restorativepractices.org

Prison Fellowship International, International Centre for Justice and Reconciliation
www.pficjr.org.www.restorativejustice.org

Kairos Prison Ministry
www.kairosprisonministry.org

Mennonite Central Committee U.S. Office on Crime and Justice
www.mcc.org/us/peaceandjustice/crime.html

BOOKS

The Spiritual Roots of Restorative Justice
by Michael L. Hadley (State University of New York Press, 2001)

Beyond Retribution: A New Testament Vision for Justice, Crime, and Punishment
by Christopher D. Marshall (Wm. B. Eerdmans, 2001)

Restorative Justice: Healing the Foundations of Our Everyday Lives
by Dennis Sullivan and Larry Tifft (Library Research Associates Inc, 2001)

Justice That Restores
by Charles Colson (Tyndale, 2001)

Forgiving and Reconciling
by Everett L. Worthington, Jr.
(InterVarsity Press, 2003)

The Little Book of Restorative Justice
by Howard Zehr (Herald Press, 1990)

20. SLAVERY, THE CONSTITUTION, AND THE FOUNDING FATHERS: THE AFRICAN AMERICAN VISION

Mary Frances Berry

Neither the U.S. Constitution nor American slavery can be fully understood without examining the proslavery compromises worked out at the Constitutional Convention in 1787. Slavery was expressly sanctioned in three places in Article I, Section 3. Under the three-fifths clause, three-fifths of a state's slaves—euphemistically referred to as "other persons"—were to be counted for purposes of representation in Congress. Another provision required that any direct tax levied in the states be imposed according to population, but only three-fifths of the slaves were to be counted in determining each state's tax levy. Counting slaves helped the South, but taxing slaves partly nullified this benefit. In Article I, Section 8, § 4, any capitation (head tax) or other direct tax had to be consistent with the provision of the three-fifths clause. This meant that slaveholders could pay less. Article I, Section 9, § 1 stipulated that the slave trade was not to end before 1808. States that needed more slaves wanted to continue importing them, whereas the older slave states would have preferred terminating importation immediately. In addition, the Constitution sanctioned slavery through the fugitive slave clause in Article IV, Section 2, and the Article V provision prohibiting any amendment of the paragraph on slave importation before 1808. The cumulative effect of these provisions was the direct ratification of slavery.

Other parts of the original Constitution were also helpful to the institution of slavery. Particularly important were the provisions in Article I that prohibited taxes on exports, because slaveholders depended on the agricultural exports produced by slaves. Furthermore, the electoral college provision on its face gave whites in slave states a disproportionate influence in the election of the president. The three-fifths ratio, which enabled slave states to count nonvoting slaves, increased a slave state's representation and thereby its influence in the electoral college, since the electors were chosen on the basis of congressional representation. The exact purpose of the electoral college is somewhat murky. Some evidence suggests that it was designed to democratize elections by having Congress choose the president. The significant point to recognize in this discussion is its impact on the power of slaveholders.

Another constitutional provision useful to the slave states was that requiring agreement of three-quarters of the states to ratify a constitutional amendment.

Slave states could refuse to ratify any constitutional amendment that curtailed or adversely affected the institution of slavery. The U.S. Supreme Court interpreted Article III's accord of diversity jurisdiction to "citizens" of different states as a prohibition on a slave's right to sue in federal court. If the language had said "inhabitants" of different states—assuming that slaves would be inhabitants and not property—there might have been a stronger basis for jurisdiction. But this assumption may be inappropriate on the basis of the evidence.

After Madison's notes became available in 1836, some abolitionists, led by Wendell Phillips, argued that the Constitution was essentially a proslavery document and pointed out still other proslavery provisions.[1] The military clauses in Article IV, Section 4, Phillips said, called on the federal government to protect the states from domestic violence, including slave rebellions; and Article I, Section 8, required the Congress to call forth the militia to suppress insurrections, including slave rebellions.

When I first read Phillips in law school, I was persuaded by his arguments that we had missed a most important proslavery compromise. I researched the debates in the 1787 convention and ratifying conventions and in 1971 published the results in a book focusing on the federal government's role in suppressing black rebellions, *Black Resistance/White Law: A History of Constitutional Racism in America*.[2] (Perhaps the title of the book was too harsh. A senior scholar in the field of constitutional history insisted I had erred, and that everyone already knew there were only three proslavery compromises.)[3] I am still persuaded that Phillips and the other abolitionists who shared these more expansive views were correct. Beyond the three traditionally cited compromises, these other features are correctly considered the framers' handiwork on the subject of slavery.

These slavery provisions have profoundly affected the predominant African American vision of the Constitution over the past two hundred years, African Americans' status, and aspirations. We know a great deal about the thoughts of free Negroes in the period before the Civil War from newspapers, letters, pamphlets, lectures, and speeches. In the first federal census of 1790, taken three years after the Constitution was approved in Philadelphia, most blacks were slaves, but about 59,000 free Negroes were counted, 27,000 in the North and 32,000 in the South. Their numbers grew rapidly between 1790 and 1810, but subsequently the rate of increase dropped sharply because of restraints on manumission and other hardships. By the time the Constitution was written, blacks in the United States were aware that the unequal political, social, and economic opportunities of their group were a consequence of whites' identification of African ancestry with inferiority and subordination. Arguing for greater opportunities for persons of African descent and for the abolition of slavery, numbers of blacks noted that in ratifying slavery the Constitution had betrayed the promises of the Declaration of Independence, which had stated that everyone had a right to life, liberty, and the pursuit of happiness. At the same time, many denounced the hypocrisy of the Declaration for not including blacks as beneficiaries of its promises.

In the years immediately after the Convention, African Americans did not have access to Madison's notes and other materials that have come to light since then, but they were contemporaries of the Constitution makers. In the absence of records of the debates at the Convention, they could, when it suited their purposes, use the very vagueness of some of the Constitution's wording to support arguments that the Constitution stood for freedom and rights. As petitioners, they noted the potential for antislavery action in the Fifth Amendment of the Bill of Rights and the clauses in the original document pertaining to interstate commerce, general welfare, and the guarantee of a republican form of government. They could—and did—assert that Congress could, therefore, manumit contraband slaves, prohibit the coastal and interstate slave trade, ban slavery from the territories and other property of the United States, enlist slaves in the armed forces, and even take private property for public use by purchasing and emancipating slaves. Although there was no doubt that the Constitution had ratified slavery in the states, it was certainly still open to debate whether some antislavery objectives could be achieved under its provisions.

Most African Americans avoided choosing emigration or attacking the Constitution, preferring instead to advance the antislavery cause by swaddling themselves in arguments emphasizing the Constitution's potential.[4] In short, these African Americans, like some literalists and original-intent adherents today, chose to base their arguments only on the words in the document, insisting that their interpretation of original intent was the only one possible. They asserted that the Constitution could be interpreted in such a way as to support abolition, or at least the containment of slavery.

In those early years of the nation, there was an overriding impression of consensus among African Americans: no matter how one interpreted the language of the Constitution, the slaveholders held the reins of power. To unseat this class would require political action and moral suasion, or, as many others eventually came to agree, it could only be accomplished through the violence of a civil war.[5] African Americans looked to other provisions of the Constitution as they considered their predicament and the means for improvement. They and their white allies were very fond of the First Amendment because it led them to hope that their right to petition the Congress and to assemble in protest would be protected. They were decidedly unimpressed with the Tenth Amendment and the federalism it promoted because states' rights then, as today, permitted discrimination and subordination in the states without interference by the national government. They found, unfortunately, that their protests were not protected automatically from state suppression because in those days the First Amendment applied to federal and not to state action.

Frederick Douglass, a former slave and ardent abolitionist, perhaps best summed up the antebellum view of the Constitution. In 1849 he pointed out that the Constitution's words could be taken to express antislavery sentiment, but that the meaning of the Constitution given to it by the framers and those with the power to interpret it made it a proslavery document. He explained:

> Had the Constitution dropped down from the blue overhanging sky, upon a land uncursed by slavery, and without an interpreter, although some difficulty

might have occurred in applying its manifold provisions, yet so cunningly is it framed, that no one would have imagined that it recognized or sanctioned slavery But having a terrestrial, and not a celestial origin, we find no difficulty in ascertaining its meaning in all the parts which we allege to relate to slav-ery. . . . [The Constitution] was made in view of the existence of slavery, and in a manner well calculated to aid and strengthen that heaven-daring crime.[6]

When, as a result of the bloodshed and violence of the Civil War and Recon-struction, the Constitution was amended to include the Thirteenth, Fourteenth, and Fifteenth Amendments, the legacy of slavery remained prominent in the African American vision of the new reality. This vision was apparent at the cen-tennial of the Constitution's writing, observed in 1887. Among the approxi-mately seven million African Americans in the country at that time, most of whom lived in the South, the badges of slavery persisted. Frederick Douglass pointed out how much they relied on the Constitution when the promise of free-dom seemed abandoned forever:

I now undertake to say that neither the original Constitution nor the Consti-tution as amended since the War is the law of the land. That Constitution has been slain in the house of its friends. So far as the colored people of the coun-try are concerned, the Constitution is but a stupendous sham . . . keeping the promise to the eye and breaking it to the heart. . . . They have promised us law and abandoned us to anarchy.[7]

Yet there was more to celebrate in 1887 than there had been in 1787. Slavery was depicted in the centennial exposition floats in Philadelphia, and despite offers of payment, organizers could not find blacks to play the role of plantation slaves. Incongruously, some of the banners in the African American part of the exposition proclaimed enfranchisement and full political rights.[8] Even so, the trend in the South, where most blacks lived, was already well on the way toward almost total disfranchisement.

Slavery was also visible in the African American vision of the Constitution as interpreted by the Supreme Court of the United States. The Court's influence permeated the *Slaughterhouse Cases* that acknowledged the one pervading purpose of the Fourteenth Amendment.[9] The *Civil Rights Cases* further weakened the ability of the Fourteenth Amendment to remove badges and incidents of slav-ery.[10] Tragically, *Plessy v. Ferguson* reduced the badges of slavery to a figment of the black imagination.[11]

Slavery was fundamental in the rationale of white Southerners for the polit-ical disfranchisement, economic oppression, and punishment of African Ameri-cans. White Southerners argued that African Americans were still not far enough removed from the slave condition to be positive participants in the political process. In the Southern states, where the majority of the black population lived, the recent history of slavery loomed large in the decisions handed down during military reconstruction. Some, for example, prohibited whites from reenslaving black children as "apprentices," and others protected blacks from disproportionately harsh punishment in the criminal justice system. Slavery as context, as definition for all that occurred to African Americans, was prevalent even in the highest state courts.

Throughout the late nineteenth century, when racial fairness appeared impossible, slavery remained an ever-present force both in legal and social affairs. The North Carolina Court, just in time to set the right tone for the centennial celebrations, struck down the statute earmarking taxes paid by Negroes only for the Negro schools and by whites only for the white schools, explaining that because of slavery, "the vast bulk of property yielding the fruits of taxation belongs to the white people of the state and very little is held by the emancipated race." The court hastened to say, however, that it was not questioning the constitutionality of separate schools, or laws forbidding the intermarriage of the races; these were made more necessary by the abolition of slavery.[12]

The centennial period notwithstanding, state courts at the highest levels, the most visible representatives of a justice system in the South, continued to hand down decisions acknowledging the ideals of slavery. The Alabama high court, in refusing to convict, as demanded by "her mistress, a colored girl, 17 or 18 years of age," for burning down the house in which she lived and worked, noted that her confession could be attributed to the fact that "her mistress" routinely disciplined her by whipping. The court did not find whipping, which was a routine punishment administered to slaves, unusual in 1887 but thought since there was no other evidence that the girl set the fire at the house, being locked up and whipped might have meant the confession was false.[13]

Cases declaring the illegitimacy of intimate relations between whites and blacks were common, indicating there were many such relationships and an eagerness to end them. White men were often involved. A case in Yazoo County, Mississippi, decided in the centennial year, involved a white man and "a colored woman" who had been jointly convicted. They had been seen together in bed; he was frequently at her house. She had two mulatto children and he "had been heard to call them his children." The court upheld the conviction. Before slavery became illegal, she could have been his concubine, as was not unusual. After the Thirteenth Amendment was passed, it became important, as the prosecutor told the jury, to maintain appropriate social relations by punishing miscegenation "as a stigma on both races."[14] As in so many things, the North had already shown the importance of strictures concerning interracial sex in a state of so-called freedom, by its laws and policies concerning relationships between blacks and whites.

The courts spoke most directly about slavery in the numerous cases from 1870 to 1900 involving legacies and bequests to freedmen. In a case decided by the Virginia high court in 1887, the descendants of slaves filed a lawsuit after failing repeatedly in their attempts to collect a promised legacy. A plantation owner in Danville had left his fifteen slaves to his heirs in an 1862 will with the understanding that they would be set free seven years after his death and taken to a free state. They were also to be given one half of what they would be worth to his estate and $3,000. He instructed his heirs to pay the money out of a surplus he had in his estate in 1865. He added this provision to this will, and shortly there-after he died. A few months later, the slaves were freed by the war's results, and they asked for their legacy. The high court decided that the end of the war did not automatically invalidate the former slaves' right to the legacy. As it turned out, however, the heirs did not have to pay them because the legacy, unlike the rest of the estate that the heirs could keep, was to be taken out of the surplus, which was in worthless Confederate money.[15]

Race and the badges of slavery entered into every type of legal matter during the centennial era and thereafter. A court describing the routine issuance of a summons emphasized that it was given to "a white person over the age of six-teen years."[16] All during the proceedings of a tort case in which the value of the life of a black man who was killed accidentally as a result of turning on the light switches for the company where he worked, the court described everyone in racial terms, as did the lawyers and the witnesses: X "a white man" was a wit-ness for the "colored widow," X "(white)" testified that the deceased whose wife was his house servant "was . . . of average intelligence for a colored man."[17] But at least blacks could bring lawsuits and appear as parties—and could sometimes win—which would have been impossible under pre-Civil War restrictions.[18]

The African American vision of the Founding Fathers, of the meaning of slavery, and of the Constitution in 1787 and 1887 was shaped by political, eco-nomic, and legal conditions. That vision was consistently suffused with both hope and suspicion of a kind that persists to this day. The Founding Fathers cre-ated a framework of government that has served many purposes. In protecting slavery and assuming racial inequality, they made African Americans outsiders from the beginning. They also provided a rationale that could be used by non-African Americans to assume the basic worthlessness, powerlessness, and inhu-manity of African Americans as a part of the nation's legacy. Even though by the time of the centennial there had been a great deal of violence and their work had been modified and improved upon, the pall of slavery's influence remained. The pall was still present at the Constitution's bicentennial, although it had dimin-ished somewhat.

An unstated premise of many discussions about intelligence and qualifica-tions is that blackness is associated with inferiority and subordination. In recent years, discussions about African Americans and legal rights under the Constitu-tion have often turned on how far away blacks are from slavery. Many a conver-sation with a white American has begun, "My granddaddy did not have any slaves, and anyway slavery was a long time ago and why do we still need to rem-edy vestiges and discuss redress." But many have also revolved around the eco-nomic disparities that continue to plague black communities. In some of these conversations, speakers emphasize the reality of legally enforced slavery, which means blacks should not expect to close the gap and become equal, except for a few extraordinary individuals who ought to be thankful instead of complaining.

The African American vision of the Constitution as it was written in 1787 can be characterized as an affirmation of exploitation and exclusion. By 1887 the Con-stitution had come to represent inclusion in language but exclusion in reality.

Today African Americans see in it a continuing struggle for inclusion. Our lives begin and end taking into account that vision of us crafted by the Founding Fathers in the Constitution. The role we have today they might not have envisioned, but certainly our African American ancestors did.

Because there was slavery, the free Negroes bore the burden of having blackness identified with subordination. Because there was slavery, the Thirteenth, Fourteenth, and Fifteenth Amendments came into being, and because some of the slaves were women, the Nineteenth Amendment was not made fully effective for women of minority groups until the Voting Rights Act of 1965. Because there was slavery, there was Jim Crow and segregation and a race-imbued justice system. Because there was slavery, there were civil rights movements; there was litigation for rights and jail for those who fought for those rights. There were lost jobs and death in the name of improving our lives and the constitutional imperatives under which we live. Because there was slavery, there is debate over remedies and correctives such as affirmative action, school busing, self-help, and black community organization designed to overcome the lingering effects of slavery. Because there was slavery, the most important features of the Constitution are the amending clause in Article V and the power of interpretation by the Supreme Court under Article III. Because there was slavery, the appointment power for Supreme Court justices under Article II, providing for a sharing of power between the president and the Senate has to be kept constantly on our minds.

We need to remember that, interpreting the same Constitution, one group of judges said forced segregation was wrong in 1954 but another said it was perfectly legal in 1896. We must worry about who is appointed to the courts and what they will say in the future. Because there was slavery, we read and hear every day that the United States is not ready for a black man to become president, not just Jesse Jackson. Because there was slavery, we have race and slavery on our minds, and we are likely to keep it on our minds until it is obviously on no one else's minds in ways that constrict the freedom and opportunities of African Americans. Therefore, when we think about everything important to our well-being, including the Constitution and the Founding Fathers, our vision, our African American vision, remains preoccupied and on guard. But perhaps it is not simply because there was slavery, but because the vision of others was shaped by slavery, and because most African Americans still experience unpleasant reminders that we are the descendants of those who were enslaved.

NOTES

1. "The Constitution—a Pro-slavery Compact," in *Selections from the Madison Papers,* ed. Wendell Phillips, 2d ed. rev. (New York: Anti-slavery Society, 1845), 5–9.
2. Mary Frances Berry, *Black Resistance/White Law: A History of Constitutional Racism in America* (Englewood Cliffs, N.J.: Prentice-Hall, 1971).
3. Staughton Lynd advances a similar interpretation in *Slavery, Class Conflict, and the Constitution* (Indianapolis: Bobbs-Merrill, 1967). Lynd also suggests that the

Northwest Ordinance, outlawing slavery in the Northwest territory, passed while the convention was in session, was part of the pattern of compromises concerning slavery. See also Staughton Lynd, "The Compromise of 1787," *Political Science Quarterly* 81 (1966): 225–50.

4. David Brion Davis, *The Problem of Slavery in the Age of Revolution* (Ithaca: Cornell University Press, 1975), 130. See also John Hope Franklin and Alfred A, Moss, Jr., *From Slavery to Freedom: History of Negro Americans,* 6th ed. rev. (New York: Alfred Knopf, 1987), 76–77.

5. Mary Frances Berry and John W. Blassingame, *Long Memory: The Black Experience in America* (New York: Oxford University Press, 1982), 60–66.

6. Frederick Douglass, "The Constitution and Slavery" *(North Star,* March 16, 1849) in *The Life and Writings* of *Frederick Douglass,* ed, Philip S. Foner, 4 vols. (New York: International Publishers, 1950–), vol. 1, 1817–1849 (1950), 363.

7. Frederick Douglass, "Speech on the Occasion of the Twenty-Fourth Anniversary of Emancipation in the District of Columbia, Washington, D. C., 1886," in *The Life and Writings* of *Frederick Douglass,* ed. Philip S. Foner, 4 vols. (New York: International Publishers, 1950–), vol. 4, *Reconstruction and After* (1955), 431.

8. Leon Litwack, "Trouble in Mind: The Bicentennial and the Afro-American Experience," *Journal of American History,* 74 (September 1987): 315–37, and notes cited on p. 315. See also Leon Litwack, *Been in the Storm So Long: The Aftermath* of *Slavery* (New York: Alfred Knopf, 1979), chap. 5.

9. 16 Wallace 36 (1873).

10. 109 U.S. 3 (1883).

11. 163 U.S. 437 (1896).

12. *Puitt v. Gaston County,* 94 North Carolina 709 (1886).

13. *Hoober v. State,* 81 Ala. 51 (1887).

14. *Steward v. State,* 64 Miss. 626 (1887).

15. *Allen et al. v. Patton Als.,* 83 Va. 255 (1887).

16. *Stolz v. Collins,* 83 Va. 824 (1887).

17. *Piedmont Electric Illinois Co. v. Patteson's Adm.,* 84 Va. 18 (1887).

18. This material on state courts is drawn from my ongoing research on how white women and black males as well as females fared in cases in the state courts in the South from Reconstruction to 1900.

21. WEEP NOT, LITTLE ONES: AN ESSAY TO OUR CHILDREN ABOUT AFFIRMATIVE ACTION

W. H. Knight and Adrien Wing

Do not be conformed to this world, but be transformed by the renewing of your minds.

Romans 12:2

Many of the authors in this volume have forcefully argued for a broad interpretation of the Constitution as a means of giving that document fuller meaning, particularly for those who find themselves at the lowest rungs of America's social and economic ladder. Although many different racial and ethnic groups are at this low end of our society, no group has waited as long as African Americans to gain admission and to be treated as recognized equals. People of African descent were on these shores for more than 150 years before this nation's founding, only since the Supreme Court's 1954 decision in *Brown v. Board of Education* have we as African Americans been a part of the constitutional discourse on how ideals such as equal protection, due process, and freedom of expression could become more inclusive. As we approach the twenty-first century, the problem of the color line remains *the* problem for America.[1]

In this essay we attempt to describe how race continues to permeate America's societal fabric and how negative connotations of color blur our collective vision of the purpose of affirmative action. We dedicate the chapter to all children, but especially to our own children, respectively, as they come of age.[3] We are sure that they will face pain and despair because of their race, and, that at times race will affect both their opportunities and their achievements. However, we hope that through these words they will better understand this nation's schizophrenia over race as it affects affirmative action. We also hope that they will be capable of leading lives that will help this society perceive race, ethnicity, and difference as positive rather than negative attributes.

While color-blindness, theoretically, might well lead this nation closer to the constitutional goal of equality, the facts remain that color-consciousness and race-based action continue to persist at the forefront of the American psyche. To illustrate the magnitude of this point, let us recount a brief experience that we are sure all African American parents have had.

In considering what we might say in this essay, we both observed that shortly after our children turned three years old, each of them began to ask questions about skin color. It seemed that race had become an issue at day care even among children at that tender age. "Why are you different?" "Can you rub that brown off?" "Black people aren't as smart as white people." At the precious age of three, our children were forced to ask questions about, and to deal with, negative comments concerning their race. By the time one child reached the age of four, he asked, "Why do black people have to have it so hard?" The so-called innocence of childhood had vanished.

As parents, our initial desire is to shield our children from the potential harm that words can and do cause (even if that harm was unintended). Each of us sought to reassure them by saying, "Sometimes kids say things they don't mean." But we could not help thinking, "Why or how is it that children become so aware of the power of race so early in life?"

While many parents are successful in teaching their children to protect themselves from many of life's physical dangers, how do parents of African American children protect them from the dangers caused by racism? We use the term "protect" because racially charged language and race-based perceptions and actions in fact harm our children in ways that demand that we shield them. We believe that it is vital to teach our children about the history and use of race not only to protect them, but also to enlarge our understanding of race in this society. Perhaps if they are equipped with a historical understanding of affirmative action and the impact of race in this society, our children will be able to treasure their own and racial differences, as well as those of others. Perhaps they will be able to see beyond the limitations that racialism now places on America.

WHAT IS AFFIRMATIVE ACTION?

Simply put, affirmative action is the name given to an array of policies designed to create greater equality of opportunity in American society. Many people think of the term in two principal arenas, employment and education. One author has described the concept as "actions appropriate to overcome the effects of past or present policies or other barriers to equal employment [and educational] opportunity."[2] The long-range goal of affirmative action programs is twofold: first, to address the effects of past discrimination by affording greater opportunities to those who have been discriminated against; and second, to create a community that values racial, ethnic, and gender diversity to a point that discrimination based on these characteristics ceases to occur.[3] These policy goals are reflected in both governmental and private initiatives that encourage parties to consider race, ethnicity, and gender as *positive* factors both in admissions decisions in higher education and in employment hiring and promotion. The addition of race or ethnicity to the decision-making calculus does not suggest that other factors are excluded; instead, the equation recognizes race as an element that should also receive weight.

Affirmative action differs from equal employment opportunity, which requires employers to treat everyone equally in employment activities; employers are not to discriminate on the basis of race, creed, color, national origin, gender or disability. Put another way, employers are not to let personal characteristics become *negative* factors in the employment decision. Affirmative action, on the other hand, requires people to go beyond mere efforts not to discriminate. The concept dictates that employers use good faith efforts to provide opportunities for African Americans and other protected class groups who either have been denied such chances historically, or who have been competitively disadvantaged by the lack of such fortune.

A number of people have the misconception that affirmative action is a recent policy designed to help "unqualified" people of color (and Caucasian women) get positions that they don't deserve at the expense of the "qualified" (Caucasian males). Critics argue that affirmative action programs lower the standards and reputations of those institutions that make such efforts.[4] These arguments are wrongly based on a vision of affirmative action as a means by which Caucasians will be discriminated against. However, common sense, court decisions, and the Equal Employment Opportunity Coordinating Council's policy statement on affirmative action all provide evidence that affirmative action does not require employers to dispense positions to unqualified job applicants.[5] Race or gender is taken into consideration only when an applicant, who happens to be a woman or a person of color, already meets the basic, stated qualifications for a job position. Employers therefore, may continue to have specific needs that are tailored to fit certain job requirements.[6] Thus, the concept of affirmative action does not lower standards, since such programs only require employers to look at race or gender as additional qualifying criteria.

Despite attempts to emphasize the need for qualifications first in affirmative action decisions, for many the perception remains that qualifications are somehow ignored when race is also used as a factor to favor a person of color. We find this perception odd given this nation's historical use of racial preference. Some Americans seemingly want to ignore the history of preferences that have been given Caucasian males in this country. Decisions often have been made to provide opportunities on the basis of some preferred set of characteristics. Education, alma mater, family history, wealth, political affiliation—all have served as criteria for selecting one person or group over others.[7] Race, however, has been foremost among the characteristics used to grant or to *deny* opportunity. The most vivid example, of course, is slavery. The history of human bondage in the United States can be distinguished from that in virtually every other society by the fact that here, race was the principal determining factor. Commenting on this fact, Professor J. Clay Smith has noted:

Our nation's founding persons proclaimed that "all men are created equal" but they also gave us a Constitution which accorded to black slaves the fractional status of three-fifths of a free person, and provided a fugitive slave clause to preserve the white master's control over his slaves. Until the arrival of the third decennium in this century, women citizens of this Republic were denied the basic political right, the right to vote. Until the middle of this century, the Equal Protection Amendment to the Constitution, enacted at the close of a civil war, meant only that blacks were entitled to separate but manifestly unequal treatment.

We cannot lay claim to a tradition of color and sex blind administration of our laws. In view of this, it does not behoove us to suddenly make the Constitution color and sex blind.[8]

Being Caucasian has been and often remains a prime basis for granting an opportunity; being of African, Latino, Indian, or Asian ancestry has been and often remains a basis for denying that same opening. Discriminatory attitudes toward non-Caucasians denied such people the very chance to compete on the basis of their actual abilities and led to preferential actions based on race that benefited Caucasians. Throughout this long period of Caucasian preference, questions about qualification were rarely raised.

Today, affirmative action represents an attempt to address this historical fact of unequal access to opportunity by opening competitive fields through the expansion of opportunities for protected classes of people. "In order to get beyond racism, we must first take account of race. . . . And in order to treat some persons equally, we must treat them differently. We cannot—we dare not—let the Equal Protection Clause perpetuate racial supremacy."[9]

The myths surrounding affirmative action clearly need debunking. Many Americans do not appreciate the value of affirmative action because they are afraid of the word "preference." People are exasperated by the word because they believe it conflicts with the concept of qualification. As Patricia Williams has noted, "Qualifications are nothing more than structured preferences"—beliefs we have come to hold about how society should go about classifying or categorizing someone.[10] Moreover,

> Categorizing is not the sin; the problem is the lack of desire to examine the categorizations that are made. The problem is not recognizing the ethical worth in attempting to categorize with not only the individual *but also social goals* in mind as well. The problem is in the failure to assume responsibility for examining how or where we set our boundaries.[11]

Affirmative action *starts* with both a societal goal of equal opportunity and a pool of capable people. The theory then asks on what basis, if any, should we prefer one able person over another? In a world of limited opportunities, people must make difficult decisions about what factors to emphasize in choosing someone to hire or to admit to an educational program. Usually, there are more people with the basic capabilities to do a particular job than there are available positions. The task for both employers and educational institutions is to select from among these individuals. Affirmative action is the one way to ensure that those who have been historically discriminated against and traditionally excluded can now be included in educational and employment opportunity. Equal competition among all people cannot exist until we include all groups of people.

THE DEVELOPMENT OF AFFIRMATIVE ACTION

Civil rights for the African American had already begun to emerge during the early years of the Roosevelt administration. The number of African American federal employees tripled during the 1930s. Roosevelt also began the desegregation of federal rest rooms, cafeterias, and secretarial pools. In addition, the U.S. labor movement began to reach out toward the African American community by emphasizing the damage done to individuals and the nation by bigotry and prejudice.[12]

The advent of World War II "stimulated blacks to demand a better deal" from American society; African Americans rushed to fill the employment void caused by the war.[13] Union membership also steadily increased during the period. The concept of affirmative action developed in response to this change in the work force. In 1941, President Franklin Roosevelt's Executive Order 8802 established the Fair Employment Practices Committee (FEPC) in the Office of Production and Management. The executive order was a direct result of pressure levied on the administration by A. Philip Randolph, president of the Brotherhood of Sleeping Car Porters. Randolph had threatened a historic march on Washington unless the executive branch stopped employment discrimination by military contractors. The establishment of FEPC was based upon two presidential precepts: (1) the power of the commander-in-chief to guarantee military supplies, and (2) the president's power, as administrative head, to establish conditions under which the government is to be run. Roosevelt's order marked the first presidential directive concerning race since Reconstruction. A vocal minority's threat to march was effective.

The establishment of the FEPC was an important turning point because it provided a means to investigate grievances. The mere fact that such an agency had been started by the executive branch signaled a change in the federal government's approach toward employment discrimination.[14] On a national level, there was the possibility that the government would be more scrutinizing of employment practices.

Despite this prospect, America moved slowly. During the war, the nation focused on defeating the German and Japanese enemies. Even among African Americans, racial equality took a back seat to winning the war. A wartime poll conducted by the Pittsburgh *Courier* revealed that 71 percent of African Americans opposed a march on Washington to protest racial discrimination.[15] By the end of the war, America's economic boom began in earnest. More than six million new civilian jobs were created between 1945 and 1950—and African Americans were among the prime beneficiaries. Given the prospect of good-paying factory jobs, it seemed that the vast majority of African Americans did not want to "rock the boat" of employment opportunity that the postwar economy brought. The absence of a mass public outcry for racial reform meant that the Truman administration felt little pressure to enact measures that would move the nation away from its culture of racial division.

America's postwar fear of Communism was also cleverly linked to civil rights calls for racial equality. White supremacists frequently charged that challenges to the racial status quo were un-American. "The fear of McCarthyism so inhibited blacks that they failed to use the Korean War as a lever for racial reform, as they had World War II. At mid-century, direct action had ceased being a tactic in the quest for racial justice."[16]

Civil rights activists thus concentrated on eradicating segregation through court challenges. The rise of black economic fortunes since World War II led many people to believe that educational opportunity was the best path toward racial acceptance. In ruling that separate schools for black and Caucasian children were inherently unequal and therefore unacceptable, the Supreme Court's 1954 decision in *Brown v. Board of Education* acknowledged the prime importance of education in providing black people with the very opportunity to compete in a society dominated. by Caucasians.[17] *Brown*, many thought, marked the beginning of a new period of race relations, a period that would erase nearly a century of professed but unrealized freedom. With the abolition of "Jim Crow" in the school system, blacks would finally obtain equality and recognition as full citizens.

But the promise of educational equality proved just that, a promise. Scarcely more than a year after the outlawing of separate but unequal public schools, the Supreme Court rejected the NAACP's request for immediate and complete school desegregation.[18] The Court refused to set a deadline and instead adopted a "go-slow" approach that had been advocated by the Justice Department. "For the first time, the Supreme Court had vindicated a constitutional right and then deferred its exercise."[19]

The administration of Dwight D. Eisenhower provided little assistance in affirming the rights enunciated by the Supreme Court. The president refused to endorse the *Brown* decision because he feared that forced and rapid integration would lead to social upheaval and conflict. Eisenhower also believed that the executive branch of government should be more administrative than proactive. This restricted view of presidential authority coupled with the Court's own go-slow attitude hindered racial progress and cast another eight-year shadow on the development of affirmative action.

It was not until 1962 and President John F Kennedy's Executive Order 10925 that the idea of "affirmative action" became a major part of governmental action.

The principal provisions of the executive order included (1) a directive not to discriminate against traditionally disfavored minorities, (2) a requirement that job advertising describe the federal government as an "equal opportunity employer," and (3) a call for special efforts to recruit black Americans for admission and training programs.[20] Kennedy's order was stirred, in part, by the growing national attention to the demands of African Americans. Student sit-ins, freedom bus rides, and nonviolent protest marches received widespread media attention and necessitated an administration response. With massive direct action throughout the nation, African Americans responded to the calls for protest by organizations like the Student Non-Violent Coordinating Committee, the Southern Christian Leadership Conference, and the Congress for Racial Equality. Even after Kennedy's order—the first executive command to consider race and ethnic origin as positive factors in the employment decision-making process—the protests did not stop. The violent Southern responses to protesters demanded that the federal government act. By the summer of 1963, the administration asked Congress to pass a civil rights law that would desegregate public facilities and move America toward racial equality. To show both black America's impatience at the slow pace of integration and support for the president's bill, a broad coalition of people at last began to trumpet A. Philip Randolph's twenty-two-year call for a march on Washington.

The August 1963 gathering of nearly a quarter of a million people demanding congressional action ultimately led to the passage of the Civil Rights Act of 1964. While often hailed as a major step, the decision to afford other races an affirmative classification was much more pragmatic than radical.[21] At the time of passage of the 1964 act, the nation had experienced an unprecedented long-term economic expansion. Race-based affirmative action programs did not present the problem of choosing to take jobs or educational opportunities away from Caucasians. The vision of an ever-expanding economic pie made it easier to offer a slice to those who previously had been denied a seat at the table.

The modern use of the actual phrase "affirmative action" came with President Lyndon Johnson's Executive Order 11246. That directive required federal contractors to adopt and implement affirmative action to ensure the hiring of blacks, women, and other minorities in the work force through the use of hiring goals. "In its early form affirmative action was seen as a temporary intervention into the processes of various competitions to insure that all individuals were treated fairly regardless of factors such as race, ethnicity, religion or sex."[22] The use of affirmative action was not limited to federal contractors, however. After the executive order, affirmative action programs grew rapidly as governments, schools, and private employers actively sought to expand opportunities for African Americans.

At first, the very promise of equal opportunity was enough to satisfy a large majority of African Americans and was not sufficiently threatening to most of the principal managers of business and government. Although working-class Caucasians may have felt threatened, the reality of seniority systems and so-called race-neutral qualification requirements worked to ensure that affirmative action would not pose a risk to their livelihoods. Consequently, affirmative action programs grew and prospered between 1965 and 1972, despite opposition in some corners. Even the Supreme Court seemed to acknowledge the importance of recognizing the long-term effects of past discrimination.

In *Griggs v. Duke Power,* the Court observed that job selection criteria had not been shown to predict job performance:

> The objective of Congress in the enactment of Title VII is plain from the language of the statute. It was to achieve equality of employment opportunities and remove barriers that have operated in the past to favor an identifiable group of white employees over other employees. Under the Act, practices, procedures, or tests neutral on their face, and even neutral in terms of intent cannot be maintained if they operate to "freeze" the status quo of prior discriminatory employment practices.[23]

The justices thus prohibited Duke Power from requiring job applicants to have a high school diploma and subjecting them to a general intelligence test where the effect was to put black applicants at a disadvantage. *Griggs* may have represented the high-water mark for affirmative action, however. Even before the case was decided in 1971, America had already begun to change both economically and politically.

Politically, the 1967 and 1968 race riots in numerous U.S. cities, the assassinations of Robert Kennedy and Martin Luther King, Jr., and the growing anti-Vietnam war movement pushed the nation toward a conservative ideology. Many Americans embraced the law-and-order rhetoric of presidential candidates Richard Nixon and George Wallace in 1968. Noting this change, historian Harvard Sitkoff writes:

> Appealing to those weary of protest, Richard Nixon rode the backlash into the White House. He campaigned against open housing and busing for racial balance. He promised to slow federal efforts at school integration and to appoint only conservative justices to the federal courts. Nixon particularly solicited the support of traditional Democratic voters disgruntled with the excesses of the black struggle. Many responded to the appeal. The Democratic nominee, Hubert Humphrey, long associated in the public mind with the civil-rights movement, won just one out of every three white votes. The ethnic working class that deserted Humphrey largely rallied to the banner of George Wallace, whose American Independent Party made the fear and resentment of blacks the central thrust of its campaign. . . .

Immediately after entering the White House, President Nixon began wooing the Wallace constituency to insure his reelection in 1972. He deliberately pursued a "Southern strategy," conceding the votes of blacks and those committed to liberalism and going after those of white Southerners, suburbanites, and ethnic workers troubled by the specter of racial equality. Rather than follow the course counseled by his domestic advisor, the sociologist Daniel Patrick Moynihan, to behave with "benign neglect" on the race issue, the President intentionally focused public attention on the matter, and in a manner hardly benign to blacks.[24]

By 1971, the twenty-five-year, postwar economic boom also had run its course. The same opportunities for economic progress—manufacturing jobs—were less available to African Americans as seniority systems worked to preserve the status of long-term workers while the number of new jobs diminished. The nation's switch to a service economy began in earnest.

The fading of America's producer base meant that fewer factory or other semiskilled positions were available. This fact was particularly devastating for African Americans who had come to realize their part of the economic American dream through factory work.[25] Many jobs were exported to developing nations where the cost of labor was substantially less. These corporate moves were often made with only the short-term goal of higher profit margins in mind. The longer-term question of what happens to the displaced worker was rarely asked. Today, nearly two-thirds of all employment in America consists of providing services rather than producing goods. Many of these service jobs require special training in science, mathematics, and economics—training that is attained principally in colleges and universities.

Threatened by the prospect of smaller economic growth, more Caucasians began to oppose affirmative action programs. This time the opposition did not come from just those who felt threatened in the manufacturing workplace; resistance also came from the governing elite. Watergate, the OPEC oil crisis, the rise of feminism, and increasing civil rights militancy all combined to threaten the political fabric of America. With both the working class and the business and government elite threatened by the future, the federal response to affirmative action took a noticeable turn. Government support for affirmative action began to diminish.

Without a forceful government voice to lead the debate on affirmative action during less than stable economic times, opponents increased their attacks through a series of clever and deceptive myths. Foremost among them was the notion of *reverse discrimination*. The term "reverse discrimination" first appeared in the popular media in 1974 after the Supreme Court issued its decision in *DeFunis v. Odegaard*. In that case the plaintiff, Marco DeFunis, argued that the admissions committee at the University of Washington Law School had discriminated against him on account of race and thus violated the Equal Protection Clause of the Fourteenth Amendment. The Court held that the issue was moot on the grounds that DeFunis would graduate with his law class regardless of his legal action. The case, however, raised a new whipping post in efforts to broaden access to higher education.[26]

Because higher education opportunities were available to only a relatively small number of African Americans (and principally through historically black institutions), a number of predominantly Caucasian colleges and universities sought to increase the number of African Americans on campus through preferential admissions policies. To combat this problem of access, schools began to take race into account positively, in their admissions decision-making process. In some instances, a specific number of seats were reserved for black and other applicants of color. In making comparisons among applicants, most schools used only two quantifiable factors: (1) an applicant's grade point average in high school; and (2) that person's college entrance examination score. Neither of these two factors are accurate predictors of a student's performance or success in college. Few, if any, schools fill their classes solely on the basis of those factors. However, the consideration of race in the admissions process permitted Caucasian applicants denied a seat in a particular school to claim victim status.

The seminal case regarding affirmative action in university admissions is *Regents of the University of California v. Bakke*.[27] In *Bakke*, a Caucasian medical school applicant sued the University of California at Davis, claiming that its minority set-aside program violated both the Equal Protection Clause of the Fourteenth Amendment and Title VI of the Civil Rights Act. Bakke successfully contended that his grade point average and medical entrance examination scores were higher than those of some persons accepted for the minority slots. No majority opinion emerged from the Supreme Court's consideration of the case. The justices wrote six separate opinions, with no more than four justices agreeing about the reasoning. Four justices gave the Davis plan intermediate review and found it completely constitutional. Four found the plan unlawful on statutory grounds but did not reach the equal protection claim. It therefore fell on the ninth justice, Lewis Powell, to form a majority. Justice Powell concurred with Justices Harry A. Blackmun, William J. Brennan, Thurgood Marshall, and Byron R. White that a university should be permitted to take race into account when considering whether to admit a candidate. However, Powell believed that any racial classification must be subjected to strict constitutional scrutiny; thus, there must be a compelling state interest in order for the program to stand.[28] In his view, the Davis special admissions program was unconstitutional because applicants like Bakke were placed at a disadvantage, even though they were not responsible for "whatever harm the beneficiaries of the special admissions program are thought to have suffered."[29] The "principal evil" of the program, Powell wrote, was the denial of Bakke's right to "individualized consideration without regard to race."[30]

In cases like *Bakke* and *DeFunis,* the legal challenges focused on the relatively few seats set aside for minorities rather than on the general admissions process that historically favored elite white males over everyone else. As a result of such reverse discrimination challenges, colleges began to retreat from their affirmative action efforts. A vast number of African Americans were simply excluded from even taking advantage of these limited educational opportunities. But the college admissions process contains a number of variables that extend beyond grade point and entrance examination scores. The process is not one that can be applied mechanically.

> Moreover, use of a pool defined exclusively by a high school G.P.A. and S.A.T results would itself disguise the fact that the substandard, segregated education of many parents of the current generation of African-American students directly impacts the G.P.A.s and S.A.T scores of . . . current black applicants. Education is a continuous and expanding process in which knowledge, skills and attitudes towards learning are communicated from one generation to another. Unfortunately, we still live in a time when many African-Americans of college age are disadvantaged in this respect because their forbears received an inferior education.[31]

Recognition of the long-term and far-ranging effects of educational discrimination is the message that proponents of affirmative action programs are trying to help people understand. "Reverse discrimination" is itself an inaccurate and misleading term. It misleads by focusing attention away from affirmative action as an effective remedy to discrimination. It is inaccurate because such programs are *not* taking something away from one group (Caucasians), but instead are varying the calculus so that others might also partake in the opportunity.

Like educational programs, affirmative action efforts in the work force met similar challenges.[32] Instead of supporting measures that called for specific outcome-focused goals with respect to racial composition, opponents successfully argued that good-faith affirmative action efforts should suffice. The problem with good-faith efforts in this area is that they permit institutional inertia—the employer simply goes through the motions of searching for someone to hire. Stiffer job or admission requirements permitted institutions, "in good faith," to tell African American and other candidates with clear potential for success in the classroom or in the work force that they did not quite measure up to the revised standards. The shifting away from stated numerical goals that were linked to timetables for their achievement to good-faith efforts rarely resulted in anything more than the hiring of a token number of people of color.

Underlying the reverse discrimination myth is the concept of tipping—the psychological notion in the minds of many Caucasians that the addition of more African Americans will change the essential nature of the institution.[33] The words "essential nature" are nothing more than doublespeak for the unstated assumption that most people fundamentally conceive of their workplace, their schools, and even *our* nation as an essentially white country.[34] Alex Aleinikoff notes that

> the stories that African Americans tell about America—stories of racism and exclusion, brutality and mendacity—simply do not ring true to the white mind. Whites have not been trained to hear it, and to credit such accounts would be to ask whites to give up too much of what they "know" about the world. It would also argue in favor of social programs and an alteration in power relations that would fundamentally change the status quo. . . . [I]t is the white version that becomes the "official story" in the dominant culture.[35]

In his book *And We Are Not Saved,* Derrick Bell tells the parable of the seventh minority candidate for a law school faculty, who despite having a superior vitae is denied a position because Caucasian faculty had reached their racial tipping point. Thus, an African American with superior credentials was still denied acceptance because of race.[36]

Though there have been few studies of the early successes of such programs, one might assume positive results because of the subsequent growth of affirmative action programs to encompass many other people in American society. Women, Hispanics, Native Americans, and many new immigrant groups have come within affirmative action's inclusive umbrella. Perhaps because so many more people from many different groups now seek affirmative action recognition, or, perhaps because others became threatened by it, affirmative action soon came under increasing attack. "Quotas," "reduced standards," "special interest politics," and "reverse discrimination" are just some of the invectives cast at programs that seek to include African American and other historically underrepresented people. Even some African American scholars, many of whom have been the principal beneficiaries of affirmative action, now suggest that affirmative action has no place in America's societal discourse because of the stigmatizing harm caused to participants. These and other writers suggest that the truest constitutional principle is that of a color-blind society.

The idea of constitutional color-blindness was first articulated in Justice John Marshall Harlan's famous dissent in *Plessy v. Ferguson*:

> In respect of civil rights, common to all citizens, the Constitution of the United States does not, I think, permit any public authority to know the race of those entitled to be protected in the enjoyment of such rights. Every true man has pride of race, and under appropriate circumstances, when the rights of others, his equals before the law, are not to be affected, it is his privilege to express such pride and to take such action based upon it as to him seems proper. But I deny that any legislative body or judicial tribunal may have regard to the race of citizens when the civil rights of those citizens are involved. Indeed such legislation as that here in question is inconsistent, not only with that equality of

rights which pertains to citizenship, national and state, but with the personal liberty enjoyed by every one within the United States.

[I]n view of the Constitution, in the eye of the law, *there is in this country no superior, dominant, ruling class of citizens. There is no caste here. Our Constitution is color-blind, and neither knows nor tolerates classes among citizens. In respect of civil rights, all citizens are equal before the law.* The destinies of the two races in this country are indissolubly linked together, and the interests of both require that the common government of all shall not permit the seeds of race hate to be planted under the sanction of law.[37]

Harlan's powerful language should perhaps be recast by changing the word "is" throughout the second paragraph to "should be"—*there should be in this country no superior, dominant, ruling class of citizens. There should be no caste here. Our Constitution should be color-blind.* Such an interpretive phrasing would force us to ask the all-important question of whether we have indeed reached a point where race does not matter.

It appears that a growing number of people have come to believe that race does not matter. The present Supreme Court has attempted to narrow the definition of permissible affirmative action programs. Contrary to these claims, America is and has always been a color-conscious and not a color-blind society. Race is such a powerful aspect of our lives that overcoming it may well be impossible; however, to claim that race should be ignored simply disregards the American reality.

The ultimate goal of affirmative action programs is to create a community that values racial, ethnic, and gender diversity to a point that discrimination based on these characteristics ceases to occur. Clearly, this aspiration is a long-term dream. Opponents of affirmative action often focus on this goal to support their claims that the only way to achieve a society that values all of its members is to ignore race completely. These critics argue that it is immoral, unprincipled, and paradoxical to have a goal of color-blindness, yet seek to reach that goal by color-conscious actions. They refuse to acknowledge the breadth and depth of the continuing legacy of racism in this country. Even though segregation is no longer the expressed law of the land, the aftermath of nearly two centuries of race-based denials of opportunity lingers to this day as disproportionate numbers of African Americans realize less of America's promise than members of any other racial or ethnic group.[38]

EFFECTS OF ATTACKS ON AFFIRMATIVE ACTION

As African Americans, we are caught between a rock and a hard place. While some few of us who have benefited from affirmative action can be pointed to as success stories, this fact cannot mask the bitter reality that the majority of our people languish economically and, even worse, spiritually. In particular, the effect on young African Americans has been devastating. Unlike those of us who benefited from these programs in the 1960s and 1970s, the generation and a half of young people who have grown up since then have seen opportunities shrink and their own accomplishments either unrecognized or minimized. The effect on their self-esteem is undeniable.

Those of us who have been the beneficiaries of affirmative action have parlayed the opportunities offered us into respectable middle- and upper middle-class lifestyles. Now, so many of us are unwilling to speak out not only in favor of continuing but also of expanding affirmative action efforts. A number of our own best and brightest have begun to question the basic underpinnings of affirmative action. Indeed, some beneficiaries even claim that "America is a meritocratic nation that permits people to rise or fall according to their quality." Hearing such declarations from our own may be even more debilitating than hearing the same from Caucasians. Disagreement over the worth of affirmative action within the African American community not only sends mixed signals to the governing elite, but, what is more important, such disagreement divides and confuses the African American community itself.

The nomination of Justice Clarence Thomas to the Supreme Court is a prime example of community division. Despite Thomas's own condemnation of affirmative action, his academic and professional career attainments were due, in large measure, to the very programs he opposed. Confronted with this irony, African Americans found ourselves split between supporting or opposing his nomination. Writing about this episode, Cornet West notes,

> Bush's choice of Thomas caught most black leaders off guard. Few had the courage to say publicly that this was an act of cynical tokenism concealed by outright lies about Thomas being the most qualified candidate regardless of race. Thomas had an undistinguished record as a student (mere graduation from Yale Law School does not qualify one for the Supreme Court); . . . and his performance during his short fifteen months as an appellate court judge was mediocre. The very fact that no black leader could utter publicly that a black appointee for the Supreme Court was *unqualified* shows how captive they are to white racist stereotypes about [African American] intellectual talent.[39]

In reality, Thomas's appointment was the quintessential *anti*-affirmative action case because it went to the very core of the conservative critique—namely, that a less-than-best-qualified person received a position through preference. This situation confused many in the African American community because we viewed the Thomas nomination as forcing us either to support someone solely because of race, or to admit that an African American candidate was not the best-qualified. Either position arguably would confirm the conservative claims about affirmative action.

The reluctance to dispute the expected qualifications of an African American judicial nominee reflects the degree of internalized oppression that exists in our community. Instead of leading the debate about how to refine, revitalize, and reconfigure affirmative action, African Americans have permitted critics to monopolize the discussion and to call into question our own sense of self-worth. Were we like Clarence Thomas—perhaps positioned where we were because of someone's benevolence; or, were we at a particular life station because of our accomplishments, because we were the best? Even among the most educated and most successful African Americans, personal doubts still exist about our place within institutions.[40]

But African Americans have no need to doubt ourselves or our accomplishments. Our successes stand on their own. Instead of harboring doubts about our achievements, let us focus on the tasks that remain. Affirmative action continues to be a misunderstood concept. We agree that society should ask whether any person can meet the basic criteria for a position. But the word "qualified" means competent or eligible, it does not mean best. Despite this fact, most people, African Americans included, believe that decisions are and should be made to favor that "best" person. Rarely if ever can one say that the person chosen is the best of all choices that could have been made. Many are differently qualified. The selection of any person of color who is comparable with, or even better than, a Caucasian is too often seen as an injustice to that Caucasian. But too often we accept the false claim that affirmative action programs result in the selection of incompetent persons.

American institutions have never operated on a completely merit-based system. There are few, if any, positions that demand that the *most* capable or credentialed person be selected. It is mere folly to suggest that capabilities can be measured so as to determine who has the most or who is the best. Race-based affirmative action merely opens doors that have been closed despite our possessing comparable or even superior credentials. It gets us to the starting gate. Where each of us then finishes is a function of our own grit and determination as well as equal employment opportunity. Thus, there is no need for us to shy away from or to question the role of affirmative action.

THE CHALLENGE FOR THE FUTURE

But what can we say to our children about the challenges awaiting us and them in the future with respect to affirmative action? One solution is to tell them to look at affirmative action over the past twenty-five years not as a failed policy, but as one that was never really tried. The Great Society programs of the 1960s were never fully funded and were insufficient to begin addressing the legacy of slavery and ongoing discrimination. We are just now coming to the point of funding programs like Head Start, an idea that Republicans and Democrats alike believe works. Imagine the result if such resources had been allocated to Head

Start from 1965 to now! Perhaps more young African American children and their families would be able to overcome the social and economic woes through greater classroom successes.

We might also tell our children that another way of regarding affirmative action is to see it as a band-aid on the cancer of racism. Racism may well be a permanent phenomenon, and African Americans may never have true equality. "Even our most successful efforts will produce no more than 'temporary peaks of progress'." A band-aid may provide some minor relief or protection from outside infection. Thus affirmative action may frustrate and retard some of the infectious manifestations of racism.[41]

Either of these alternatives may be too pessimistic to convey to our children. Instead we need to give them hope. We can give them hope by teaching them the history of this centuries-long struggle for racial equality and just opportunity. We can give them hope by teaching them about all those African Americans who came before them, who suffered and even died without losing sight of this quest. We can give them hope by telling them that their and our efforts must continue to be directed at reconfiguring this society in a way that will lead us and others to see race, ethnicity, and difference as positive rather than negative attributes. Such a society, we must tell them, will permit all of us to be confident in ourselves, our capabilities, and in those same attributes we find in others. We must tell the children that affirmative action should be one of many tools that help us grow beyond "the accumulated effect of the black wounds and scars suffered in a white dominated society . . . a deep seated anger . . . a boiling sense of rage, and a passionate pessimism regarding America's will to justice." Like Cornel West, we believe in the politics of conversion, politics that emphasize love, care, and the rebuilding of African Americans and all society.[42]

In the next century our children will become part of the majority as America becomes a nation principally comprised of people of color. If this country is to survive and perhaps even flourish in the future, it must overcome, or at least honestly confront, its fear of race. We must be bold enough to utilize tools such as affirmative action as sources of growth and reconciliation that will spiritwarm rather than spirit-assault.[43] The memory of our ancestors should hearten us for this effort; their hopes and dreams have not yet been realized. The sweet faces of our children will inspire us; what legacy will we leave for them? We are a nation inextricably bound together—black, brown, red, and white. We must work together to build a tomorrow filled with hope. We must work now, and we must not fail.

NOTES

1. W. E. B. Du Bois, *The Souls of Black Folk* (Chicago: A. C. McClurg, 1903), 1.
2. J. Clay Smith, "Symposium: Perspectives on Equal Employment Opportunity Litigation: Review: Affirmative Action," *Howard Law Journal* 27 (1984): 496.

3. Boxill, *Blacks and Social Justice* (Lanham, Md.: Rowman and Littlefield, 1992), 148. See also Smith, "Symposium," 496. Boxill states that affirmative action can be seen in two ways, either through a "backward looking" argument that aims at compensation for past wrongs or through a "forward looking" argument that seeks to achieve greater status, education, and income for blacks. We embrace this forward-looking model as a means to achieve greater distributive justice and not simply a method of compensation that will elevate the status of some select few.

4. See Allan Bloom, *The Closing of the American Mind* (New York: Simon and Schuster, 1987); Steven Carter, *Reflections of an Affirmative Action Baby* (New York: Basic Books, 1991); Dinesh D'Souza, *Illiberal Education: The Politics of Race and Sex on Campus* (New York: Free Press, 1991); and Shelby Steele, *The Content of Our Character: A New Vision of Race in America* (New York: St. Martin's Press, 1990).

5. See Equal Employment Opportunity Coordinating Council Policy Statement on Affirmative Action Programs for State and Local Government Agencies, 41 Fed. Reg. 38, 814 (1976).

6. See Smith, "Symposium," 500–1.

7. Children of alumni in Ivy League schools have approximately a 50 percent acceptance rate, as compared with a 17 percent acceptance rate for the children of nonalumni. But Caucasian alumni children do not suffer a stigma because of their preferred treatment; indeed, many regard it as their birthright to matriculate at the institution that their parents attended.

8. Smith, "Symposium," 518.

9. *Regents of the University of California v. Bakke,* 438 U.S. 265, 407 (1978) (opinion of Blackmun, J.).

10. Patricia J. Williams, *The Alchemy of Race and Rights* (Cambridge, Mass.: Harvard University Press, 1991), 103.

11. Williams, *The Alchemy of Race and Rights,* 102 (emphasis added).

12. Harvard Sitkoff, *The Struggle for Black Equality* 1954–1992, rev. ed. (New York: Hill and Wang, 1993), 11.

13. Sitkoff, *The Struggle for Black Equality,* 11. Some two million blacks found employment in defense-related industries.

14. James E. Jones Jr., "The Development of Modern Equal Employment Opportunity and Affirmative Action Law: A Brief Chronological Overview," *Howard Law Journal* 20 (1977): 75–77.

15. Jones, "The Development," 13.

16. Jones, "The Development," 17.

17. 347 U.S. 483 (1954).

18. *Brown v. Board of Education* (No. 2), 349 U.S. 294 (1955).

19. Sitkoff, *The Struggle for Black Equality,* 23.

20. Steven J. Witosky, "Beyond Reverse Discrimination: The Quest For a Legitimizing Principle," *Nova Law Journal* 4 (1980): 63.

21. See, for example, Sitkoff, *The Struggle for Black Equality,* and Franklin and Moss, *From Slavery to Freedom,* 436–94.

22. LaNoue, *The Demographic Premises,* 421.

23. 401 U.S. 424, 429–30 (1971).

24. Sitkoff, *The Struggle for Black Equality,* 212.

25. Andrew Hacker, *Two Nations: Black and White, Separate, Hostile, Unequal* (New York: Scribner's, 1992), 101.

26. 416 U.S. 312, 319–21 (1974) (Douglas, J., dissenting).

27. 438 U.S. 265 (1978).

28. 438 U.S. 265, 289 (1978). For Justice Powell, the curing of past intentional discrimination on the part of an institution using such a plan would be the only interest the Court should find sufficiently compelling. However, Powell's opinion also recognized that educational benefits could flow from a racially and ethnically diverse student body and that such a goal is constitutionally permitted as long as race is not the sole factor considered in the admissions process.

29. 438 U.S. 265, 310 (1978).

30. 438 U.S. 265, 318, n. 52 (1978).

31. *Podberesky v. Kirwan,* 838 F. Supp. 1075 (1993). 1993 WL 482923 (D. Md. Nov. 18, 1993), 10. *Podberesky* had to do with the University of Maryland's use of race-based scholarships.

32. See, for example, *Martin v. Wilks,* 490 U.S. 755 (Oct. Term, 1988) (permitting Caucasian firefighters to sue the city of Birmingham alleging that "less qualified" African Americans were promoted).

33. For a description of the tipping phenomenon, see Ankur Goel, "Recent Developments," *Harvard C.R.-C.L. Law* Review 24 (1989): 561.

34. Derrick Bell, *Race, Racism, and American Law,* 3d ed. (Boston: Little, Brown, 1992), 7.

35. Aleinikoff, "A Case for Race-Consciousness," 1069.

36. Derrick Bell, *And We Are Not Saved: The Elusive Quest for Racial Justice* (New York: Basic Books, 1987), 140.

37. 163 U.S. 537 (1896) (emphasis added).

38. Nationally, the high school dropout rate of African Americans is twice that of Caucasian American school children. See Gerald D. Jaynes and Robin M. Williams, Jr., eds., *A Common Destiny: Blacks and American Society* (Washington, D.C.: National Academy Press, 1989), 20. In nearly every economic or social measure, African Americans are significantly worse off than their Caucasian American counterparts. The median income for African American families is 57 percent of that for Caucasian American families.

    With respect to crime and punishment, African Americans also constitute one-half of all prison inmates, despite the fact that we make up only 13 percent of the population. African Americans are six times more likely to be victims of violent crime than our proportion in the general population, and seven times more likely to be the victims of murder (the leading cause of death among African American men between the ages of fifteen and twenty-five). See Jaynes and Williams, *A Common Destiny,* 464–65, 498.

39. Cornel West, *Race Matters* (Boston: Beacon Press, 1993), 23.

40. See Carter, *Reflections,* and Cose, *Rage.*

41. Bell, *Race, Racism, and American Law,* 62, n. 56.
42. West, *Race Matters,* 18–19.
43. Professor Patricia Williams has coined the term "spirit assault or murder." Patricia Williams, "Spirit-Murdering the Messenger: The Discourse of Fingerpointing as the Law's Response to Racism," *University of Miami Law Review* 42 (1987): 127.